DALIT WOMEN'S AUTOBIOGRAPHIES: A CRITICAL APPRAISAL

DALIT WOMEN'S AUTOBIOGRAPHIES

A Critical Appraisal

Edited by

Dr Bijender Singh

KALPAZ

ISBN: 978-93-5128-200-6
Price: ₹ 890/-

First Published 2016

Published by

Kalpaz Publications
C-30, Satyawati Nagar,
Delhi - 110052
E-mail: kalpaz@hotmail.com Ph.: 9212142040
Laser Typesetting : Rajender Vashist, Delhi
Printed at : G. Print Process, Delhi

Cataloging in Publication Data--DK

Courtesy: D.K. Agencies (P) Ltd. <docinfo@dkagencies.com>

Dalit women's autobiographies : a critical appraisal in India / edited by Bijender Singh.
pages cm
Contributed articles.

1. Indic literature--Dalit authors--History and criticism. 2. Indic literature--Women authors--History and criticism. 3. Women authors, Indic--Biography--History and criticism. 4. Autobiography. I. Singh, Bijender, editor.

PK2907.U56D35 2016 DDC 891.409 23

Contents

Foreword 9

Introduction 15

Notes on the Contributors 31

1. Sex Knows No Caste: A Study of P. Sivakami's *The Grip of Change* 39
Professor D. Amalraj

2. Dalit Experiences of Social Rejection and Creativity in Urmila Pawar's Autobiography *Aaydan / The Weave of My Life* 47
Dr Irum Alvi

3. Articulation of Social Injustices, Gender Discrimination and Patriarchy Tradition in Bama's *Sangati* 57
Dr Archana Bhattacharjee

4. Role of Marriage in Shaping a Dalit Woman's Identity: A Study of Dalit Memoir *Viramma: Life of an Untouchable* 69
Dr Sigma G.R.

5. Voice of the Voiceless: A Study of P. Sivakami's *The Grip of Change* 79
Dr Himanginee Kaushik

6. Marginalisation and Subordination of Dalit Women in Mukta Sarvagod's *Closed Doors* 87
Dr Deepika Rani

7. Breaking the Margins: Analysing *The Prisons We Broke* as a Testimony of Oppression and Resistance 99
Guni Vats

8. A Doubly Oppressed Voice in Urmila in Pawar's *The Weave of My Life: A Dalit Woman's Memoir* 109
Suruchi Sharma

9. A Reading of Subjugation of Dalit Women in Baby Kondiba Kamble's *The Prisons We Broke* 119
Kusum Kanger

10. Bama's *Karukku*: (Re)-reading Dalit History in South India and (Re)-interpreting the Identity of a Dalit (Wo)-man 129
Ramanuj Mahato

11. Little-Narrative of Infinite Pain: C. K. Janu's *Mother Forest* and Socio-economic Deprivation 141
Saikat Guha

12. Multiple Facets of Dalit Patriarchy in P. Sivakami's *The Grip of Change* 151
Dwaipayan Mitra

13. Bama's *Sangati*: The Autobiography of a Dalit Community 161
Mohd. Anwar Husain Khan

14. Powerful Clamp of Caste in Kumudtai Pawde's *Antaspot: Thoughtful Outburst* 173
Himanshu Sharma

15. Demystifying the Curse: Reading Kausalya Baisantri's *Dohra Abhishaap* as a Journey of an Untouchable Woman — 183
Guni Vats

16. Poverty, Tyranny and Fear in *I, Phoolan Devi:* The Autobiography of India's Bandit Queen — 193
Pradip Sarikhada

17. An Exploited Serf and Patriarchal Chains: A Study of Viramma's *Viramma:* Life of an Untouchable — 203
Dr Namita Panda

18. Reflection of Dampening Down of Persona in Urmila Pawar's: The Weave of My Life — 211
Dr Sumitra Singh

19. Selected Dalit Women Autobiographies: The Unheard Agonies — 219
Dr M.B. Gaijan

20. Casteism, Classism and Sexism: (Re) Examining the Intergenerational Syllogism in Baisantri's Dohra Abhishaap (Twice Accursed) — 229
Dr Aparna Lanjewar Bose

21. Religion, Caste and Identity: A Study of Bama's Karukku — 247
Dr Narendra Kumar

Index — 255

Foreword

Women have been invisible on the pages of history. This situation of invisibility arose when patriarchy got replaced by matriarchy. Female characters of Ramayana and Mahabharata are the mythological characters. In real life one can find rare examples of women who have independent existence. Since Vedic Era Gargi, Maitreyi etc. names can be cited as illustrations. In fact, Maitreyi was threatened to shut her mouth by Yagyavalk at the time when she had to show her wisdom and knowledge. Many Buddhist nuns have written their autobiographies that show their independent existence and these autobiographies are a slap on their critics.

In Maharashtra, the Queen of Jhansi, Ahilya Bai Holkar, Rani Tara Bai etc. a few names can be cited who ruled over the kingdom to maintain their independence by showing their potential after the death of their husbands. In nineteenth century, the Britishers opened Missionary Schools and other institutions. After that women started getting education; though at large they studies at their homes. Mahatma Phule opened a school in Pune in 1948, then his wife, Kashi Bai Kanitkar and many other women like Laxmi Bai Tilak, Rama Bai Ranade, Baya Karve etc. declared their own existences from the cruel Brahminical clutches after getting education. It was a strange experience for men at that time.

In the historic background if we think about Dalit women, then we find that they are still invisible or have been described nowhere. In fact, Dalit women have been pugilist and combatant enough to tackle any problem. They were always ready to embattle for their rights. When Mahatma Phule opened his school in Pune then Mukta Mang wrote her first essay about the Dalits and Dalit women. Then she was in fourth class and she narrated the pains, sufferings and woes of the Dalits and the Dalit women. Due to casteism, poverty and Dalit patriarchy, Dalit women were thrown away at the lowest level of the society. Thus, they faced disparaging snags and hitches. I have tried to show their existence in historical times.

Dalit literature emerged in 1960s in Marathi language. The term "Dalit Literature" was used in 1958 for the first time by influential Dalit personalities including Jyotiba Phule and Dr B.R. Ambedkar in a conference of Maharashtra Dalit Sahitya Society. The trend of Dalit autobiographies commenced with Daya Pawar's autobiographical work *Baluta*. After that there came the flood of Dalit autobiographies. Due to atrocities of upper caste, the low caste people were infuriated. Dalits started writing their woes, sufferings, humiliation, torture and exploitation of their community and it was like the eruption of a volcano. Even the people who were merely studied up to first or second standard showed their anger and protest in written form. Generally, an autobiography is written at the old age to have a look on the whole doings in one's life. Women's responsibility is of their households, children and so many other works. They hardly get time to write about themselves and about their society. It can generally happen when they cross fifties. These women know the importance of education. I have met many women who did efforts to educate girls.

Women autobiographers have written about the hurdles in getting education due to casteism. On the school black-board, Mahar caste was written when a Dalit teacher entered in the class. Mukta Sarvagod criticised it, "It is shown on board, public place is prohibited for Dalits." The society banned on Baba Saheb to read Sanskrit. The attitude of the society was same even after 30-40 years. Kumud Pawade was restricted to choose the same subject as a teacher. The upper caste students showed their anger that they were not ready to learn Sanskrit from a Dalit teacher. Babytai Kamble, Shantabai Kamble, Janabai etc. all endured this autonomy.

Being women, the female autobiographers are attached to every pain of a woman. They themselves bear every atrocity and humiliation. Thus, every autobiography by women writers represents the pain and agony of their lives. Babytai Kamble, Janabai Girhe, Sushila Patkar etc. have represented the lives of illiterate women of village Khera, atrocities by their men, poverty, hunger and orthodox views. It seems that these women are now asking for justice.

Aaydan (in English *The Weave of My Life*) my autobiography got published in 2003. Meanwhile Pawar's *Baluta* completed twenty-five years. *Aaydan* was critically analysed with the reference to condition of women during twenty-five years. From all over Maharashtra the autobiographies of Dalits were published except Konkan region. There were a few male Dalit writers in Konkan region. The life of a Dalit woman was introduced to people in my autobiography.

I was born in a village in Konkan region. My father was a teacher and due to his efforts we four siblings were brought to study in a small city, Ratnagiri. Most of our time was spent in village. My father passed away when I was in third standard. We were brought up by our mother by selling bamboo baskets. The women of the village used to go to city to sell grass or cashews. These women loved us. Occasionally, I accompanied with them. On the way I listened to their tales of woes and humiliations. My sister-in-law (brother's wife) has suffered like them. When I started writing, I got acquainted to their pains as a woman. Neither my mother nor the other women could write. Thus, I decided to write, to give words to their sufferings and their agony. Dr Baba Saheb Ambedkar was my inspiration. I wanted to express the pitiable conditions of Dalit community. The decision of change of my religion was of Dr B.R. Ambedkar. We followed him and thus, it changed our lives. How we abandoned Hindu religion and how we embraced Buddhism, I decided to write everything. Thus, I wrote about every experience of poverty, humiliation and education.

Every woman has some such events in her life that after these incidences the life starts like a rebirth for her. Decision of change of religion was my first step towards a big change of my life. The idols kept in the house were immersed in water. The fear of God and phantoms faded away that day. Hereafter I developed a scientific attitude in my life.

Some of my school teachers also had distorted mentality. They ordered me to collect cow-dung and sweep the floor etc. One day when I denied to these assigned tasks, the teacher slapped me. My mother was a daring woman. She threatened the teacher in harsh words and warned not to repeat the same. The reaction of my mother realised me about her bravery and this incidence inspired me not to get frightened from anybody. It was the second incident. Since 1976 I joined Dalit and Woman Liberation Movement that changed my life completely.

Woman is an independent entity. She has her own thinking power to take decisions. She should speak and write her views openly and frankly. If she will talk freely, it is only then the society will understand her. This is my own judgment. I believe that a society of a country like India where people of various castes and creeds live in harmony, in that country there is nothing like personal. Everything is related to society. Due to this belief, I wrote my personal experiences also frankly like experience of menstruation cycle, experience of first night, experience of delivering a baby etc. I made critics also when some denigrators disparaged my frank writing. In spite of many critics, *Aaydan* got translated into English, Hindi and Kannada languages. It was included in syllabus of SNDT Nagpur, Jalgaon, Vardha (Hindi) etc. universities. My book *The Weave of My Life* is now in the library of Columbia University, USA. It was selected as a subject for study in M.A., M. Phil, and Ph.D. Due to this autobiography; I got an opportunity to deliver my lecture in Sweden and England. I, a simple Dalit girl of Konkan region and many other Dalit women writers like me, are raising our voices against casteism. It is not only our voice but of all the women of the past centuries also who have remained invisible on the pages of history.

This anthology entitled *Dalit Women's Autobiographies: A Critical Appraisal* edited by Dr Bijender Singh endeavours to examine and explore Dalit women's autobiographies very scrupulously and meticulously. It is an exhaustive compilation of almost all the requisite Dalit women's autobiographies available in English till date. Strength of the book also lies in its voluminous nature that makes the book more charming and exquisite. It endeavours to add a new critical chapter in the pool of knowledge in the field of Dalit literature. This anthology is a collection of twenty-one scholarly articles written in a judicious, practical and precise manner by the learned contributors.

Last but not the least; I salute the unflagging and unfaltering enthusiasm of the editor, Dr Bijender Singh to bring out such a careful, painstaking, punctilious and precise critical study in the realm of Dalit literature. His enthusiasm, perseverance and eagerness in this arena are decidedly commendable. I wish him all the success — today and always — in his life for all his moves towards new horizons.

Urmila Pawar
A Dalit Writer and Activist
Writer of *Aaydan : The Weave of My Life*

Introduction

Dalit literature is not simply literature; it is associated with a movement to bring about change. It represents the hopes and ambitions of a new society and new people. (Dangle, 266)

Indian society is an evidence to the centuries-old social and textual subjugation of dalits and Dalit writers. The *bhadralok* of our society did not consider them fit enough to become the protagonists of the mainstream literature. The Dalit characters were found grovelling in obscurity on the margins of Brahminical literature. However, in the recent past, this 'indispensable' yet the 'invisible' populace refused to accept the age-long humiliation and the Caliban has eventually begun to answer back to the Prospero. The 'modern' Eklavya chose to fight back with the weapons of 'pen' and correct the 'history' by re-writing 'his story'. The authenticity which missed the mark in the 'established' (and accepted) Indian literature found place in the works of Dalit writers. Thus, the hegemony of the Brahminical literature was disrupted with the advent of Dalit writings.

Dalit writers started sowing the seeds of Dalit Literature in 1950s in Marathi. Subsequently, Dalit writers also wrote in other Indian regional languages also like Tamil, Telugu, Kannada, Malayalam, Gujarati, Punjabi, Hindi and English.

Before this, literature was the heritage of only high caste people as they had the right of education and dalits were not allowed to get education. When some Dalit people got education, they started writing about dalits and in this way, the Dalit literature germinated. Dalit literature is a saga of sufferings and pains, atrocities and exploitation, humiliation and degradation. According to Arun Kumar Yadav, "Dalit autobiographies have been described as "capsules of agony" and "narratives of pain" (Yadav, 1).

Daya Pawar, with his autobiography *Baluta: Social Claim* (1978) bears the credit of having inaugurated the Dalit autobiography. In the beginning Dalit literature flourished mainly through Marathi autobiographies. Apart from *Baluta*, other Marathi autobiographies also emerged on the Dalit literary scene like Laxman Bapu Mane's *Upara: An Outsider* (1980), Laxman Gaikwad's *Uchalya: The Branded* (1987), Kishore Shantabai Kale's *Kolhatye Chepor: Against All Odds* (2000), Vasant Moon's *Vasti: Growing up Untouchable in India* (2001), Narendra Jadhav's *Outcaste: A Memoir* (2003) and Sharankumar Limbale's *Akkarmashi: The Outcaste* (2003). These are prominent Dalit autobiographies in Marathi but there are several other autobiographies written in various other regional languages also. Bama's *Karukku* (1992) and K.A. Gunasekaran's *The Scar* (2009) are Tamil autobiographies. Aravind Malagatti's *Government Brahmana*, Siddalingaiah's *Ooru Keri*, Ramayya's *Ma Neyara* and Govindareya's *Manavilled A Varamadhye* autobiographies are in Kannada. Mohandas Namishray's *Apne Apne Pinjre* (1995), Omprakash Valmiki's *Joothan: A Dalit's Life* (1997), and Suraj Pal Chauhan's *Triskrat* (2002), Kausalya Baisantri's *Dohra Abhishaap* (2012) and Sheoraj Singh Bechain's *Mera Bachpan Mere Kandhon Par* etc. are Hindi Dalit autobiographies. Balbir Madhopuri's *Changiya Rukh: Against the Night* is a Punjabi Dalit autobiography.

Preferring the mode of personal memoirs above other genres, Dalit writers announced their arrival on the Indian literary scene. Charged with the element of legitimacy of lived-experiences, autobiographies encapsulated the story of the entire Dalit community. Dalit testimonios involve a constant shuffling between the 'I' of the author and the 'We' of the community. Despite the torture of 'relive(ing) all those miseries, torments, neglects, admonitions' (Valmiki, *Joothan*, viii), the dalits favour personal narratives with the aim of inspiring the future generation. Arun Prabha Mukherjee refers the Dalit autobiography to be 'a report card on the condition of people who are now routinely called 'erstwhile untouchables' or 'ex-untouchables'' (*Joothan*, xi). The purpose is not only remembering of the past things as in the mainstream autobiographies, but also shaping and structuring them in such a way as to understand autobiographer's life and the social order that shaped it in order to 'arouse a passion for change' amongst the dalits.

En route the corpus of Dalit literature enlarged with the inclusion of other genres too. Till date, writers have explored almost all possible literary genres — novels, short-stories, poetry, (although drama still is in the cradle) — we have a considerable corpus of Dalit criticism too. Equally laudable is the growing volume of 'translation' of this new body of literature. Due to inaccessibility to English language and also to maintain the authenticity of the narration, the Dalit writers preferred to write in their native tongue. It helped them in reaching out to their people but the age of globalisation demands global readership too. And also it would help the dalits in connecting with the 'dalits' (read 'subalterns') abroad as well their counterparts within India.

It was a happy scene to celebrate the triumph of the once-silenced and erased section of our society. However, the battle was only half-won with their women still bearing the brunt of triple exploitation — caste, class and gender. The 'Dalit among Dalits' as Ruth Manorama labels the Dalit women, expose the lacunae of the Feminist Movement on the one hand and the Dalit Liberation Struggle on the other hand. The former remained confined to the upper class/ caste women and eventually turned out into 'Brahminical Feminism' whereas the Dalit Movement homogenised the caste issue and by ignoring the gender concerns, was essentially patriarchal in approach. In brief, 'The women's movement has in its enthrallment of 'sisterhood' failed to note the 'caste' factor while the Dalit movement has remained patriarchal and sees the Dalit women's oppression merely as a caste oppression' (Anupama Rao, *Gender and Caste*, 4). The politics of caste and gender prevented the Dalit women to get united to make their social and political presence felt. The 'Manuwadi Sanskrit' of the Dalit males and the 'brahminism of the feminist movement' compelled the Dalit women to talk 'differently'. It was due to the incessant efforts of Jyotiba Phule, Dr B.R. Ambedkar and Periyar that the Dalit women realised their haplessness and organised themselves under the banner of various organisations such as Dalit Mahila Federation, National Federation of Dalit Women, All India Dalit Women's Forum, Maharashtra Dalit Women Sangathan, Bahujan Mahila Mahasangha etc. Phule initiated the cause of Dalit women; he not just educated his wife Savitribai but also opened the first school for girls in 1848 in Pune. In the south, Narayan Guru and Periyar worked relentlessly to bring back dignity and self-respect in the lives of Dalit women. Ambedkar too inspired and stirred Dalit women to be the active part of Dalit liberation movements. His speech at the Mahad Satyagraha stimulated much the Dalit women:

> ...The problems of living have to be tackled by men and women together. If men alone undertake this task (annihilation of caste) they will, I have no doubt, take a longer time. If women, however take this up, I believe that the task can be successfully completed sooner...Therefore, you must attend the Parishads. The task of ending Untouchability is a woman's

> question...You must think and realise that you have as much character and purity as a brahman woman. In fact, the courage and will to act that you possess, even the brahman woman lacks...So take a vow that you will not live with the stigma. Give up your old habits,...It is these customs that mark the stigma of untouchability...All those things that mark you as untouchable – you must drop them. The way you drape your saris marks you as untouchable...Similarly, the neckful and handful jewellery marks you...Clothes bring more grace than jewellery...Knowledge and education are not for men alone. They are essential for women too. (Rege, "Debating the Consumption of Dalit 'Autobiographies'", 53-54)

Motivated by such moving words, Urmila Pawar and Meenakshi Moon came up with *Aamhihi Itihaas Ghadavlaa (We also Made History)* in 1989 narrating the struggles of Dalit women involved in the Ambedkarite movement. As in society, in literature too, Dalit women were silenced and made only the 'guest appearance' (Rao). Gopal Guru's seminal essay "Dalit Women Talk Differently" argues for a distinct literature for Dalit women as 'Beneath the call for women's solidarity the identity of the Dalit woman as 'dalit' gets whitewashed'. This proposal was seconded by stalwarts like Sharmila Rege and Anupama Rao. Rege further explicates her dictum of 'casteless gender' and 'genderless caste' explaining how 'the larger identity of sisterhood among all women' subsumes the caste identities (*Writing Caste/Writing Gender*). And conversely, the Dalit male literature severely suffered from the 'excess of caste concern and scarcity of woman question'; the Dalit woman being a 'woman' is neglected, her only identity remains of being a 'Dalit'. To respond and to counter their stereotyped images of the 'victimised sexual being' and a 'sacrificing mother', women like Baby Kamble, Urmila Pawar, Bama, P. Sivakami, Hira Bansode, Meena Gajbhiye etc. declared a war against the biased Feminist and Dalit Movements in India. In their writings, they question their absence as 'individuals', as 'women' caused by 'the unholy nexus between caste and masculinity' (Karan Singh, *Dalitism and Feminism,* 131), contradicting Kancha Illaiah's proposition of 'Dalit patriarchy'.

Using the platform provided by Dalit Women Writings, Dalit women writers explored the various literary genres with autobiographies such as Kumud Pawade's *Antasphot,* Baby Kamble's *Jina Amucha,* Shantabai Kamble's *Majya Jalmachi Chittarkatha,* Urmila Pawar's *Aaydan,* Bama's *Karukku;* short stories like Rajat Rani Meenu's "Sunita" in Hindi, Kusum Meghwal's short stories in Rajasthani; the novels of Kaveri, Sushila Takbhore, Raj Bharati and Tara Parmar in Hindi, P. Sivakami and Bama in Tamil, Daxa Damodara in Gujarati are a few names to be mentioned. However, among all, it was once again the mode of writing personal memoirs that was the favourite. Despite the sameness of the mode, the approach was different. Whereas their males were preoccupied with the caste concern, the women personal narratives to be 'more inward looking as they tend to interrogate the evil practices of dalit community' (Guru, *The Prisons We Broke,* 160). Their memoirs are the protest against 'Dalit patriarchy' and 'social patriarchy'. While Dalit men take the readers outside the community and blame the upper castes for depriving them of their rights, Dalit women conversely adopt a 'look within' approach; they give the readers a clear picture of their community, 'subjugating their selves to a secondary status' (Jain, 286). They are writing against the trend of 'masculinisation of and *savarnisation* of womanhood' which eventually leads to 'a classical exclusion of Dalit womanhood.' Moving out of the four-walls of the household and their personal lives, the dalit women made their community their family and focused upon the edification of the entire caste as a whole. Their female characters are not depraved women but valiant, dynamic not static who 'end the journey of deep darkness and behold dreams of sunrise...they revolt to protect their self-respect...the revolt of Dalit women is not person-centred but society-centred...the courage to fight, resoluteness, rebelliousness are the very essence of their life.' (Lanjewar, 193)

It is indeed commendable to see the writers/readers/critics and researchers taking serious note of Dalit literature and the increasing number of books in the market are evidence to the same. The present book is another significant contribution in the large body of Dalit studies. The exclusive approach to Dalit women autobiographies narrows down the area of reading, simultaneously providing ample opportunity to delve deep into the lives of Dalit women and produce significant results. The contributors of this book have succeeded in doing justice with the topics undertaken for study. Their papers cover a wide-range of writings exploring the various facets of dalit women — from being the 'crushed earth' to being the 'balls bouncing back', from being 'objectified' to the 'ferocious tigresses'. C.B. Bharti writes that "The aim of Dalit literature is protest against the established system which is based on injustice and exposes the evil and hypocrisy of the upper caste." (Bharti, 34)

Present book is an anthology of twenty-one well-crafted and scholarly articles by erudite scholars. First paper by Professor D. Amalraj deals with how illiterate Dalit women have been taken for granted by patriarchal system belonging not only to the higher caste but also to the Dalits. In this regard, the hapless and unfortunate Dalit woman becomes a prey to the patriarchy. Thangam in P. Sivakami's *The Grip of Change* has become a victim of man's lustful snare for being a Dalit woman. Thangam, the protagonist, is not an individual but a type and there are many Thangams in the Dalit community facing disgraceful treatment for being a childless widow and Dalit woman. She has to cope with the situations in which she is placed by reconciling herself to her fate. She has no other option except living as a sexually abused woman and as the third wife of her Dalit leader, Kathamuthu.

Second paper is written by Dr Irum Alvi. She explores Dalit women's experiences of social rejection. It deals with these social experiences and the connection between social rejection and creativity. It posits that creative Dalit women writer embrace notions of sovereignty and indulge in creative writing following such experiences of social rejection by searching for evidence from their autobiographical works. The paper focuses more specifically on Urmila Pawar, a Dalit woman writer; concentrating on the text of her autobiography *Aaydan* which is an account of three generations as well as her own experiences which the paper posits fueled her creativity helping her become a renowned feminist Dalit writer.

Third paper, written by Dr Archana Bhattacharjee, explores various issues such as social injustices, patriarchal tradition and gender discrimination and its impact on the marginalised Dalit community, particularly women in *Sangati*, the autobiographical work of Bama. As a member of the Dalit community, she herself has gone through the entire order she talks about so convincingly and explicitly. But her experience has also shown her that despite all exploitation and discriminations, women of her community are still capable of fighting for their rights and creating a respectable position of their own in the society if they are provided with the tools of education and awareness. She ends her work on a positive note and gives out a clarion call to all members of her own community to wake up and demands for a life of dignity and respect in the present society.

The fourth paper by Dr Sigma G.R. is a critical study of a Dalit autobiography *Viramma: Life of an Untouchable*. She has analysed in her paper how marriage plays an important role in shaping the identity of a Dalit woman. Viramma has to suffer since her birth as she was not accepted whole-heartedly in her own home and after her marriage she has to face many problems. Gender issues, problems of child marriage, and subsequent problems have been studied by Dr Sigma G.R. in her paper.

The fifth paper is written by Dr Himanginee Kaushik. Her paper is about the outcaste women and their exploitation not only by the high caste people but also by their own community. It explores how a woman is suppressed in male dominating society after the death of her husband. It is about the struggle of a widow woman, Thangam for her rights in her husband's property but she is denied by her brothers-in-law as she bears no child but she does not succumb and continues her struggle for her rights.

The sixth paper of this anthology is written by Dr Deepika Rani. Her paper seeks to explore the crushed identity and hellish status of Dalit females and it attempts to reach to their soul-numbing incidents through the critical study of Mukta Sarvagod's autobiography *Closed Doors*. A Dalit woman has to bear all the tortures of upper caste society and she is a prey of patriarchy in her own community. She is marginalised and subordinated by upper class men, upper class women and males of her own community. Thus, she finds herself in the clutches of unjust taboos and imposed identity as secondary being as well as a triple marginalised being. Some women of her community are conscious and aware of this condition of Dalit women and they want to liberate themselves from the lowest social stratum. Mukta Sarvagod, with some women, efforts to deconstruct the imposed customs and imposed identity so that Dalit woman could live her life with dignity.

The seventh paper by Guni Vats entitled "Breaking the Margins: Analysing *The Prisons We Broke* as a Testimony of Oppression and Resistance" attempts to look beyond the established prison bars and screams with Kamble of the injustice inflicted by the self-acclaimed superior section of society on the very natives of the land of Maharashtra. *The Prisons We Broke* is a work carved by a strong headed untouchable woman who changed the meaning of 'self' with her autobiography, she spoke for her entire community. The autobiography does not attempt to gain sympathy but commands respect for the darkest section of society which rose to an intellectual standard with its hard work and resilience. It is the true saga of oppression and resistance and the paper analyses it precisely. It is the first autobiography of a Dalit woman that changed the face of Dalit women in Indian literature forever.

The next paper i.e. eighth one written by Suruchi Sharma entitled "A Doubly Oppressed Voice in Urmila Pawar's *The Weave of My Life: A Dalit Woman's Memoir*" is devoted to assess the real problems of the Mahar women at Adgaon village in Konkan Region of Maharashtra. She explores the lifelong struggle of Urmila Pawar since her childhood. After the death of her father, her mother had to weave baskets from bamboos and she and her siblings had to sell the baskets bunking from their schools. The problems of utter poverty, destitute, caste discrimination and male dominance after her marriage also have been explored in her paper.

Kusum Kanger's paper is the ninth one that takes up the issues of Dalit subjugation and patriarchy in Baby Kamble's *The Prisons We Broke*. In this paper she has observed the pains and sufferings of the Mahar Dalit men and women in Baby Kamble's village, Veergaon, in Maharashtra. It foregrounds the hegemonised state of the Dalit women who make up leeway for their liberty but they don't have better life than animals. Baby Kamble has to work for Dalit women's emancipation and she raised voice against the patriarchal setup, exploitation and suppression of women.

Next paper entitled "Bama's *Karukku*: (Re)-Reading Dalit History in South India and (Re)-Interpreting Dalit-(Wo)Man Identity" written by Ramanuj Mahato highlights Dalit history in South India in Bama's eyes, penetrating the deeper issues of a Dalit woman's individual struggle, representing all marginalised Dalit-women against the patriarchy, the mainstream society, the Christian authority and intra-dalit dogmatism. Bama's fight which is tantamount to Daedalus and Icarus's flight unveils the transgression as well as empowerment of a dalit-woman for breaking the labyrinth of existing dogmas of present mainstream ruling culture.

Saikat Guha's paper registers infinity of pain of the Dalit or tribal classes in the pastoral setting of the Malabar in C.K. Janu's unfinished autobiography *Mother Forest*. It investigates the problems of C.K. Janu and her mother after the death of Janu's father leaving behind five children. Janu's working as a babysitter at the house of a school teacher in Vellamunda and toiling in the agriculture field at a low wages has been explored in his paper. It highlights that Dalit women's conditions were worse than their husbands. They had to do all the household chores, taking care of the kids and hard manual labour like digging, sowing, preparing the fields etc.

The twelfth paper of the book is written by Dwaipayan Mitra. His paper analyses and assess the saga of a Dalit woman, Thanagm's exploitation. In *The Grip of Change* P. Sivakami retrieves the voice of a Dalit woman suppressed under the tripartite marginalisation of being a woman, a Dalit and a subaltern. She inveighs against the various atrocious and obfuscated systems that hardly offer any scope of emancipation for the Dalit woman. Through this text Sivakami fires a salvo at multiple facets of dominations. Yet the autobiography does not end up being a blackish documentation of untold sufferings but chalks out the path for salvation that is still available within the citadel of Dalit patriarchy.

The next paper written by Mohd. Anwar Hussain Khan explores gender-based prejudices in the Dalit community as depicted by Bama in *Sangati*. It studies the hierarchy of social status with special reference to Dalit women. At the workplace a dalits woman has to face casteism from the upper caste landlords and at home, the Dalit patriarchy tortures her. This double subversion displaces her situation from mainstream feminism and necessitates a new theory solely dedicated to the Dalit women.

The fourteenth chapter written by Himanshu Sharma tries to explore Kumud Pawde's autobiography *Antaspot: Thoughtful Outburst* and through this paper he has narrated how being a Mahar, Kumud has to face many problems in the purported casteist mentality of the caste-ridden society. Kusum Pawde's problems in her choosing Sanskrit as an elective subject for her studies and getting a job after doing her M.A. in Sanskrit have been explored in this paper. The exploitation of dalits from the upper caste people also has been analysed in this paper.

The fifteenth paper of the anthology is written by Guni Vats. She analyses in her paper that Kausalya Baisantri's *Dohra Abhishaap* — a social narrative — criticises the hypocrisy of society which marginalises a part of its own and further corners the weaker sex. Through her words Baisantri goes on a self-introspective journey which does not blame but strives to carve a place for the Dalit women in Indian society. Her autobiography is modern in every sense of the word. She does not shy away from depicting the filth in all its ugliness and the use of colloquial language brings her closer to the common man whom she wrote for. Kausalya sets a platter where she serves what she received without any ornamentation. Kausalya's autobiography is not a chronological social narrative but an unprohibited string of events that find a place in the order she remembers them. Her autobiography is the innocent memoir of a girl who learns her caste and its place in the society and struggles to establish a respectable place for herself.

The sixteenth paper is contributed by Pradip Sarikhada. He has explored the problems of Phoolan Devi how she lived in utter penury, under constant fear both in her home and outside and under the shadow of tyranny of the people of her village. She had to become a bandit to avenge her enemies who had made her life a hell. Poverty, fear, rape, tyranny and revenge etc. themes have been analysed by him in this paper.

The next paper by Dr Namita Panda tries to explore the Viramma's narratives of life in her autobiography *Viramma: Life of an Untouchable*. She explores how the landlords exploited the serfs under *jajmani* system. She has explored how Viramma's family lived in astute poverty without the basic amenities in their lives. Child labour, patriarchal chains, dalit women's molestation, caste prejudices, dalits' exploitation etc. themes have been explored in her paper.

The eighteenth paper to this anthology is contributed by Dr Sumitra Singh. In her paper she explores the struggle of Urmila Pawar and her community how they had to live a life of subjugation and exploitation in the utter poverty. The hardships of her family and Dalit community have been explored by her in this paper.

The next paper of the book goes to Dr M.B. Gaijan. His paper is an attempt to explore Dalit women's autobiographies from two perspectives. He discusses the selected Dalit women's autobiographies and the sufferings of dalits at different levels. The paper includes two categories of autobiographies. The first part includes the first generation of works. In this part Shantabai Dani and Kaushalya Baisantri's works are considered for study. The second part includes contemporarily Dalit autobiographies by Sushila Tankbhoare and Bama.

The twentieth paper by Dr Aparna Lanjewar Bose is a study of three generations of women represented by her maternal grandmother, her mother and the writer herself. She explores the Dalit patriarchy and beautifully delineates how dalit women are doubly accursed in Koshalya Baisantri's autobiography *Dohra Abhishaap*. She finds it a true Dalit autobiography that lashes out at the anathema of casteism, sexism and classicism. The three generational women not just become the building blocks and pillars, cementing women to women bonding, but also education and awareness in the community that till date is a hapless victim of nepotism, jabber and deceit of the caste Hinduism.

The last paper of the book is written by Dr Narendra Kumar. He explores the themes of religion, caste and identity in Bama's *Karukku*. The paper is an effort to explore the corruption, caste prejudices, untouchability and gender discrimination in this autobiography. Dr Kumar throws light on the nepotism on the basis of religion and at the life for the Dalit women through this autobiography. The paper analyses how life even for children is very difficult and they have to work in order to fill their empty stomachs.

Though no introduction can sum up the contents of any book fully, yet I have tried to cover it to the most possible extent. This anthology paves way to some other Dalit women's autobiographies like Shantabai Kamble's *Majya Jalmachi Chittrakatha*, Shantabai Dani's *Ratran Deen Amha*, Gunabai Gadekar's *Samritigandha*, Janabai Girhe's *Maran Kalan*, Mangla Kevle's *Jagayach Pratyek Sekand*, Vimal More's *Teen Dagdachi Chul*, Sushila Patekar's *Farfat*, Yashdara Gaikwad's *Majhi Mi*, Vibha Rahi's *Vish Kanya*, Sunita Arlikar *Hiraknicham Binhad*, Asha Thorat's *Angatha Te Sahi*, Sujata Lokhande's *Majh Narshing, Shodh Astitvacha*, Rajasbai Gaikwad's *Me Ahe Hi Ashi Ahe*, Shanta Gawai's *Mati Bhide Aabhala*, Lalini Ladke's *Satyashodhakachi Varas*, Najubai Gawit's *Aador*, Parvatibai Bhore's *Eka Ranranichi Katha* etc.

I hope that this book will be very advantageous and helpful equally for teachers, researchers, students and Dalit activists both India and abroad and will prove a distinctive work that offers a comprehensive and in-depth critical analysis of many Dalit women's autobiographies. I express my sincere thanks and deep sense of gratitude to Mr Amit Garg, Managing Director, Kalpaz Publications, New Delhi and the whole publication team for the fastidious copy-editing and prudent shepherding and judicious scrutinisation of the manuscript. Thanks a ton again to Mr Garg to give me a privilege to publish this book by his reputed publishing house and for his expert assistance at the different stages of the book handling in the course of publishing. There are some debts which can never be paid. I, from top to toe, am indebted to my mother, wife and siblings for their unfailing and unspoken tree-like support. A shower of paternal affection to Soumya, my heart!

Last but not the least; let me acknowledge an internationally acclaimed Dalit writer, Urmila Pawar. She has published many books on dalits literature and she has won many awards and honours like Sahitya Sanskriti Mandal Maharashtra Rajya Puraskar, Asmitadarsh Puraskar, Shakuntala Neme Puraskar, V.C. Gujar Puraskar, Priyadarshani Academy Award, Padmashri Vikhe Patil Puraskar, Matoshri Bhimabai Ambedkar Puraskar, Maharashtra Foundation Granth Puraskar, Dalit Mitra Award, Soi Sammaan etc. I would like to place on records my heart-felt gratitude to her for writing the foreword to this book from her hectic schedule.

Dr Bijender Singh
Email:drbijendersingh@india.com
Mob. 91-9992873801

Notes on the Contributors

1. **Professor D. Amalraj** is a retired Professor of English. He began his teaching career at Kandasamy Naidu College for Men from October 1969. He retired in May 2004 as a selection grade faculty member. He has served as Head and Research Supervisor in the Department of English, Vivekanandha College for Arts and Sciences (W), Elayampalyam, in district Namakkal in Tamil Nadu. He has worked as a part-time Professor in the Department of English at Bishop Appasamy College of Arts and Science in Coimbatore. He has published his research oriented articles in international journals of repute. Thirty-two scholars have successfully completed their M. Phil. degree under his guidance. His areas of interest are Dalit Literature, Indian Writing in English, Diasporic Literature and Gender Studies. He has brought out many Zazzler Study Aid Series on English Literature. The revised edition of his book *Research Methodology for Literary Research* has been published from Innovation Scientific Research Publications, Salem in 2015.

2. **Dr Irum Alvi**, M.A. (Gold Medalist), Ph.D. is presently working as Faculty in HEAS (English) Department, and Assistant Dean, Applied Sciences, Rajasthan Technical University, Kota. She is In-Charge, Professional Communication Skills and Faculty In-Charge, Training

and Placement Department and has organised several lectures and workshops for the students. She has a professional experience of more than ten years in Academics and Training in the areas of Professional Communication Skills and Soft Skills. She has published several papers in different journals, presented papers at National and International Seminars, Conferences and Workshops, as a Resource Person, Guest Speaker and Keynote Speaker. Her research interests include Post-Colonial Writings, Diaspora Studies, Professional Communication Skills, Technical Communication Skills, Soft Skills and American and Indian Literature. She is Editorial Committee Member of University Newsletter, College magazine, brochure etc. She knows several languages including Persian, Urdu, Hindi and English.

3. **Dr Archana Bhattacharjee** is an Associate Professor and Head in the Department of English, Kakojan College Jorhat, Assam which is affiliated with Dibrugarh University. She did her M.A. in English Literature from Gauhati University and M.Phil. from Vinayaka Missions University, Tamil Nadu and holds a Ph.D. Degree in English Literature. She has presented 66 papers at various National and International Seminars and Conferences both within and outside the country. She has published more than 30 research papers also in various journals and books. She is the joint editor of an ISSN journal "Emerging Echoes." She is also in the Editorial and Advisory board of four international journals. Her areas of interest are Gender Studies, Post-Colonial Writing, Indian Writing in English and British Literature.

4. **Dr Sigma G.R.** is an Assistant Professor at Department of English in VTMNSS College, Dhanuvachapuram, Trivandrum, Kerala. She has nine years of teaching experience both in national and international colleges. She worked for three years as a lecturer in English

under Ministry of Manpower in Sultanate of Oman. Dr Sigma's few poems were published by American Literary Press in Wordchimes Anthology. She has also published few articles in Journals and Newspapers. She is currently working as an Editorial Board Member of TJPRC Journals, as a Reviewer in 'The Criterion' journal and as an Advisory Board Member in 'The Expression' journal.

5. **Dr Himanginee Kaushik** is an Assistant Professor in RJLB Govt. Polytechnic College, Loharu. She has done her B.Ed. (Spl.), M. Ed. (Spl.) and M.A. in English from Kurukshetra University, Kurukshetra. She has done her Ph.D. in English from M.D.S. University, Ajmer. She has published some papers in different international journals and edited anthologies. She is an Associate Editor of *The Expression: An International Multidisciplinary e-Journal.* Her areas of interest are Diasporic Literature, Gender Studies and Indian Writing in English.

6. **Dr Deepika Rani** (M.A., M.Ed, and Ph.D.) is presently working as an English mistress in Government Sr. Sec. School, Abulkhurana, Malout, Punjab. She has rendered her services as a lecturer in English in Dashmesh Girls College, Badal and D.A.V. Sr. Sec. School, Malout, Punjab. She has seven years teaching experience. Her publications include seven research papers and six poems and review of a book. She is a member of an international e-journal, 'The Expression'. Her areas of interest are Indian English Writings, Postcolonial Writings, Feminism and Dalit literature. Her active participation in National and International Seminars has enriched her knowledge. She has won many prizes in academics as well as in cultural activities at various levels.

7. **Guni Vats** is an independent researcher and a professional writer. She has completed her Master's degree in English Literature from Central University of Rajasthan and she has earned the Bachelor's (Honours

in English Literature) from the University of Delhi. She is a keen reader, budding researcher and an enthusiastic writer who takes immense pleasure in looking at diverse aspects of life from a psychoanalytical bent. She loves to experiment with themes, subject and writing styles. She is keen to research on the Indian women writers and carves a niche for them in the predominantly masculine world. She is currently attempting a thesis tracing the feminist waves in Indian literature and analysing them through translations. She has a few publications to her credit.

8. **Suruchi Sharma** (UGC-NET) is an Assistant Professor in R.K.S.D. College, Kaithal, Haryana. She has done her P.G. from K.M.V. College, Jalandhar, Punjab. She is pursuing Ph.D. from NIMS University, Jaipur. She has presented her papers in many national and international seminars and conferences. Her papers have been published in national and international journals and seminar/conference proceedings and edited anthologies.

9. **Kusum Kanger** is an Assistant Professor in B.A.R. Janta College Kaul, Kaithal, Haryana. She is a Ph.D. Research-scholar in NIMS University, Jaipur. She has earned her M.Phil. from Kurukshetra University, Kurukshetra. She has presented and published her papers in many national and international seminars and conferences. Her papers have been published in many national and international journals and edited anthologies.

10. **Ramanuj Mahato** is a Lecturer in Chitta Mahato Memorial College, Jargo under Sidho-Kanho-Birsha University, Purulia, West Bengal. With excellent academic background, he did his M.A. from Banaras Hindu University, Varanasi and he has qualified in UGC–NET twice. He has already published many national and international journals. His areas of interest are Cultural Studies, Indian English Writing, Diasporic Literature and Postcolonial Literature.

11. **Saikat Guha** has submitted his M.Phil. dissertation on the poetry of Northeast India at the Department of English, University of North Bengal, India. He has been a Guest Lecturer in English at a general degree college. His articles have been published in various journals including *Rupkatha, Muse India, Labyrinth, Lapis-Lazuli, The Literary Voyage, Singularities, Rock Pebbles* and *The Apollonian,* and some edited volumes. His two edited anthologies have been published on Feminist and Postcolonial approaches to Literature. His areas of interest include: Poetry, Indian Literature, Postcolonialism and Postcolonial Literature, Feminism, Folklore, Cultural Studies and Philosophy.

12. **Dwaipayan Mitra** (CBSC-NET and JRF, West Bengal SET) is an M.Phil. Research Scholar at Jadavpur University, West Bengal. He has completed his M.A. from Rabindra Bharati University. He is a budding scholar who has keen interest in research. He has attended many UGC-sponsored seminars. His areas of interest are Postcolonial Studies, New Literature, American Literature and Indian Dalit Literature.

13. **Mohd. Anwar Hussain Khan** (CBSE NET and JRF) Ph.D. Research Scholar at Punjabi University, Patiala. He did his M.A. from Punjabi University regional centre. He has served as an English lecturer at Punjabi University, Baba Jogipeer Neighbourhood campus, Ralla, Mansa. His area of interest is social marginalisation. He has several research publications under his name.

14. **Himanshu Sharma** has done his M.A. in English from Regional Campus, GNDU, Jalandhar. He has done M.Phil. in English Literature from Department of English, GNDU, Amritsar. He is submitted his Ph.D. thesis in Himachal Pradesh University, Shimla. His areas of interest are Indian Diasporic Literature, Linguistics, Literary Theory Especially Deconstruction and Post Colonialism.

15. **Pradip Sarikhada** is a Ph.D. English Scholar at Rai University, Ahmedabad, Gujarat. He has done his M.A. from Saurashtra University, Rajkot. His areas of interest are Indian Writing in English, Diaspora Literature and Dalit Studies. He has published his research papers in a few national and international journal of repute.

16. **Dr Namita Panda** is currently working as an Assistant Professor in English at KIIT, Bhubaneswar. Dr Panda obtained her Ph.D. from Sambalpur University in 2013. She has over eleven years experience in teaching at different Engineering and Management colleges. She has published many articles in national and international journals. Her areas of interest are Indian Writing in English, Diaspora Literature, Eco-criticism and Dalit Literature.

17. **Dr Sumitra Singh** is an Assistant Professor at Amity University, Noida, India. She is Editor of International Research Journal of Humanities, Engineering and Pharmaceutical Sciences. She holds Ph.D. in Afro-American Literature. She has presented her research papers/articles in around 65 national and international conferences/seminars and workshops. She has published many papers in various national and international journals of repute. She is also associated with various Community Outreach activities.

18. **Dr M.B. Gaijan** is the Head, Department of English, Samaldas Arts College, Shri M.K. Bhavnagar University, Bhavnagar, Gujarat. He is teaching English language and Literature at U.G. Level since last 25 years. He is also a visiting faculty for P.G. Department. He is a Ph.D. guide. He is a counsellor of Dr Baba Saheb Ambedkar Open University, Gujarat and IGNOU. He has also worked as the coordinator of IGNOU. He has presented more than 60 of his papers in various national/ international seminar/conferences especially on Dalit Studies, Women Writings, ICT, Diaspora Literature and

Indian Writings. His more than 58 papers are published/reprinted in reputed journals/books. His poems and translations are also published in Gujarati/Hindi and English. He has contributed four books. He is the member of the editorial board of the journals, *"Shyamal"*, *"Hayati"*, *"Unheard Melody" Sangharsh e-journal* and *Creative Space: International Journal*. He is the author of *"Dalit Literary Tradition in Gujarat: A Critical Study"*. He has co-edited books are *"Dalit Literature: Critical Exploration"*, *Pristine Land: Gujrati Dalit Literature"*, *"Indian Women writers: A Critical Reinterpretation."* Dr M. B. Gaijan is a poet, critic, translator, editor and teacher. His translations are published in Hindi and English. He has guided and evaluated M.Phil. and Ph.D. theses. He has chaired the sessions in different conferences.

19. **Dr Aparana Lanjewar Bose** (b. 1971) is an Associate Professor in the Department of English, English and Foreign Language University, Hyderabad (A Central University). She is a trilingual writer, poet, translator and activist. She taught English literature at University of Nagpur for seven years and then for a decade at the Postgraduate teaching Department of Mumbai University before joining EFL University, Hyderabad. She specialises in American Literature, British Literature, African American Literature, Revolutionary and Marginal Literatures and Contemporary women's writings. She also has a degree in law. She participated as a resource person in several major national and international platforms both in India and abroad. Her study tours, research and social activism led her to visit severally countries like Germany, France, England, Switzerland, Sweden, Zimbabwe, South Africa and Thailand to speak on both literary and social concerns. Widely travelled both in India and abroad, she was invited as a member of the Sahitya Academi's writers and scholars' delegation to Moscow and Istanbul at the Moscow International Book Fair 2009. She has published several papers and

three books which includes a collection of her book of poems in English titled 'In the Days of Cages'. She has written a collection of Hindi-Urdu poems titled "Kuch Yu Bhi" and a collection of translations from Marathi to English titled "Red Slogans on the Green Grass." She is primarily a poet who writes poetry in Hindi, Urdu and English. She is the daughter of renowned Marathi poet and critic Dr Jyoti Lanjewar.

20. **Dr Narendra Kumar** is a Principal at Stani Memorial P.G. College, Jaipur, Rajasthan. He has worked at many reputed institutes at different capacities like an Assistant Professor, Head of Department and Principal like Shankara Institute of Technology, Sri Balaji College of Engineering and Technology, J. D. College of Technical Education, Jaipur and Rajasthan P.G. College, Chirawa, Jhunjhunu, Rajasthan. He has published his papers in many international journals and edited anthologies. He is a multi-talented personality who has many degrees at bachelor, master and doctorate level like B.A., B.Sc., BJMC (Journalism), MBA (HRM and ITM), M. Sc. (CS), M. Ed. (CE-UK, USA, Ph.D. in three subjects — English, Education and Management. He has good command on English, Hindi, French, German and Russian equally. He has guided many Ph.D. and M. Phil. candidates and has evaluated many theses and dissertations.

1

Sex Knows No Caste: A Study of P. Sivakami's *The Grip of Change*

Professor D. Amalraj

All human beings are God's noblest and highest creations and as such, all are equal to one another. Shakespeare has greatly glorified God's creation of man in his play *Hamlet*:

> What a piece of work is a man! How noble in reason!
> How infinite in faculty, in form and in moving!
> How expressive and admirable in words and deeds!
> How angelic and god-like in appearance!
> He is simply the beauty of the world and the paragon of animals! (3:2.41-45).

Social set-up, attitudes, the ways of living, and cultural habits have caused discrimination among human beings in their status. As a result, people are discriminated as the superior and the inferior, the high and the low, the great and the small, and the rich and the poor. It is not divine but man-made. It has been inerasable from the faces of Indian societies since time immemorial. It has become more and more prominent and acute even in this computer age.

People born in higher caste do not realise that no one has any right to prevent the other from enjoying his rights of living in dignity and happiness. Neither have them any superiority to claim over the other the socially unfortunate. But they consider themselves superior in all respects. They always look down upon the people born in lower caste as the inferior, treat them as untouchables and keep them at distance. Swami Satchidananda in his *Biography of Swami Satchidananda* has also echoed the attitudes of the people of highborn:

> No person is an untouchable during his sojourn on earth; nor is one human being inferior to the other in his status and his position. Differences come, not with the work which man does, not with the caste into which man is born, not with the status which man occupies, but with the attitude of his mind. (qtd. in Jaisre p. 129)

People who belong to the higher strata of society do not still consider the people as their equal just because they were born in lower strata of society. Gone are the days during which the higher caste people had not allowed the people of lower caste, the Dalit in particular, even to cross their streets. Even if they were allowed to walk through the streets, they were not permitted to go wearing shirts on their bodies and having chapels on their feet.

Nowadays, such restrictions have gone with the wind as the modern day Dalit men and women are equally educated, professionally well-settled, and economically advanced and independent. If these people are neatly dressed, it is very difficult to identify and fix their social status. There are still some constraints on the freedom of these socially marginalised people. They are not allowed to participate on equal terms along with others in social and religious functions conducted in public if they are identified as Dalit. Nor are they allowed to enter into the temples of worship because they are considered to be untouchables. The great sufferers among them are the uneducated Dalit men at the hands of the upper caste people. But the worst affected of all the Dalit people are their women at the hands of patriarchy of both castes. The physical and mental suffering meted out to the Dalit women is purely sex oriented.

Through the ages, fictionalising the Dalit and their social predicament has been left to the writers belonging to the higher strata of society. As these writers could give only the second hand information about the plight of the Dalit, the bitter reality of the lives of the Dalit people has not reached the reading public and so there has not been any awareness in their minds. This kind of situation has necessitated the Dalit literary artist both men and women to take to writing and highlight the problems of the Dalit. Their literary contribution in English has paved the way for the birth of Dalit Literature in Indian Writing in English.

Many Dalit writers of both the genders have brought to limelight the greatest predicament of the Dalit through their fictional works. Martand Kaushik in his article titled *Dalit Literature Goes Global,* which appeared in *Sunday Times* of Times of India, has stated the popularity of Dalit Literature all over the world:

> Over the past few decades, a Dalit Literary Movement has been giving the readers a first-hand experience of how the Dalit community lives in the society. It has in turn made the Dalit writers re-script the conceptions of Indian society and history while challenging the prevailing literary conventions. (5 April, 2015)

P. Sivakami is one of such reputed Dalit women writers. Being a woman and a Dalit, she has given truthful account of real happenings in the lives of the Dalit people. She has shown in all her novels her great concern to the untold plight of the Dalit women and their status of misfortunes in the society. The novelist has focussed her attention mainly on the attitudes of Patriarchy belonging to both the higher caste and the Dalit towards the body of the Dalit woman in

The Grip of Change, an English translation of her Tamil novel *Pazhaiyana Kazhithalum*. The writer of the article has pursued his study on the topic "Sex Knows No Caste" with particular reference to a Dalit woman character Thangam, the protagonist of the novel.

Man considers every woman only as a sexual object. He does not make any differentiation among women as far as sexual relationship is concerned. It does not matter to him whether the woman with whom he is having sex is an Indian or American or whether she is born in a higher caste or lower caste, and whether she belongs to his religion or some other different religion. She should be a woman of sexual appeal with all her bodily assets intact. Naomi Wolf in her book *The Beauty Myth* has endorsed this view about women:

> Men are visually aroused by women and her bodies. They are less sensitive to their arousal by women's personalities . . . while women are less visually aroused but more emotionally aroused. . . . Men look at women's bodies, evaluate and move on but their own bodies are not looked at, evaluated, and taken or passed over. (1997, n.pag.)

A higher caste man treats the Dalit man and woman as unequal beings and he always keeps them at a distance. But when he feels attracted sexually towards a woman, he does not see whether she is a higher caste woman or an untouchable. He is more concerned with the assets of her body than with her caste. He always waits for a chance to go ahead with his sexual exploitation of any helpless woman. Since such an immoral act is carried out in secrecy, the woman affected goes silent accepting her fate for want of economical support. Every Dalit man should be a real protector of the woman of his caste, but he also appears to be a wolf in sheep's clothing.

All men are not Jekylls and sexually starving. But the fact cannot be denied or hidden that there are also Hydes, indulging in sexual abuse for pleasures outside their homes. Happening in real life is indigestible and it is quite contrary to the expected belief. Men of both castes take advantage of the helplessness of the uneducated women, in particular Dalit women, and fulfill their sexual urge. Such men are only exceptions but exceptions become more prominent in society because of their lustful activities. P. Sivakami brings home this truth through the predicament of Dalit women character in *The Grip of Change*. Though it is a fiction, it is based on real life incidents and as such, it is only the reflection of life being lived in society and how a woman for being a Dalit is taken for granted.

Thangam is a childless and an illiterate Dalit widow. After the death of her husband, she has every right to her husband's property. Her brothers-in-law should be for her welfare but they are not. They are after her body for their sexual gratification. When she demands her right to be fulfilled, they are ready to give her the right, provided she sexually satisfies their needs as and when they desire. She refuses to concede to their unethical demand. As she longs to have an economic independence without the support of her brothers-in-law, she comes out of her house. She then begins her earning as a labourer in the fields of Paranjothi Udayar, an upper class landlord. But Udayar abuses her sexually after seeing her 'an orphaned like status.' Hence, her life is like 'falling from frying pan into fire.' She has to remain silent, reconciling to her situation in life.

However, Thangam's brothers-in-law come to know of Udayar's sexual relationship with her and bring it to the knowledge of the wife of Udayar. As a result of this revelation, the brothers of Udayar's wife beat her black and blue. She escapes from them and seeks refuge in the house of Kathamuthu, the Dalit leader. She apprises him of her predicament at the house of her husband, at the place of her work and her beatings at the hands of Udayar's brothers-in-law:

> My husband's brothers have tried to force me [for sexual relationship] but I have never given any room for it. They refuse to give me my husband's land for being a barren woman, but they have wanted me to be a whore for them! I would not give in . . . Udayar has also raped me in his sugarcane field. I have to remain silent because Udayar is my paymaster. (7)

Thangam should have stayed in the house of her husband accepting the conditions of her brothers-in-law. Had she remained where she should be, she would not have gone through sexual torture outside her home and met with public disgrace. Udayar should have remained content with his marital bliss but he did not. He looked at Thangam not as a Dalit woman but as a sex object to be handled emotionally and physically, and enjoyed satisfactorily.

> The place of shelter of Kathamuthu turns to be a place of her further sexual abuse. Instead of being a protector of the woman of his Dalit community, Kathamuthu has raped her while she is asleep in the kitchen. Even her words, "You are like a brother to me" (93) fail to prevent him from raping her. Since then, she has no courage to see his face at all. It is only his daughter Gowri who is educated identifies in her father the real character. She reveals her inner self, saying "Dogs! Dogs in this house! Shameless as dogs!" (93).

Regarding Thangam's hapless situation as a Dalit widow, Ginni Rani in her article "Articulating the Voiceless: A Study of P. Sivakami's *The Grip of Change*" has summed up:

> The protagonist of the novel Thangam is a poor parachi widow and she suffers not only for being a Dalit but also for being a woman, an OTHER too. Ironically, she is victimised even by her own Dalit community. Thus,

> she faces triple marginalisation such as economic oppression, gender subordination and cast discrimination. Being helplessly caught in the jaws of patriarchy, she is abused, raped and beaten rapidly. (684)

Kathamuthu first finds fault with Thangam for her mute surrender to her being sexually exploited by the higher caste man. But he does not feel guilty when he rapes Thangam who sees his house as a haven and in him a compassionate saviour. He is a man living with two wives in Kangavalli and Nagamani. Because of his constant sexual abuse of her, she cannot but be his third wife. Passivity in the Dalit uneducated women is mainly responsible for their sexual predicament.

Men who want to enjoy premarital and extra marital sexual relationship with women of their choice willingly or by force do not decide their women partners on the basis of caste. Their immediate sexual need is greater than searching for women belonging to their caste. Hence, sex knows no caste, no nationality, and no religion but it needs two souls of opposite genders. Man should neither give too much importance to a woman belonging to his status nor to a woman who is higher than his status. He should not also take a woman belonging to the lower strata of society for granted in his love making just because she will not become vociferous over his violation. But at the same time, he should not violate the cultural norms of society, and religion in enjoying sex with any woman he prefers. Time is the greatest healer and all women should wait for time to get rid of the ills of the society.

Works Cited

Jaisre, V. "Untouchability: Man-made Discrimination among Human beings in Mulk Raj Anand's *Coolie*." *Language of India.* 12.4. (2012): 128-134. Web.

Kaushik, Martand TNN. "Dalit Literature Goes Global." *Sunday Times: The Times of India.* 5 Apr. 2015. Print.

Rani, Ginni. "Articulating the Voiceless: A Study of P. Sivakami's *The Grip of Change.*" *Research Scholar: An International Refereed e-Journal of Literary Explorations.* 2.11. (2014): 683-687. Web.

Sivakami, P. *The Grip of Change and Author's Notes.* Trans. P. Sivakami. Chennai: Orient Blackswan, 2006. Print.

Wolf, Naomi. *The Beauty Myth: How Images of Beauty are Used against Women.* Toronto: Vintage Canada, 1997. Print.

2

Dalit Experiences of Social Rejection and Creativity in Urmila Pawar's Autobiography *Aaydan/The Weave of My Life*

Dr Irum Alvi

Many Dalit Literary Women writers have given an expression to their experiences of social rejection in their autobiographical works. The present paper intends to deal with these experiences and search for the correlation between such "social experiences" and "creativity" if any. As the evidence of this connection is subjective, the paper deals with the psychological processes that might help in comprehending this connection. Although a great deal of research has been done on social rejection which points out the various harmful and injurious effects of social rejection on one's performance, this paper posits the implications of the notion that there exists an association between social rejection and creativity using the text of a renowned Dalit woman writer's autobiographical work in the light of modern researches.

Urmila Pawar, a Maharashtrian literary writer of numerous novels and short stories, portrays several incidents of social rejection due to casteism. Her autobiography *'Aaydan'* (2003), translated by Maya Pundit as *'The Weave of My Life: A Dalit Woman's Memoir'* is replete with such accounts. The 'Preface' sheds light on the theme of social rejection and the need to transcend it, as Maya Pundit refers to the text as "'a complex narrative of a gendered individual who looks at the world initially from her location within the caste but who also goes on *to transcend the caste identity...(my emphasis)*(XVII).

Pawar portrays her desire to transcend the caste identity and need for the individuation of self which seems to motivate her to partake in endeavours of a creative nature, social rejection even initiating a psychological course that encourages her to indulge in acts of a creative nature like literary writing, instead of suppressing it. Pawar depicts social rejection and the consequences of social rejection faced by the members of her caste especially the women. The images of social encounters permeate her entire work and she displays they are critically important in a Dalit individual's daily life. She states "What the writer writes about is social reality and not his/her individual life" (342). Social rejection is a common social reality for Dalit women. She narrates one such incident of social reality and rejection when she was asked to carry the baskets made by her mother to the members of the Upper caste and forced to stand outside the house. She recalls how the baskets were washed when she put them down, by sprinkling *"water on them to wash away the pollution, and only then would they touch them"* (65). She narrates another incident of social rejection when coins were dropped *"in my hands from above, avoiding contact as if their hands would have burnt if they touched me"*.(65)

Pawar recalls with great poignancy an incident of social rejection when after her marriage, she went to Ratnagiri and was forced to vacate the house and the cause was *"one point: caste"* (206). The negative consequence experienced by her after being rejected is seen to be prevailing and immediate. Initially, she narrates how for her rejection, regardless of who is rejecting her, was enough to produce negative outcomes. Williams and Zardo state Rejection "evokes a strong immediate warning" (22).

Pawar notices the differences between herself and the other girls; she cannot but become conscious of the differences between them. Insignificant yet "novel items" in tiffin boxes compel her to ask questions which she calls "the stupid question" regarding social rejection. The realisation dawns on her, "We were aware, without anybody telling us, that we were born in a particular caste and in poverty, and that we had to live accordingly" (96). Pawar also notices the variations in the degree of social rejection between the male and female members of her community and the fact that the Dalit women also suffer rejection from the male members of their own community. She notes separate dishes are prepared for male and female members of her community. According to Baumeister and Leary (1995), "A need to belong, that is, a need to form and maintain at least a minimum quantity of interpersonal relationships, is innately prepared (and hence nearly universal) among human beings" (499). The experiences of rejection encountered by the Dalit women hence frustrate their need to belong.

Pawar depicts the humiliation and embarrassment suffered by the female children and women of the community who occupy the periphery of the society and are compelled to live on the fringes. She narrates an experience, when she along with her two nieces sat down to eat and began asking rice time after time. She recalls the humiliation, "The cook returned with more rice but being called monster was not easy to digest and we politely declined" (117).

Pawar in her autobiographical work sketches images of her native place "Adgaon" as well as "Ratnagiri", where she pursued her education. Pawar recollects rejection she confronted during her school days, her classmates at school decided to prepare a meal. She recalls everyone discussed what they should bring, rice or lentils etc but Pawar was instructed not to bring anything. She was told, "You must bring some money" (107). Pawar recalls poignantly that they didn't allow her to touch anything. The humiliating news regarding her eating habit "had become the hottest topic for juicy gossip" (110) which led her to have thousand deaths experiences, indeed so harrowing were the effects of the rejection on her sense of self-esteem. James, W. in *The Principles of Psychology* describes the feeling of being ostracised as "every person we met cut us dead" (293). She shows the opinion of those she felt closer to her had a greater impact on her self-esteem than those whom she considered merely acquaintances.

Williams postulates in his model of *Ostracism* four needs which are shattered by ostracism: "The core theory of the model is that ostracism, in comparison to other aversive interpersonal behaviours, has the unique potential to threaten up to four fundamental needs. These needs are the need to belong, the need for self-esteem, the need for control, and the need for meaningful existence."(59-60). Pawar shows how the exposure to ostracism resulted in lowering of four fundamental needs she felt, the need to belong, for self-esteem, for managing things and last but not least the need for meaningfulness existence. She narrates incidents after incidents in her life which deal with the need to belong, for self-esteem, for managing things and for an existence that has meaning. She becomes a target of ostracism time and again and acutely conscious of every minimal rejection scenarios. Such ostracism functions the same as rejection. Pawar shows the negative effects of ostracism, when the villagers abandon all Gods and Goddesses. Pawar narrates, "We put all of them in a basket...we have firmly resolved to discard the gods with all the accompanying paraphernalia."

The "same traditional invocation" is chanted with an entirely different set of words:

O ye Gods;
Yes that's right, Maharaja,
Go back to your own place.
"Yes that's right, Maharaja
You never did well to us."

Pawar portrays not only the images of social rejection that she herself had to undergo but also those of other members of her community with the same realism. She depicts the fate of Sushi, her elder sister after her marriage who died with misery and pain. She narrates the case of Parvati, brother's wife, who has no voice of her own. Pawar depicts the embarrassment to which she was subjected to by her English language her teacher who used to abuse her for her poor language skills but the worse she felt were related to sexual exploitation, wherein her uncle tried to play dolls with her imagining being her husband, dragging her and pressing her hard (125). These incidents of rejection resulted in anxiety and depression, making her feel unhappy and less in control. The intensity of her negative responses depended on who she was rejected by. Her being close to her rejecter intensified the negative outcomes associated with rejection. Pawar shows the anxiety resulting from rejection by close others compared to rejection from someone who is not close. She reports her feelings when she is thus treated by her close maternal uncle than by a stranger. She also narrates the experiences of her wedding night when she felt the groping hands of her husband and was called 'frigid', which made her feel negative about herself. She talks about the fate of other women of her community at home when she describes incidents of domestic violence, especially the incident of a pregnant woman being beaten realistically. Williams in *Ostracism* stated, that "few events in life are more painful than feeling that others, especially those whom we admire and care about, want nothing to do with us." (1)

Pawar also records how her husband Harish Chandra was made the target of social rejection emanating from caste differences when he joined the office of District Superintendent. He was treated like an untouchable. This experience forced him to leave his job and go to the city complying with the call given by Dr Babasaheb Ambedkar to youngsters. The incident shows the effects of social rejection as the being rejected lowered the levels of belonging and self-esteem, and meaningful existence for Pawar, her husband and the other members of her community.

Pawar shows the effect of experiences of social rejection on her but then goes on to deal with them. She portrays her inner transformation which began with partaking in stage shows at the school/college and reading books, about Babasaheb Ambedkar and other Dalit women writers. She feels strongly that woman have to make sustained efforts to achieve self-respect. She portrays her own efforts for self-regulation which began when she started to develop her writing skills in a Mumbai office while at work, by writing short stories and articles and her making efforts to come closer to women/friends. Her motivation is to fit in and maintain harmony with the society, as seen in her efforts to adopt self-strategies like strengthening friendships. She recalls her husband Harish Chandra's resistance to her doing M.A. course who expected her to do the homely chores like a typical Dalit wife. She received no support from anyone and felt that no one cares about her wellbeing. According to Baumeister and Leary (1995), "To satisfy the need to belong, the person must believe that the other cares about his or her welfare and likes (or loves) him or her"(500).

Pawar voices the frustration of her need to belong poignantly. While it is true she shows a very strong motivation to form and maintain relationships but her need to belong is not the only focal point of the autobiography nor is it the most salient. Indeed, the need to individuate is seen to be an equally, if not stronger, motive. Through her friend Heena Bansode she received information about "Maitrini", she met renowned women, Usha Mehta Chhaya Datar, Vidya Bal, etc. She opposed the distinction between male female titles, any man become a 'Bhaushaeb' or 'Raosaheb' while a woman merely remains a 'Bai' without the title of Sahib. She raised the issues of Hindu Code Bill and daughter's rights to property. She mentioned the Marathi Sahitya Kokan conference where she met Ramakant Shadan Chadrahas Gadre, Prakash Karat, and P V Shashikant Lokhande. Further, she decided to write a biography on Dr Ambedkar. She also decided to meet the women who had worked with Dr Ambedkar, including Laxmibai Kakade, Tayabai Pawar and Chandrika Ramtake. She published her first storybook "sixth finger", despite the resentment shown to her by her own husband recalling, "His attitude towards me was full of contradictions. On the one hand, he was proud of my writing, he admitted to his friends and relatives. However, on the other, he immensely resented my being recognised as a writer, my speaking in public programmes and my emerging as a figure in the public domain."(246)

Pawar's independent self-concept blunts some consequences of social rejection. With the passage of time she seems to be less sensitive to rejection because of the reduced value placed on being part of a group, which is considered untouchable. For Pawar, her individuality can be seen as a positive distinction; and therefore, rejection in her case only functions to reinforce her sense of self-determination. She takes upon herself the literary work after she has lost a son. She introspect her literary career and realises that her children have experienced rejection due to her job as a writer. She gained name and fame but at her children's expense. The connection between social rejection and creativity is seen when she mentions she was exposed to the lashes off the sharp and caustic tongue. She also recalls her experiences of social rejection as a Dalit woman attached to the Dalit movement and as a woman supporting women's liberation movement. This further confirms the fact that writers are more often than not sufferers of social rejection due to their non-confirmatory attitude towards the established norms of the society, Pawar more so being a Dalit woman. Pawar's enthusiasm to distinguish from others seems to have played significant implications in her performance of creative tasks. For Pawar who has an independent self-concept, rejection serves to increase her creativity by conferring upon her the willingness to take on ideas from all places and make the most of them. Social rejection she confronts only reinforces her desire to differentiate herself from others and her mindset leads to more creative solutions.

The study shows for creative persons like Pawar the experience of social rejection promote creativity. Urmila Pawar deals with rejection both from family, relations and friends courageously. She narrates the incident when she lost her son but her colleague and friend showed a negative attitude towards her. Pawar chronicles the fact that not only uneducated but also educated people indulge in the activity of unfairly rejecting others instead of accepting them for what they are. She refers to her creative writing, comparing it to her mother attempts to weave the basket. Sharmila Rege writes, "Memoirs of humiliation and resistance delineate the reproduction of caste as a form of modern inequality both in the village and the city" (336). Pawar depicts not only experiences of social rejection but also conveys her own awakening consciousness and self-concept that fueled her creativity. She reveals that the harmful consequences of social rejection are not predictable and are dependent on the extent one relies on one's concept of the Self. This concept of the Self is important and forms the basis on which reactions to social rejection are generated. Urmila Pawar concludes her Memoir, stating, "Life has taught me many things, showed me so such. It has also lashed it me till I bled, I don't know how much longer I am going to live, nor do I know in what form life is going to confront me let it came in any form; I am ready to face it stoically. This is what my life has taught me. This is my life and that is me."(320)

'Aaydan' implies weaving of baskets made of cane, which happens to be the main occupation of the community to which Pawar belongs. The weave of memories give a detailed narrative of how Dalit men, women and children encounters with social rejection- in the school, in the city, in the family, in literary societies and in other spaces. Pawar shows that males and females react differently to social ostracism and it is more threatening to Dalit females because they are more likely than males to be blamed for their own poor abilities as motive for the ostracism. Being accepted and belonging are very important for psychological and physical wellbeing of the Dalit women, and social rejection results in many negative consequences for them but her account and her spirited struggle displays her bolstering independence, which helps her to manage some of the consequences of social rejection and even open opportunities for increased creative expression, offering her a constructive alternative to other negative outcomes faced by others. Colin Wilson in *The Outsider,* (1956) asserts that extremely creative people live on the margins of society and speaks of the way a writer has to reject the traditional values in a society and "evolve a set of values that will correspond to his higher intensity of purpose" (142). The literary endeavour was for Pawar, a Dalit writer, living on the margins of society a means to evolve and her creativity the best way to fight against the social rejection she has suffered corresponding to a higher purpose which is to end a social evil.

Works Cited

Baumeister, R. F., and Leary, M. R. "The need to belong: Desire for interpersonal attachments as a fundamental human motivation". *Psychological Bulletin,* 117:1995, 497-529. Print.

James, W. *The Principles of Psychology.* New York: Cosimo Classics, 1890. Print.

Pawar, Urmila. *The Weave of My Life: A Dalit Woman's Memoirs.* New Delhi: Columbia University Press. 2008, Print.

Williams, K. D. *Ostracism: The Power of Silence. Emotions and Social Behavior.* New York, London: Guilford, 2001, Print.

Williams, K. D., and Zardo, L. Ostracism: The Indiscriminate Early Detection System. In K. D. Williams, J. P. Forgas, and W. von Hippel (Eds.), *The social outcast Ostracism, social exclusion, rejection, and bullying.* [*The Sydney Symposium of Social Psychology,* Volume 7] New York: Psychology Press, 2005, pp. 19–34. Print.

Wilson, C. *The Outsider.* Boston: Houghton Mifflin, 1956, Print.

3

Articulation of Social Injustices, Gender Discrimination and Patriarchy Tradition in Bama's *Sangati*

Dr Archana Bhattacharjee

The Dalits, called by different names like Dasyu, Dasa, Atisudra, Panchame, Tirukutdba, Adikarnataka, Adi Dravida are actually the 'Depressed Classes' of Indian society. They are the people who are economically, socially and politically exploited since centuries. They have been systematically pushed to the periphery by the traditional Brahaminical structure of oppression. This exploitation is due to the discrimination followed by age old caste hierarchical tradition in the Hindu society. It has subjected them to a life of poverty and humiliation. Even after independence Dalits have not been allowed to live a life of dignity and equality. It is this idea of 'equality' which sparked the beginning of the Dalit Movement in India, as a protest to the age old atrocities committed against them.

Jacques Ranciera (2011, p. 53) observes that rather than create works of art, contemporary artists want to get out of the museum and induce alterations in the space of everyday life, generating new forms of relations. If this is true of the most forms of contemporary art, it is even more so in the case of the artistic expressions of communities that have been historically subjected to all kinds of painful experiences due to political, social or cultural reasons, such as literature of the Indian Dalit women, the lowest rung in the hierarchy of the Hindu caste system. Narratives for them are spaces in which they can become "[] both the observing subject and the end the object of investigation, remembrance and contemplation" (Watson, 1).

According to Ruman Sutradhar at a time when there was no means of communication to support the Dalits, pen was the only solution. The media, newspapers were all under the control of the powerful class – the Brahmin. The Brahmins never allowed the Dalit voice to express; as they thought it a threat for their own survival. Dalits began their own magazines and began to express their own experiences. Their pain wrote not with ink, but with blood, of their own cuts – the cuts being basically mental, with instincts of physical in them.

Keeping this in view, this paper will examines *Sangati,* autobiographical work of Indian Dalit writer Bama to see in what manner, her literary narrative articulates social injustice, gender discrimination, casteism and all other difference and serves as a social document that tries to counter-attack the social-cultural hegemony of the upper castes.

Cielo Griselda Festino rightly opines that the literary narratives like all kinds of narratives are deeply intertwined with the life of the community where they originate. In the same way, that there are no communities that do not tell their stories in some way or another. Because these stories are either told or silenced, they reveal all. What the community does or refuses to do, what it believes in or considers a prejudice; its virtues and also its deep injustices. (http://www.uem.br/acta). In other words, literature has the power, as Morris (1996) adds to validate or invalidate, human suffering by recognising 'literariness' in some narratives and denying it to others.

Nevertheless, if literature expresses the values of the community within which the narrative exists, subjugated communities can also challenge established modes of literature by creating their own aesthetics and narrative traditions. This actually happens when, what is considered as having 'literary value' is reinvented in order to give visibility to what counts as other forms of suffering.

Within Dalit literature, autobiography as a literary and cultural expression has created a praxis, which has challenged existing literary structures through their articulations of cultural and caste discriminations, "It focuses on the question of otherness, difference, marginality cannon and the categories of aesthetics. In order to voice the protest of the marginalised Dalit literature often follows the subversive historiographic paths of personalising history. It is therefore, perhaps, that autobiography is the most potent and often exercised form of fiction produced in Dalit literature." (Devy, 272)

According to Shweta Singh, Dalit woman's personal narratives not only challenged their absence in Dalit men's narratives, but also voice the concerns shared by women across all strata. These alternative accounts openly criticise the patriarchal structure in their society thus reflecting on women's problems with specific issues in a Dalit society. The hardships faced by these women under the patriarchal order are thus articulated. Dalit women's autobiographies are very candid about all kinds of exploitation and oppression that these women had to endure both within and outside their society. They also give lucid accounts of their contribution to the larger cause of the Dalit community.

Dalit men's autobiographies do not mention domestic violence. It is quite evident from Dalit women's autobiographies that this was a major issue among the women. Its complete dismissal in the men's narratives shows their apathy and the complete denial of violence at home. Dalit men like men of all classes and caste thus espouse the beating of wives and the general physical, mental and emotional trauma which the womenfolk have to bear within a household. In the narratives of Dalit women the everyday is a very important theme. The day-to-day private life as depicted in the autobiographies reveals the dark side of a patriarchal structure. We get a women's perspective on things – what makes her world, her take on societal evils and her anguish, hopes and fears and also a remembrance of the past. The autobiographies are different not just because they reveal different experiences and different views but also because they unravel the bigger questions of memory, experience, general relations and familial structures which are the same across all societies and classes. Dalit autobiographies help us to think about the genre itself and its deployment by the two sexes. (DU Journals, 42-43)

The writer whose work is to be examined in this paper, Bama Faustine, Mary Fatima Rana is one of the first Dalit women writers to be widely recognised and translated. Born as Faustine, Mary Fatima Rani in a village called Puthupathi in Tamil Nadu, South India, Bama is the leading voice of the suppressed class – Dalit. She has committed herself to impart the values of self-respect and social consciousness among the Dalit section of the society. Her works include Karukku in 1992, a well-known autobiography, *Sangati* an autobiography of her community and Vanman.

Sangati (1994) is the second work of Bama that is translated into English by Lakshmi Holmstrom nearly after a decade of its publication in Tamil. The title "Sangati" means incidents or events of daily life and the episodic plot covers a set of interconnected incidents that happen in the lives of the characters in the novel. The plot covers a span of three generations starting from Vellaiyamma Kizhavi to that of the narrator. Lakshmi Holmstrom, in the introduction of his book, makes its theme clear, "Sangati" moves from the story of the individual struggle to the perception of community of Paraiya women a neighbourhood group of friends and relations and their joint struggle. In this sense *Sangati* is perhaps the autobiography of a community" (Page XV). M.S.S. Pandian argues that Bama verbalises her own life story, depletes the autobiographical "I", which he calls an "outcome of bourgeois individualism...and displaces it with the collectivity of the Dalit community." The story is not her own but that of others too.

In Bama's case nobody can interpret her story. It is something that is very personal. Her life is related to the people of her community. What has happened to her could have happened to many of other people of her community. She had the opportunity to tell something that others in her community did not have. She documents the reality of all the people of her community who were not allowed to voice their own story. In Karukku, the "absence of the self" and the presence of the "collective 'we'" is evident. Bama's text instead of privileging her own voice, functions as a site for the criss-crossing of multiple voices from within her community.

She places every detail in the context of Dalit life. She gives detailed generalised description of life in her village, the activities and jobs the men and women perform. The act of naming is considered as an exercise of power. So she deliberately does not name her village, the priests, schools and colleges, the nunnery, the Dalit headman etc. The lack of distinctiveness harmonises better understanding of the message. Bama's text is also marked by absence of adherence to grammatical rules. She conveys a sense of remorse and guilt when she talks about the material benefits she had enjoyed, an elusive dream for others in her community.

Bama's shared testimonial typically unfolds her growing up story in episodes, and throughout she displays indomitable courage, conquering the dominant forces.

In the opinion of Nayar *Sangati* is built around women's conversations events are narrated through women's stories and opinions delivered through them. Bama highlights the fact that in her work the female characters suffer from double discrimination; they are oppressed by both the high class people as well as the Dalit males. They constitute the majority of labourers doing hard manual labour and engage in agricultural activities. But they are paid much less than their male counterparts. This unequal division of labour becomes a major issue in *Sangati*. The Dalit community is also under the reigning patriarchal system whereby Dalit men who themselves are marginalised by the upper class land owners, in turns marginalise Dalit women.

It is not the same for women of other castes and communities. Our women cannot bear the treatment of upper-caste masters in the fields, and at home, they cannot bear the violence of their husbands (65).

Invidious patriarchal distinctions are initially inculcated in children within the first ten years of their lives. Gender games act as effective tools to achieve this goal. Bama as a young girl understands the crafting nature of gender games they play. Girls are not allowed to play the games of boys, while games like 'Kabadi' and 'marbles' are meant for boys, girls play at cooking, getting married and other domestic matters.

Even when we played 'mothers and fathers' we always had to serve the mud 'rice' to the boys first. They use to pull us by the hair and hit us saying, 'what sort of food is this, die without salt or anything!' in those days we used to accept those pretence blows and think it was all good fun. Now-a-days, for many of the girls, those have became real blows, and their entire lives are hell[s] (31).

Dalit women are oppressed in multiple ways by upper caste men who have evil designs on them as Patti tells: "If upper caste fellows clap eye on you, you are finished. They will drag you off and rape you that's for sure. If you go on a little further, there will be escaped criminals lurking in the plantation" (8).

Again wife beating and cases of domestic violence are found scattered all over the novel. Two of the stories that Bama reminds is that of Mariamma and Thayi whose marital disharmonies are revealed in an attempt to stereotype the Dalit predicament. They are beaten up daily by their husbands. Mariamma is humiliated by her father; assaulted by the landlord and later tormented by her husband. She is a true representative of the entire community of the submissive Dalit women. Thaayi is badly beaten with chappals and belts by her husband. When he is interrupted by Karuthamuthu, he resorts aggressively: "Who are you to speak for this munde? She is my wife. I can beat her or kill her if I wish. You go and mind your own business" and then turns to his wife to abuse and beat her saying, "You common whore, you, any passing loafer will come in support of you, you mother fucker's daughter. You will go with ten men" (43). Bama describes in *Sangati* how the female sex is stripped off from self-respect and deprived of all rights which can help them to uplift themselves. Bama's cry on the grounds of gender discrimination is audible in her autobiography *Sangati*:

> Why can't we be the same as boys? We are not allowed to talk loudly or laugh noisily; even when we sleep we can't stretch out on our backs nor lie faces down on our bellies. We always have to walk with our heads bowed down, gasing at our toes. You tell us all this rubbish and keep us under control. Even when our stomachs are screaming with hunger, we must not eat first. We are allowed to eat only after the men in the family have finished and gone. What, Patti aren't we also human beings?" (29).

In the novel, Bama's conversation with her Patti sheds light on the issue of economic exploitation by the superior people on the part of Dalit men and by both on the part of Dalit women. Their women are real wage earners but they do not get their wages. They do the hard work inside or outside the house but "whatever work they did, were paid less than the man. Even when they did the very same work, they were paid less". Their plight is evident as Patti explains that, "We have to labour in the fields as hard as men do and then on the top of that, struggle to bear and raise our children. As for the men, their work ends when they've finished in the fields...We only toil in the fields and in the home until our vaginas shrivel."

It is worth noticing here that Bama has slotted in all those issues which are complimentary to each other, that is, one problem overlaps another, for instance, above discussed economic exploitation is the result of caste, class and patriarchy. Patriarchy (a society, system or country that is ruled or controlled by men) is the patron of gender discrimination or better to say, gender discrimination is the central feature of patriarchy. In *Sangati,* from beginning to the end, Bama has dealt with gender issues at large so the term 'gender' needs to be conferred. The book *Sangati* encapsulates the author's experience of working within a heterogeneous and oppressed society and the series of several interconnected anecdotes, experiences, news, and events as narrated in the book, form an autobiography of a community. Bama clarifies her acknowledgement of the work:

> My mind is crowded with many anecdotes: stories not only about the sorrows and tears of Dalit women, but also about lively, rebellious culture their eagerness not to let life crush or shatter them, but rather to swim vigorously against the tide...About their hard labour. I wanted to shout out these stories." (Limbale, 119)

There are various other instances scattered throughout the novel which reflect the psychological trauma, stresses and strain faced by all Dalits one way or the other. But the incorrigible optimist that she is, the writer still believes that all is not lost. A time will come when the Dalits will no longer be victims of humiliation in the hands of the upper castes. They will be able to raise their voice against Caste, Class and patriarchy in general and 'male' sex in particular. The very last line of the novel reveals her belief for a better future of her community: "I am hopeful that such a time will come soon" (123).

Bama suggest that it is the sharp tongue of a woman that can protect her against her oppressors. The characters often break into a song or a chant when the situation demanded and there is a song for every occasion. But what is thought provoking in Bama's literary sketching is a positive identity for the Dalit women. An alternate to her story as opposed to the mainstream is drawn with vivid descriptions of a marriage ceremony, attaining of puberty ceremony, joy of happiness, singing songs, cooking and sharing food. In most rural homes, the Dalit women is an earning member, widow re-marriages are possible and the sacred thread worn as a chain during the marriage is not this binding symbol as in other communities. It is interesting that the Dalit women cannot be suppressed in spite of caste and gender oppression. Anam Ragamalika rightly opines that by discussing narratives of many women from the Dalit community Bama places before us the rural Dalit women's identity. Though the struggle is much owing to the double oppression of caste and gender, we notice that their strength is also revealed when the women stand by each other to help each other where there is injustice meted out not only in society but in family circles as well. Bama does not shy away from describing violent, domestic or street quarrels. In *Sangati* we hear the voices of many women some in pain, some in anger, some in frustration and some out of courage.

Sometimes the language is full of exploitive, with sexual undertones.

To conclude it may be said that through her memorable heart-touching autobiography, *Sangati,* Bama has given a clarion call to all women of her community to wake up from their slumber collectively so that they can live with dignity and self-respect which is their birth right. But to live with dignity, the only thing required is power. To attain power, the first thing required is knowledge. Phule and Ambedkar gave the main emphasis on the education of the Dalits, which will not only bestow them with reason and judgment capacity, but also political power and lead to improvement of their socio-economic status. If this turns into reality, the subalterns will speak and their voice will definitely be heard and they will go all out to remove traces of sorrows, miseries, servitude, misfortunes, sexual exploitation and assaults of Dalit women from the face of Indian society and a new world order will reign and prevail.

Works Cited

Ambedkar, B.R. *Writings and Speeches*. Vol. 3. Government of Maharashtra Education Department, Mumbai, 2008, p. 429.

Amstrong, S. "Testimonios: An Indian Perspective", IRWLE, Vol. 6, No. 1, January, 2010.

Bama. *Sangati*. Trans. Lakshmi Holstrom. New Delhi: Oxford University Press, 2005. Print.

Devy, G. *The G.N. Devy Reader*. Hyderabad: Orient Longman, 1992. Print.

Dalit Women Life Narratives and Literature as Experience. Act a scientiarum_http://www.uem.br/acta

Pandian, M.S.S. "One Step Outside Modernity: Caste, Identity Politics and Public Sphere", Economic and Political Weekly. Rep. Vol. XXXVII, No. 18, May 4, 2002.

Rangalika, Anam. "Caste, Gender, Dichotomy: A Dalit Feminist Perspective: A Study of Bama's *Sangati*." *Impressions: Bi-annual*

Refereed E-Journal. 6.1. (2012) Vol. VI, Issue I, January, 2012 (www.impressions50webs.org/Jan12/ar_annamr.html)

Singh, Shweta. "Representation of Dalit Women in Dalit Men's and Women's Autobiographies." *The Delhi University Journal of the Humanity and Social Sciences.* Vol. I, 2014, pp. 39-47.

Sutradhar, Ruman. "Dalit Movement in India: In the light of four Dalit Literature." *IOSR Journal of Dental and Medical Sciences.* Vol. 13, Issue 4, April, 2014, p. 95.

http://www.museindia.com/regularcontent. asp?issid=53&id = 4716

4

Role of Marriage in Shaping a Dalit Woman's Identity: A Study of Dalit Memoir *Viramma: Life of an Untouchable*

Dr Sigma G.R.

Different types of people live on the vast land of India from many caste, communities and classes. According to Hindu *Varnashrama Dharma* (social duties based on works) society is divided into four varnas. Our scriptures describe that in the Purshasukta of the Rigveda there is a mention that men on this world were born from the different organs of the Lord Brahma (RV 10.90.11-12) and that's why they are classified in different categories. According to it, the Brahmins were born from mouth, Kshatriyas from shoulders, Vaishyas from thighs and Shudras from feet. Here god has been called as Purush or Virat in visible form. The word 'Dalit' has many meanings and it has Sanskrit roots. Its root 'dal' means to crack, break, or split into parts. Dalits are those persons who are downtrodden, degraded, exploited, crushed, underprivileged and downtrodden. These people are economically and socially backward and have fewer facilities in their homes. There are many religious-mystical, biological, socio-historical etc. theories about its origin. And the varna system is generally found at its base. Annabhau Sathe said, "Dalit literature is a struggle of new life. It is a soul of humanity. It is a life story which faced the states of death." (Awad, 4)

The first chapter of this autobiography is "A Childhood in Velpakkam" and in this we come to know that Viramma belongs a serf family and her grandfather, Samikkannu was a staunch worker and loyal to his masters. He was a sorcerer also. One day he goes to see a famous sorcerer and when he returned at his home he surprised everyone. He had brought a new wife for him who was pregnant then. Her grandmother said nothing to see her *sautan* as she feared that he might cast a spell on her if she argued. He got a boy and girl from his second wife. After that at the advice of his friend he went to Madras where he worked as a worker in coconut plantations. He thought that his children will also be able to earn something in the city. But the life was very difficult there at Velpakkam. She described their life, "But at least we had the sky, the clouds, water all of nature. Water gushed out everywhere in those days!" (2) When he was there then her grandmother felt very lonely and heartbroken:

> The separation was heartbreaking for the grandmother though. She was always crying and lamenting and wishing that the boys would come back, or at least her son Nadeshan. Night and day, she tried to think of ways to bring him home and she decided to talk about it to her sister who lived in Ranganam. (2)

Viramma's mother Pattu had seven children. She tells an instance of her life. It was the month of Markaji and at that night they observed fasting and stayed awake at night and actors entertained then till morning. Her mother was in her gestation period and her labour pains started. Her grandmother and aunt Kanikkai conducted delivery with the traditional methods and a baby girl was born. The people awoke in the morning and they saw that Viramma's father, Nadesan was sitting near the door with "his head in his hands" (3). They did not feel the importance of even asking from him about the sex of the child and understood everything. The men understood it automatically and women also uttered to hear the sharp cries of the child, "Hey, here's another little bitch been born!" (3) Viramma calls it an auspicious day as it was the day of the gods' worshipping, "Be that as it may, I was born on a lucky day, when we worship the gods, and I was given a divine name, Viramma" (3). The second chapter "The Marriage is Arranged" tells about the story how Viramma was married in a tender age when she was just a child:

> I was still a little child, innocent, happy and flat chested when it was decided that I should get married. Big sister Ellamma, one of my much older cousins, had been given to a family from Karani. When she heard that my future parents-in-law were looking for a daughter-in-law she let them know that an ideal little girl in Velpakkam the village where she was born. (15)

Her sister loved her mother very much and she wanted to show her concerns and affection to her by bringing this marriage proposal. When she came with her proposal at home, her mother's joy knew no bounds, "I can still see my mother weeping with joy on the tinnai and big sister Ellamma comforting her." (15). She thought that Viramma will be happy at her new house and if she faces any problem then her sister Ellemma will be an easy reach to her to help her out. Her mother brought fresh fish and palm wine for the occasion. When Viramma's father came after his work she was very anxious to tell her this good news. Viramma was listening to everything silently and she heard fragments of the conversation, "I knew they were talking about me, but I only heard snatches of sentences, "She will be happy... She will work well...Ellemma will be there to look out for her...Karani's not far, we'll be able to go and see her a lot..." (15-16)

> There is a strange thing to note at the time of the marriage of a daughter. If the marriage proposal is turned down from the other side, it is considered that it will be a big blow on the fate of their daughter and the respect of the family. Viramma's mother was also in this doubt and not only this, the other family was thinking about the same thing. "I was going to leave home, leave my family, my friends and the village where I'd been born, to go and cook for strangers. From then on, I would only belong to them. (16)

Viramma was not happy with her marriage in this tender age. She requested her mother not to marry her. She sobbed day and night. She told her mother that she would prove a good daughter for them and she would not play any game, she would work hard and bring a lot of money in the home but nobody paid any attention to her pleadings.

The text is an attack on the institution of marriage, "I sobbed day and night. I begged my mother not to give me away in marriage. I would be good. I would stop all the games, I'd work hard, I'd bring home lots of money" (16). She called Nayaki and other friends so that they might help her in this situation. In fact, her mother was also not happy as she knew that Viramma's marriage would separate her from her family. But she was also forced in front of the circumstances as every girl has to go to her new home. The girls have to accept this reality that she has to go to another home and this is their fate. "That was the fate of women. Leaving is terrifying, you believe that everything is coming to an end but everything is only just beginning when you get married. You become a woman and you blossom in the light of your new household."(16)

The girls are burdened with family responsibly as soon as they get married. They have to cook food for the members of their in-laws' house. All of her dreams to play with the other children are shattered after her marriage. Viramma tells Sinnamma, "That's how we learned to work, Sinnamma. We would rather have carried on playing and getting up late. We would have loved to stay children all our lives, and we tell ourselves that if it wasn't for these bloody stomachs which we always have to fill, we'd live innocently and happily" (12).

Viramma's attained her puberty after three years of her marriage. Her husband, Manikkam was much senior to her. There was a big age-gap between them. Viramma was sent to her in-laws' home after she attained puberty according to the custom of the Parayas.

Chapter three "Becoming a Woman" is a frank description of how Viramma attained her puberty and she attained the womanhood. One day when she saw blood on her thigh without any injury or wound, she was very frightened. When she told the other members of her family they seemed happy to see her in this position. It was only she who was alone worried about it:

> I lifted my underskirt and found, to my horror, blood, fresh blood. Fear seized me. I hadn't cut myself, I hadn't scratched myself. I must have been ill to be bleeding like that. But I didn't hurt anywhere. Seeing what was happening, grandmother, Subbu didn't panic at all. Quite the opposite she told me that it was a happy event and that she was proud to witness it. (29)

After that a ritual bath was performed for her and she attained womanhood. This ritual was performed with the turmeric paste. When her father came he became very happy to get this news. He immediately arranged borrowed some money from the Reddi. This money was asked for her cleansing as it was thought that the evil spirits get attracted by the reek of menstruation, "... evil spirits are attracted by the strong smell of periods" (31). Her father sent a message to her in-laws house about this news.

Viramma's life was going smoothly. She kept going to fields for work, going for evening walks with her friends and listening to grandfather Munissami until she got the news one evening that the family of her would-be husband is coming to see her. This news was like falling of a lightening on the palm tree. She could not sleep whole night. She was in that age in which a girl does not know what a marriage is. She was thinking like her kidnapping news with the consent of her family members.

She considers her husband a stranger and finds him dominant over her. She hated her when he forced her to have sexual relationships with her. She did not know about the relationships of a husband and wife. When he touched her she told him that she had no right to touch her being a stranger. She even did not know that he was not a stranger for her. Even after many years of her marriage she kept the memory of her first night as fresh as a flower in her mind:

> I know how it's done with the Reddi ... The elders lead the married couple into the bedroom and shut the door. Then the young ones have a whole day to talk, win each other over and make love gently. It's too crude with us, too brutal. It's true we don't have the time or the space to do it like that. But my experience was too awful! (44)

She did not find the men of her community sensible and humane in their sexual appeals. No any family planning method was adopted in her community. Thus, there was no control on the population. Viramma herself gave birth to twelve children and only three survived out of them — only a son and two daughters. Children were considered the source of income. There was very poor care and attention for the children. There was no any health facility was provided to them due to which many children died due to lack of nutritional food and health facilities.

Paraya women had double responsibilities in their life. They had to work as labourers in the fields as well as they had to attend all the domestic chores of their house. Men worked hard all the day and at the evening time they reached to wine shop to drink. After reaching home staggering they demanded good dishes without giving any money to their wife. The women would cook food with the available eating material at their home. Thus, there were quarrels on many petty issues in their homes.

The life of the Paraya women was very hard and they had to go out of their homes to work. They were socio-economically weak and that's why they were the easy targets for the upper caste men. They molested them whenever they got any chance. They threw money to them and thus, they made them an easy prey to satisfy their bodily hungers. Another strange thing is that the upper caste people did not touch the people from their caste and they did not feel any shame to exploit them in such a way. They enticed the upper caste men than their own wives. Viramma comments that their bodies attracted them more than their own wives:

> Those gentlemen of the *ur* talk a lot about the uncleanness of Untouchables, but our holes always turn them on. We're the ones they get up to all their dirty tricks with; it makes you think our juices taste better than their wives'! It is the same in the hospital. All of them make passes at us, from the doctor to the sweeper. "Aye! What do you say? Are you coming?" (52)

Poverty is a curse for the poor. They have to see very bad days in that condition. When they don't have money everybody wants to exploit Dalit women just for a few coins and the same was happening with these Paraya women. They had no money and that's why they had to go to the cheaper hospitals for to their treatment. From doctor to sweeper, everybody looked for an opportunity to exploit them, "The doctors pretend to listen to our hearts so they can feel our breasts. Others just go ahead and get their packet out and tell us to touch it. That's happened to more than one of us. We're harassed nonstop down there" (52). But they had no any option left for them to bear all their sufferings just because there was no any source of income for them and if they object it then nobody believed them. Moreover, they could not get any chance for their treatment in the hospital.

Bhaskar Jyoti Gogoi writes, "The main thrust of dalit writing has moved from poetry to autobiography. These autobiographies are an exclusive insight into the dalit's daily life" (Gogoi, 170). Viramma's autobiography also tells her story of sufferings. Chapter Six "A mother to twelve children" tells Viramma's experiences how she came to know that she is pregnant. When her menstruation stopped for the first time, she was a bit happy to get rid of her that bad experience as well as worried about its future consequences. Her sister, Ellemma told her sick about her pregnancy when she got sick after taking her supper. Her sister went running to her husband and told him, "Hey Manikkam, your wife is pregnant" (61) and his friends also seemed congratulating him in the humorous tone, "Hey! Manikkam, you have done your work well" (31).

The life in the hospitals has also been described in this autobiography. At the time of Kaliyamma's delivery they were given a female baby by mistake and there male child was given to them only after checking the register. Doctor confirms it from the delivery register, "He looked at the register. It was clearly marked 'boy' for Kaliyamma" (72). Women did not prefer to go to the hospitals just because they faced this kind of problems. Moreover, they had fears that doctors would tore their hole and dislocate the bones of their children. Viramma gave birth to all of her children at her home and she did not take much time in the delivery. It was not much painful to her like other women.

Viramma goes to Velpakkam when her mother dies. This incidence has been described in Chapter Thirteen "A Family

Funeral." She went there after a long period and she did not feel like home then in that house, "The village I grew up in has almost become foreign to me now, even though my brother still lives there"(131).

Thus, Viramma's life has been a journey of struggle since her childhood. She focuses in her autobiography how Dalits are considered untouchable and they are deprived of their education and basic amenities. Child marriage and problems of Dalit women have been beautifully explored in this autobiography. Viramma feels alienated and oppressed under the patriarchal pressure. Over all, the text is a beautiful depiction of the Dalit women's problems and caste-based discrimination in Tamil Nadu.

Works Cited

Awad, Eknath. *Jeevnath Ghetlela Parivartnach Varsa...*, Dainik Vishw: Savidhan Samrat. ed. Nirmal, Friday: 2nd August, 2013.

Gogoi, Bhaskar Jyoti. "Dalit Autobiography: Troubled Times, Troubled Stories." *Indian Dalit Autobiographies: Marginalised Voices*, Ed. Singh, Bijender. New Delhi: Authorspress, 2015: 163-175. Print.

Omvedt, Gail. *Buddhism in India: Challenging Brahmanism and Caste.* Sage: New Delhi, 2013. Print.

Viramma; Racine, Josiane and Racine, Jean-Luc. *Viramma: Life of an Untouchable.* London and New York: Verso, 1997. Print.

5

Voice of the Voiceless: A Study of P. Sivakami's *The Grip of Change*

Dr Himanginee Kaushik

Discussion about minorities and 'down-trodden' people is the latest burning topic in literary scenario. Even after social, economical and political development, Dalits are still neglected. Although many movements were started by the social workers in the mid-nineteenth century for the upliftment of these voiceless people but it is a matter of sorrow that Dalit women are still neglected. So, Dalit women have to face both caste discrimination and gender inequalities; and the exploitation increases as they are economical weak also. They are not treated like human beings. This paper aims at gender inequalities, caste discrimination and also the exploitation of the poor by rich people with special reference to P. Sivakami's novel *The Grip of Change*. This paper also tries to break the silence of voiceless Dalits in an oppressed society.

Palanimmuthu Sivakami is the first Dalit woman to write full length semi-autobiographical Tamil novel *Pazhaiyana Kazhithalum*. She is the most celebrated Tamil writer. She was the first Dalit woman IAS officer in Tamil Nadu. She came into limelight with the publication of her first novel *Pazhaiyana Kazhithalum* and this work is also translated into English by Sivakami herself under the title *The Grip of Change* in 2006. She gave up her job of IAS to become a full time writer in 2008. The main subject of her first book *The Grip of Change* is patriarchy in Dalit society. P. Sivakami believes that caste is the main hurdle in the progress of our country. She highlights the exploitation of Dalit women not only in outer world but also in family environment. They have to suffer in every role as a daughter, wife or a beloved. No one is there to listen to their cries and sobs. But with the help of her work Sivakami wants to give voice to these women and also encourages them to fight for their rights. Vaishali Shivkumar says:

> A very famous statement 'Woman is a Dalit from beginning to the end' seems really a naked truth at this stage just because of this struggle of the Dalit women against the society, against their own outset and against the traditions their men follow. The patriarchy crushes down the originality, warmth, delicacy, tenderness and even beauty in them. (Shivkumar, 3)

The present autobiography, *The Grip of Change* starts with the story of Thangam, a Dalit woman and ends with Gowri's decision to remain unmarried for whole life as she does not find any answer to patriarchy. The novel opens with Thangam, a Dalit Parayar woman who is badly beaten up by her upper caste lover's relatives. She is a widow and is harassed by her brother-in-law. She is also sexually exploited by her Hindu landlord. Her husband dies and she becomes a widow. She wants her right on the property of her husband but she is refused on the basis that she is a barren woman and can't give birth to a child. Her fertility is linked to the land and she is denied to give the share in her husband's property by her brother-in-law. Her brother-in-law wants to exploit her physically and sexually both. He wants to keep her as his mistress. He asks her to accept all of the terms and conditions devised by him, only then she will get her share in the property. But she denies to accept these terms and conditions. She says to Kathamuthu:

> My husband's brother tried to force me, but I never gave in. They wouldn't give me my husband's land, but wanted me to be a whore for them! I wouldn't give in.... (Sivakami, 7)

Thangam never loses her heart and tries to face all the situations very boldly. She starts to live alone and works as a labourer in the farms of an upper caste Hindu landlord named Paranjothi Udayar. But he also proves a very selfish and cruel person. He rapes her but she does not complain to anyone due to shame and fear. She also knows that no one is there to listen to her inner pain. That's why she does not share this to anyone. Paranjothi Udayar takes advantage of it and repeats his shameful act. She again describes:

> I didn't want it. But Udayar took no notice of me. He raped me when I was working in his sugarcane field. I remained silent; after all, he is my paymaster. He measures my rice.... (Sivakami, 7)

Thangam maintains her silence due to her economic requirements and continues to fulfill his lustful demands. But when Thangam's brother-in-law comes to know about her illegal relationship with her landlord, he plans to take revenge to Thangam and reports about all this to Udayar's wife and brothers. When the relationship between Thangam and Udayar is disclosed, Udayar's brother-in-law attacks on Thangam and beats her brutally and also threatens to kill her. Only because of poverty a poor widow has to bear the sexual, physical and mental exploitation silently. After all these incidents Thangam takes refuge in Kathamuthu's house. Kathamuthu is considered a leader of lower castes.

It is the bitter truth of Indian society that Dalits are considered untouchable and impure also and the same situation is with Dalit women. They are also considered untouchable and impure. Dalit women have to face very contradictive situation in Indian society. On one side, they are considered impure and untouchable and on the other side they are sexually harassed. If these women are impure how high caste people can touch them to satisfy their physical lust. At the night, high class Hindus enjoy their company and have sex with them. But in the day, the same women are considered untouchable. The main reason behind their exploitation is that they are an easy approach to molest and rape as these women are weak both socially and economically. They don't raise their voices against their exploitation and if anyone tries to do so, no one is there to listen to them and their voice is suppressed. When relationship between Thangam and Udayar is disclosed, he abuses Thangam and says:

> Ungrateful whore! Even if she was hurt, she was hurt by hand adorned with gold! A Parachi could never dream of being touched by a man like me! My touch was a boon granted for penance performed in her earlier births! And then the dirty bitch betrays me! How can I face world with my name thus polluted. (Sivakami, 31)

Thangam recollects her courage at the right time and raises her voice against the violence imposed upon her. She is a helpless widow and has no one to help her. Paranjothi Udayar finds Thangam helpless and exploits her regularly. But finally she takes a right step by filing a police complain against Paranjothi Udayar. He also gets surprised by her step and courage. He always considers Thangam as a helpless and poor widow whom he can buy easily with his money. He never expects her to take such step against him. He underestimates Thangam. She again takes a bold step by asking Kathamuthu to go to court for her matter of property and her share in her husband's property. She becomes an inspiration for all the widows of her community and other communities. B. Mangalam observes:

> Sivakami's fiction documents violence against women within the domestic space. Her fiction exposes caste and gender hierarchies outside and inside the home that renders the woman an outcaste in her community. (Mangalam, 111)

When Thangam files a complaint against her landlord, the issue takes a serious shape. Now it becomes the issue of workers, wages, prejudices, casteism and revenge; it is not only limited to Thangam. But the problem rises and the huts of lower caste people are brunt as a warning to Thangam to take her complain back against Paranjothy Udayar. But she does not take her complain back and fights against injustice of high class people with her full strength. The other lower castes people also fight against the injustice under the skillful leadership of their leader, Kathamuthu and continue their case and finally get the compensation in back. Their demand to increase their wages one rupee more in addition to old wages of three rupees as the prices are rising day by day is settled by fifty paisa only. Because of increment in their wages high class people already have their own ways:

> Arunachala Peddiar, displeased over the decision to raise the wages, joined Paranjothi Udayar and ask, we should not have agreed to higher wages. Don't worry. We'll make them work an extra hour. When we pay more, we have the right to demand more work from them. (Sivakami, 75)

Dalits get happy and consider it their victory and go to work in the fields next morning happily thinking about their earning an extra fifty paisa for their labour. But their happiness is just for few hours when their supervisors don't allow them to leave the fields at five in the evening and ask them to work continuously while this condition is not discussed later. By this high class people want to teach poor people a lesson and now they come to know about the hard realities of the life. Sivakami says, "In continuance with the traditions of the society they lived in, the lower caste had learned to tolerate the intolerable" (Sivakami, 75).

Upper caste people have no sympathy for lower caste people and they know many ways to take back their money with interest. They accept to give twenty-five thousand rupees in compensation for fire to the poor people, that is just a plan.

> We haven't given in to Kathamuthu's demands, we have only agreed to the Tahsildar's suggestions. Later we will be able to apply to the Tahsildar for permission to cut that huge banyan tree next to the school. The auction proceeds will make up for what we are paying now. (Sivakami, 75)

Thangam even doesn't get justice and the compensation given to her out of the court is unjustified. She wants and deserves respect and her right but she is given only ten thousand rupees. No punishment is given to those high class people. She says, "Sami, these hooligans who beat me up. They should be jailed for at least a day and tortured. The pain is killed me" (Sivakami, 5).

Thangam has to face so many sufferings. She even does not able to sleep properly after that night. But no one is concerned about her psychological condition after that incident. She says:

> Whenever she remembered her life in Puliyar, she wept. She equated the incident in the sugarcane field with the repulsive experience of stepping on shit while walking on a river bank. She could not recover easily from the troubles she had suffered. The shock of being dragged out by her hair in the middle of the night to be beaten up like an animal had affected her mind deeply. She would gasp awake at night at the slightest sound. (Sivakami, 87)

Thangam's sorrows and struggle do not end here. She is not exploited only by high class people but is also exploited by the rich people of her own Dalit community. Kathamuthu, who first appears as a well-wisher and helper to her also, wants to take advantage of Thangam. He wants to gain political importance among his caste people and for this he interferes and changes Thangam's story. He does not care about Thangam and her dignity. He also gets ready for out of the court settlement by taking cash from Paranjothy Udayar. Then he asks her for that money and promises her that he will give it back when she wants that. His intention is also not good towards her. He also exploits her sexually and uses her as an option to make his wives jealous. One afternoon he enters in kitchen and abuses Thangam sexually and physically without her wish and also disfigures her face.

The present work depicts the real condition of outcaste women. Gouri, the daughter of Kathamuthu, appears as a bold woman character. She is well aware about all the situations happening with Thangam and her mother. So to avoid all these situations in her life she takes a bold step and decides to live unmarried for the whole life. With the help of his father she gets a chance to get study and knowledge and with the help of that knowledge she becomes aware about her rights. She protests against marriage and denies and decides to live single for whole life. She declares that she does not want to live a terrible life like her mother after marriage. She says, "The sufferings that my mother underwent in her marriage! I don't want to be tortured like her by some man" (Sivakami, 124). So, she concentrates on her examinations. After completing her education in village school, she decides to go to a city college for higher studies. When she crosses the threshold of her home, she thinks that she has crossed the man made boundaries and now she is free to live her life freely. She feels:

> During floods, waters from overflowing wells mingle with the waters of huge water bodies, transgressing their boundaries. Gowri felt that she had crossed over human-made boundaries her father, her caste and her village – and merged with the ocean of people. (Sivakami, 95)

Gouri never appreciates the dominating nature of her father and she also dislikes when her father exploits dalits women. She also protests against her father when he sexually exploits Thangam and shouts: "Dogs! Dogs in this house! Shameless as dogs!" (Sivakami, 93). Gouri does not stay quiet and rebels against her father and society. She also fights for Dalit women and their right to live free like men. Her voice is the voice of all outcaste women. K. Sachidanandan observes, "Dalit literature empowers the marginalised by retrieving the voices, spaces and identities silenced or suppressed by castiest power" (Sachidanandan, 14).

Though her autobiography, *The Grip of Change*, P. Sivakami highlights the social structure of Indian society. She also discusses how outcaste women are denied to give their natural and birth rights and treated like slaves. But in the end, the writer also shows how women and their roles are changing and they also know to fight for their own rights.

Works Cited

Mangalam, B. "Caste and Gender Interface in Tamil Dalit Discourse." Signifying the Self: Women and Literature. Delhi: Macmillan, 2004. Rpt. 2007. Print.

Sachidanandan, K. *Indian Literature: Positions and Propositions*. Delhi: Pencraft International, 1999. Print.

Shivkumar, Vaishali. "A Dalit Woman under A Strong Clutch of Patriarchy: A Comprehensive Study of *The Grip of Change*." *Language in India*. 13.4 (2013): 3. Web. 3 Jan, 2014. Print.

Sivakami, P. *The Grip of Change and the Author's Notes*. Trans. Sivakami. Chennai: Orient Blackswan, 2006. Print.

6

Marginalisation and Subordination of Dalit Women in Mukta Sarvagod's *Closed Doors*

Dr Deepika Rani

Autobiography is a literary genre which expresses the personality of its writer. It portrays the realities and vicissitudes of one's life. The personality of the writer remains at its core. An autobiography claims our attention and interest chiefly because of its reflection of the individual personality in it. Writing an autobiography is the process that leads to self-discovery, self-assessment and self-assertion. For Dalit writers, autobiography is a strong tool to narrate their stories, events and situations of hardships of life. Autobiography is an attempt to reach to maximum people and to let them know of their grievances and exploitation. Self assertion is the prime feature of an autobiography.

Dalit autobiographies are the record of suffering and pitiable living conditions of Dalits. These texts highlight the plight of Dalits and their segregation from the society. The word 'Dalit' itself expresses its painful meaning. This very word is rooted in Sanskrit and it means broken, ground-down or oppressed. Dalit literature in India emerged in the 1960s. It aimed at the liberation of Dalits from the oppression and injustice meted out to them by upper caste. Many Dalits had written autobiographies that lead to self-expression and paved a way for them to get them acquaint to the world. These autobiographies explain their pitiable conditions due to casteism, marginalisation, subordination etc. Dalit autobiographies project the saga of sufferings and humiliations of the Dalits. *Why I am not a Hindu* by Kancha Ilaiah, itself shows that the writer raises question regarding its birth in a lower caste and wish to get birth in an upper caste as Hindu. Laxman Bapu's *Upara: An Outsider* explains its pain as a human who has been taken as an outsider from the society. Om Prakash Valmiki's *Joothan* reveals the pain of a Dalit who has to eat the leftover food of upper caste. In this series, Mukta Sarvagod's *Closed Doors* is an autobiography and the title reveals itself that Dalits find doors closed for them everywhere whether it is a school or an office.

Closed Doors by Mukta Sarvagod occupies a prominent place in Indian Dalit literature. It focuses on the realistic picture of inhuman treatment meted out to Dalits. The theme of exploitation and social exclusion are dominant in the work. The various incidents highlight the pathetic condition of a Dalit whose life was full of oddities and hardships. *Closed Doors* articulates the voice of Dalit women. Their pathetic life reveals the bitter truth of their social status as a human being. They were deprived of basic amenities. *Closed doors* projects the harsh realities of the Mahar community. Mukta Sarvagod not only projects her story of exploitation and harassment but also raised her voice in favour of pathetic condition of Dalit women.

It can be said the fate of a person to take birth as a woman in a patriarchal society where she has no right to live her life at her own. The story of Mukta Sarvagod is full of subordination, marginalisation and humiliation. Taking birth in a caste upper or lower, is not decided by a child to be born. The innocent soul does not know that it is a crime to take birth in a lower caste. Then why that child has to pay for it? But it is its destiny that it had to struggle for identity even as a human being, especially when it is a female and secondly a female of a Dalit community.

Mukta Sarvagod narrates many incidents of her life that lead a person to think on the categories of society on the name of caste. Although humanity comes first and foremost but the social animal has divided human beings into so many categories. In her childhood, Mukta Sarvagod faced discrimination and she had crossed so many hurdles to get education. Her father worked for the Indian Railways. In the town of Puntambe, Mukta went to school when she was five years old. She faced discrimination not only from the students but teachers also realised an innocent child about her lower caste status. Her teacher closely examined the slates of every student to check their spellings. For this, she called every student to her table but Mukta was not allowed to come close to the table of the teacher. She was supposed to throw her slate from a height onto the table so that she could not touch that table with her body or her hands. Mukta was very intelligent in her studies. She used to get full marks in dictation. Instead of any reward or appreciation, she had to collect her slate from the floor on which the teacher slid it back after marking. Thus, Mukta was learning her identity as an untouchable. This was not enough. This tender girl was not allowed to touch the vessel filled with water. Whenever her classmates used the water to clean their slates, any of them sprinkled water on her slate, only then she could clean her slate with the help of them. She was not even allowed to sit on the bench with other students. Thus, a child was made to believe that her birth in a lower caste has restricted her to enjoy her life as a common child. Many of the parents of Mahar and Mang communities did not allow or dare to send their wards to school to get education. It was this because they were aware of the discrimination and the rude behaviour of teachers towards their wards. The teachers often threw the sticks at Mahar and Mang children from a distance so that they could save themselves from touching them. It was believed that if they touch them, they will get polluted. The same partial and rude behaviour of teachers has been recorded by many Dalit autobiographers. It shows their pain as well as their power to bear the atrocities at school to get education. Omprakash Valmiki has recorded his pain as untouchable in his autobiography, *Joothan*. His headmaster tried a lot to rusticate him from his school only because of his caste as a Chuhda or Mahar. Dr Deepika postulates in her paper:

> When Valmiki's father took him to school for admission, he was not got admitted because he has nothing to do with education. The logic behind this was his caste, 'Chuhda'.... Once the headmaster came to know his caste, Valmiki was instructed to sweep the huge ground by making a broom from tree. The process of cleaning was on for three days until his father noticed him. The rationale for the punishment was only the thinking of that headmaster that a Chuhda has to do only those things in his future i.e sweeping, cleaning sanitary, sowing seeds and harvesting. (261)

The reading of the various anecdotes from the autobiography fills the heart of the reader with anguish. Every incident is a proof of the marginalisation as well as enduring power of the Dalit women. As ours is a patriarchal society, it is very difficult for a woman to live her life peacefully. The monster of traditional patriarchal society still has its effect on the women. Talking about previous times, when such practices were at its youth, one cannot imagine the pitiable condition of women. Mukta's father got transferred to Agra and she with her mother had to vacate the railway quarters. But they still continued their life at Puntambe. While going to school she observed the men sitting free. Their wives were the only members who worked for earning. These women took care of their households as well as worked outside to earn. Sweeping the roads of the town was their mode of earning. Mukta Sarvagod often wished to make the men folk to understand the importance of the women. She wanted to make them understand their duties. If they cannot do hard work to earn their livelihood; at least they can clean their homes and children before returning of their women. Mukta Sarvagod had a strong desire to do something for such women but she was too young to do anything then. The illiterate women abused this little girl when she passed from the lanes. The reason of the abuses was her dare to study in a school as their only motive was to get married the girl child at an early age so that she can birth to children. Mukta Sarvagod was doing a shameful act by going to school. Mukta records her pain of discrimination and oppression. She was a double victim. Her own caste and upper caste both tortured her mentally and physically. Baby Kamble also writes her mother's position in her autobiography *The Prison We Broke*, "My father has locked up my aai in his house, like a bird in a cage (Kamble, 5) Bama delineates in *Karukku* that she had to wear the same clothes for a whole week due to her utter poverty conditions, "For a whole week, I went around in the same skirt, jacket and davaani. All my classmates looked at me as if I was some outlandish creature" (Bama, 74). Thus, Dalit women's real position has been depicted very pertinently in their autobiographies.

They were exploited by upper class people. These women did all odd jobs for them to get a little food in return to feed their children. Many women used to collect rags and scraps and sold them to wholesale merchant. Even the merchant did not spare them without exploiting them. He gave them less wages and used to cheat them. Some of the women used to go to private homes with the hope of getting food to fill the hungry bellies of their children. In order to save the life of their children from starvation; some Mahar and Mang women used cow dung to make cakes so that they would supply it in homes to get some food in return. How pitiable life they had to live! Just to save their lives from starvation, they did many little jobs. Mukta's father narrated many pathetic stories of Dalits. The oppression goes on to this extent that Mahars were assigned to do dangerous tasks that would risk their lives. The reason behind accepting that dangerous task was just to get hollow and rotten grain which would save their children from starvation. Issues of labour, food and hunger have been discussed in the autobiography. Starvation also gets birth with a Dalit and continues until its death. Hunger is that phenomenon that makes a Dalit disrespectful. Many soul-numbing incidents have been narrated by various Dalit writers. The empty bellied person choose wrong path to fill its stomach. Sharankumar Limbale in his autobiography, *The Outcaste* describes the pathetic conditions of Dalit women who served themselves to get food for the survival of their children. The Patils were known to their helplessness. They took its benefit and assaulted the Dalit women physically as well as sexually. They were beaten also. Thus, their life was as a slave. How ridiculing it seems that after getting independence from Britishers, the practices of slavery continued in the country, but at present this heinous task is done by their own neighbouring people.

Woman is taken as a passive and patient creature. Male tests her capacity of endurance. On the other hand, a woman knows trust and surrender and with her rationale she takes decision from the gut. She is conscious about reason of her existence in the world. But male cannot recognise her power of endurance and patience. He takes woman as other and treats badly with her. Thus, whole woman community is considered as secondary but for a dalit woman, it is a grave problem. It has been destined that if a child gets birth as a dalit female, then she has to face triple discrimination. She has to face subordination as a female in male dominated society, as a Dalit and as a Dalit woman. She should be ready to walk through the burning desert of casteism and to survive in the patriarchal society. She has to fight for her true identity. She has to suffer a lot as a Dalit woman is a Dalit amongst Dalit. She is marginalised amongst marginalised. Due to casteism Dalit women were being molested. Brutal patriarchy has been a major issue in their lives. The principle of gender equality is enshrined in the Indian Constitution, in its preamble and fundamental rights and duties. The constitution grants equality to women but practically they are depriving of equality. There still exits a wide gulf between constitution and its implementation.

Occupations were based on caste in previous era. A lower caste person was assigned lower ranked works. These people were discriminated everywhere. A person was known by its caste not by karma at school, offices, competitions, social gatherings etc. Even Karna, a character of a legendary epic Mahabharta was ridiculed and insulted many times because of his lower caste of a charioteer. Everyone was unknown to his divine roots and everyone just knew that he was a son of a charioteer. Thus, he was called *sootputra* and was ostracised by high caste people. Even Mahrashi Parshuram took back all his powers given to Karna as his disciple only because of his lower caste. Thus, casteism is deeply enrooted in India. Upper class enjoyed good status and was given high profile jobs whereas Mahars, lower caste people were assigned to pull and slay dead cattle, to clean the drains, to clean the roads and sewage. They were taken as equal to animals. Their death is of no importance. They were taken as those worms that were born to serve the upper caste. It was believed that Mahars' duty is just to clean the garbage or excreta of the road. Mahars were only welcomed when they came to ask for alms during solar eclipse. It was so because of the myth of serving poor people during solar eclipse. Mukta Sarvagod felt disheartened at this very state of her community.

The subordination of Mahar women was too worse to describe. These women were ordered to do many works and almost all those works required physical strength. The list of the works is endless. These women with empty bellies did every assigned work in order to get some food for their children. How pathetic state they had to live in just to survive. These women were subordinated by upper caste men who use them sexually and upper caste women who use them physically by giving works. Bama, gives a description of the endless list of works that a woman had to do:

> From the moment they wake up, they set to work both in their homes and in the fields. At home they are pestered by their husbands and children; in the fields there is back-breaking work besides the harassment of the landlord. When they come home in the evening, there is no time even to draw breath. And once they have collected water and firewood, cooked a kanji and fed their hungry husband and children, even then cannot go to bed in peace and sleep until dawn. (Bama, 22)

The autobiographer expresses the pain at the poor condition of Dalit women in a village. Although male was considered head of the family but it was just for namesake. The bitter reality is that women of the house did all assigned tasks to get food for the family members. These women had to go to Patils' or any other upper class house for work. They directly entered the animal pen and after cleaning its floor, they collected all leftovers. Then they cleaned the gutter which overflows with their urine. They collected the excrescence with the help of a big shovel and made its cakes; then kept them for drying. That was later on collected and stacked.

If any tree has been cut, they chop up their branches into neat little pieces, arrange them in stacks. Then grind whatever the mistress wants ground; and then, if they are lucky, they are free to go. By this time, it is already afternoon. They collect all the leftover....this is the life, if one can call it by that name, of all Mahar women! (qtd. in Rege, 148)

Each of the Dalit women underwent humiliations as an untouchable and as a female who is considered as 'other'. Various writers cite many examples how they tried to get education as they were aware of importance of education. Many dalit women tried to raise their status by earning their livelihood. Mukta tells in her autobiography that she organised literary classes for women and children of their community. To make them ready for the literary classes, she and her friends offered some prises like comb and mirror to some women whose houses were clean. By these efforts they were trying to establish relations so that these women could join literary classes with their children. Dr B.R. Ambedkar influenced the lower caste people to revolt against the exploitation and injustice. His views influenced Mukta and left a great impression.

To raise the status of Mahar women Mukta joined a mahila mandal, which was established to do something for women. After Mukta's involvement in mahila-mandal, there comes a new life. She is full of enthusiasm and strong determination. The mahila mandal decides to do some business. Sharmila Rege writes:

> Most of the women were uneducated, but their husbands were clerks and supervisors working in government offices...The mahila mandal decided to order leaves from Kajrat and make containers for wholesale merchants. Encouraged by their husbands, the women worked hard and made the containers, stringing them on the walls from the ceiling to the floor. Their tiny homes were crowded with these containers. When 80,000 such containers were ready, a wholesale merchant from the main vegetable market was invited to see the goods, and discuss prices. (Rege, 151)

One of the merchant came to see the hands of the women who had made the containers. But when they saw most women's arms were tattooed with pictures of trees and flowers, and a portrait of Babasaheb hung on wall, he realised that they were untouchables. Immediately he rushed out by replying that he will tell later about the containers. Rege records in her words:

> ....later, Muktabai contacted the merchants and sought to bring pressure upon them through the Mayor and editor of a local newspaper. However, they argued that the containers were used for distributing the Prasad and no one would buy the containers if they came to know that Mahar women had made them. (Rege, 152)

Mukta tried her best to sell them to others but no one agree to buy them. Thus, at last the containers had to be thrown away. The only reason behind not to purchase the containers was that those were made by Mahar women — the untouchables. O! What destiny these women had had. In spite of getting good wages of their hard labour of making containers, they had to throw them by their own hands. Ruchi Tomar writes, "Not only patriarchy and caste but also class divides Dalit women by bringing the embourgeoisment and Sanskritisation. Dalit feminism must respond to the complexity of salience of class and the differences create by the caste-ridden society." (Tomar, 2)

Dalit women were considered as impious but it is really ridicules when these impious women were sexually harassed by the upper caste people. In the dark these people not only touch these untouchables but sexually harassed them; and at day light they give cold look to these untouchable women. Dalit males also treat their women brutally. They beat them mercilessly and treated like animals. Dalit women were enslaved. *Closed Doors* is the result of Mukta Sarvagod's inner cry and her desire of liberation from her being double subaltern, as a woman and as a dalit. The autobiography raises various aspects of untouchability, humiliation, subalternity and marginalisation. A Dalit woman is a triple marginalised being. She is marginalised and subordinated by upper class men, upper class women and males of her own community. *Closed Doors* is an autobiography that brings the pain and agony of Dalit women from the deep waters on the surface so that it should be realised by others. It is a work that records the sufferings and humiliations of Mukta Sarvagod from her childhood to adulthood. She seems to be spokesman of her community. With her efforts, she tries to change the condition and status of Dalit women. Her efforts to deconstruct the imposed identity will bring a new change to the social status of Dalit women and the closed doors will be opened to them to welcome them in a liberated world and they would be able to live their lives with dignity.

Works Cited

Bama, Faustina. *Sangati: Events*. Trans. Lakshmi Holmstrom. New Delhi: Oxford India Paperback, 2014. Print.

Kamble, Baby. *The Prison We Broke*. New Delhi: Orient Blackswan, 2009. Print.

Limbale, Sharankumar. *Towards an Aesthetic of Dalit Literature: History, Controversies, and Considerations*. New Delhi: Orient Longman, 2004. Print.

Rani, Deepika. "Omprakash Valmiki's *Joothan: A Saga of Sufferings and Humiliations*". *Indian Dalit Autobiographies: Marginalised Voices*. Ed. Singh, Bijender. New Delhi: Authorspress, 2015, pp. 260-267. Print.

Rege Sharmila: *Writing Caste/Writing Gender, Narrating Dalit Women's Testimonios*. Zuban: New Delhi, 2006. Print.

Sarvagod, Mukta. *Mitleli Kavaade* (Marathi). Amalner: Chetashri Prakashan, 1983. Print.

Tomar, Ruchi. "Dalit Feminism: A Transformation of Rejection into Resistance." *The Criterion: An International Journal in English*. Issue 12, February 2013. 1-8.

7

Breaking the Margins: Analysing *The Prisons We Broke* as a Testimony of Oppression and Resistance

Guni Vats

> You have always been treacherous to us but we never deceived our mother... we dreamt and floated among the clouds, waiting for one little ray of hope to lace our dark dreams. (Kamble, 38)

Centuries ago Aryans colonised the Indian lands and claiming themselves to be the superior issued literary book of rules. Rig-Veda, one such guide of social hierarchy divides the all existing humankind in a well defined *Varna Vyavastha*. The division wraps the society while dividing the labour according to the *Varna*, Brahmins were the teachers, Kshatriyas the warriors, Vaishyas the artisans and merchants and Shudras the labourers and service providers. The division that rules the society and defines the code of conduct thus forgets the section of people who are forced to the margins of village, who eat dead animals and wear the shroud. This section of people are the natives of the village from which they have been dragged out; they are the 'Dalits', the oppressed, the marginalised, the pollutants, the filthy, the slave, the untouchable and the other. Baby Kamble's foreword to her Marathi autobiography grieves:

> Today, our young educated people are ashamed of being called a Mahar. But what is there to be ashamed of? We are the great race of the Mahars of Maharashtra. We are its real original inhabitants, the sons of the soil. The name of this land is also derived from our name. I love our caste name, Mahar- it flows in my veins, in my blood, and reminds me of our terrific struggle for truth. (Kamble, 3)

With Indian literature experimenting with new genres of prose in the nineteenth century came the genre autobiography. Since now this genre was only popular in the west as they celebrated a 'self' which could demand documentation. India was yet to explore a self-amidst the chaos of society and family. Even when autobiographies touched the horizons they were limited to the upper caste, Rashasundari Debi's *Phaniyamma* is a work which drifts towards the tradition of Bhakti poetry as it is all about her belief in God, autobiographies by Nehru and Gandhi also reverberate about their 'self' and the society they moved in. None of the upper caste writer took the pen to explore the boundaries of the village where they dump their waste and it was primarily because of this exclusion from the literary scenario that Dalit writers took to tell their own tale. The autobiographies of Dalit men would eclipse the picture of Dalit woman completely, either behind the doors of the house or as a portrait of the ideal mother. To fight with such a demeaning scenario, Dalit women took the initiative of writing their stories, the stories that convey every breath of toil that a Dalit goes through and Kamble's effort is probably the beginning of such a literary revolution, as Maya

Pandit asserts in her introduction to *The Prisons We Broke*, "It is the first autobiography by a Dalit woman not only in Marathi but in any Indian language"(3).

Baby Kamble's *Jina Amucha* is a social narrative that was compiled after a rigorous toil of note making and hiding the manuscripts from everyone of the community. She took notes over years and then hid her papers under the old newspaper and her notebooks at the alcove. She remembers that she "used to be scared of both my son and my husband, scared of their reaction" (Kamble, 147). The fragments of Kamble's memories weave a precise scenario of the cultural, social, economical and historical existence of a community that was thrown to the margins and well forgotten. Gopal Guru argues Sharmila Rege's calling the autobiography a 'testimony' and ultimately settles categorising Kamble's autobiography in three contexts:

> First, Baby Kamble's autobiography *The Prisons We Broke* is an important text which offers us an insight into the possibility of understanding the tension between tradition and modernity. Second, it shows us that it is through the everyday response to this tension chart out their journey to modernity, which according to the author is epitomised in Ambedkar. Third, Baby Kamble informs us about some of the important social practices that indicate resonance with modernity and its sphere of influence (Guru, 163).

The autobiography opens with the mystic of Baby's birth which was enwrapped in the superstitious Hinduism. The instances of devout Hinduism and the blind following of traditional rituals lead the readers to a darkness that raptures the oeuvre in the era when medicines meant chanting the God's name and rubbing ash. Furthering in the work the text leads to the streets of Maharwada with fifteen or sixteen houses and big clay pot, *keli* kept at the entrance of houses for drinking water. The genius of depicting the ritual of drinking water, the burnt out *tawa*, the holy threads hanging above the grinding stone and the description of people covered with dirt and tangled hair, bodies wrapped in rags and scratching their heads rigorously with lice sticking in the crevices of their clothes does not demand self-pity but portray a self-critical view of the community that celebrated existence and ignored self. Every poverty-stricken home was decorated with a mandatory 'god's place' which was a raised platform with stones situated on it. It was the height of these platforms that sang the ode of family's reputation.

The autobiography could be read as a cultural journal for depicting every face of life. The month of Ashadh and the Buffalo fair seem to be the two occasions for which the poor Mahars put up till the rest of eleven months. As Kamble recites, "Ashadh for them was the burgeoning of happiness. A blessing for their starved bodies-when the tongue was satiated with the taste it loved" (12). The food that was eaten; a gummy mixture of *bhakris* and jaggery and the meat of buffalo would seem barbarous to the middle class but it was the delicacy that still lingers at the heart of a Mahar. The Hindu philosophy was dearest to the hearts of the Mahar women especially since they treasured their *haldi kumkum* more than any wealth they could have in spite of the mainstream Hindus throwing them into their "dirt and garbage pits" (Kamble, 18). Women were the pioneers of these households who would take control of the domestic matters, collect firewood or fresh grass and sell it in the village and get possessed to announce the fate of Maharwada. The men would either do nothing or beg for alms or discuss in the *chawdi*. The children were a bunch of naked bodies loitering through the village and imitating their elders as a part of the game play which would at times cost them their life. Travelling to the deepest corners of these homes and inside the huts brings across another interesting fact, they always had a longing to become rich or at least the middle class of the upper caste:

> The moral of the story is that so far we have been calling our huts, royal palaces; our poor husbands, kings; and the leftovers we got, rich dishes...we love to dream. For it is in our dreams that all our hopes come true! (Kamble, 41).

Clothing plays an essential part of culture. The children were left naked till they matured and even when boys grew to become potraja they would only tie a waistband across their loin. Mahar women would hardly have a piece of rag that would be of some length achieved by stitching tatters together. They would not even have ample cloth to curb bleeding at the time of delivery. On the special day of Ashadh women would give their saris to their daughters to wash. Daughters would invest hours in killing lice that were stuck in the pleats of sari. At the time of monthly periods, women would wash one part of their sari wrapping themselves with the other end and repeat the procedure with the other end once dry. The shrouds would give women a chance to show off the styles of tying saris like the upper caste women. The hegemony did not spare clothing:

> There were caste rules even for how one tucked the pleats. Mahar women had to tuck them in such a way that the borders remained hidden. Only high caste women had the privilege of wearing their saris in such a way that the borders could be seen. A Mahar woman was supposed to hide the borders under the pleats; otherwise it was considered an offence to the high castes. (Kamble, 54)

The women who were the pall bearers of tradition and managers of household were vigorously 'doubly marginalised', they were the 'other of the others' and were strangled till their voices choked. As Uma Chakravarty understands, they were suffering from a 'Graded Patriarchy' (580) where they were being subjected to what the Brahmins were subjecting their husbands towards. Their identity was clouded under the burdens of class, caste, gender, poverty and illiteracy. They had a history of suffering whatever they were subjected to because the religion that they prescribed to bound a woman under the fetters of *kumkum*, "for the sake of the kumkum mark, we lay our lives at the feet of our husbands" (Kamble, 41). A woman in a patriarchy is recognised as a social being only after her marriage and this obligation was exercised on the Mahar women when they were mere girls. The marriage meant baking *bhakris* at three in the morning, bearing the insults and beatings of the in-laws, leading a life of slave in the house of slaves, child bearing that would involve lack of medical precision and risk their lives and any attempt of eloping would result in chopping off the nose, literally!

Any form of hegemony could be achieved with the pre-requisite of binary opposition. This opposition between the castes synthesised a gap that tore man from man and designated part of land and filth. Hindu religion not only created but made sure that this gap remains intact. Through the stories of Ramayana, Mahabharata, Eklavya, Sati Savitri, Vrinda and Narada the Brahmins tied Dalits in the history of oppression and made it seem as natural as the birth of man. The practice of this oppression is not only portrayed but questioned in this autobiography when through the high walls of upper caste Mahars settle for lesser bargains for their toil of collecting firewood and are then dragged to the backyards picking out every strand of their hair or sari that might have remained stuck to the firewood. Kamble voices her aggression and protests thus:

> What a beastly thing this Hindu religion is! Let me tell you, it's not prosperity and wealth that you enjoy - it is the very life blood of the Mahars! Mahar women's sweat would have soaked the firewood. Sometimes when thorns picked them, blood trickled and dripped on the sticks. Sometimes they cut their own limbs instead of the wood and blood poured down, drenching the wood

> with blood...it was the very essence of the Mahar woman's life that was found sticking to the wood. And yet the Brahmin woman objected to what they found sticking there! (56).

The rage against oppression that burns the soul of Kamble gets expressed in her work since the first chapter but the scattered aggression gats streamlined only under the leadership of Dr Babasaheb Ambedkar. He shook the cradle of filth and woke the Mahars to make them realise their existence and place in society, "You don't worship god; you worship your ignorance! Generations after generations of Mahars have ruined themselves with such superstitions" (Kamble, 64). He commanded the oppressed not to clean the filth of the village, to let the upper castes clean their own filth. He appealed the women to lead the endeavour towards change and educate their children. Walking on the path directed by Ambedkar, Baby along with a few other girls enrolled themselves to a girl's school where they were subjected constantly to oppression; they were thrown towards a corner of the room where they were reminded continuously of their untouchability:

> The teachers used to be awfully worried about our polluting them and harassed us a lot as if we were their enemies. They treated us like lepers, really. They wouldn't even look at us. (Kamble, 140).

Ambedkarite movement changed the face of Mahars; women would send their children to school even if they had to arrange for money through borrowing, girls would gather the strength to enter the temple, boys started living in hostels and arranging rallies, change was now the topic of discussion at *chawdis* instead of the superstitious practices, the life bathed fresh, weddings did not require a Brahmin priest anymore, the occupation of selling firewood was replaced by establishing small scale business in the untouchable locality. The Indian face of revolution was coloured with the Dalit

Panther movement. The changes introduced majority of women participating in the unions when the older women would take care of the household in their absence. The women now had a voice and they made sure they were heard.

Women may have transgressed the boundaries laid by Hindu religion and adopted Buddhism but the limitations laid by patriarchy were non-transgressable. The walls of patriarchy were higher than those of the upper caste. Kamble might have written an autobiography but her mother was still not allowed to step out of the house. Kamble's autobiography does not talk much of her personal life and thus, it is only through her interview with Maya Pandit that we witness her being subjected to patriarchal subjectivity. We learn this through her need of hiding her writings for a long time, "Firstly, because of my husband. He was a good man but like all the men of his time and generation, he considered a woman to be an inferior being. He would not have tolerated the idea that I had taken to writing. I used to be scared of him. So I had to hide my writing" (Kamble, 147). This fear of the man still poses a big question in the era of development, half of the population stays in fear of the other half.

The educated Dalits got lured by the Congress in lieu for a few seats. They then replaced the upper castes and occupied the top position in the government. Since they no more suffered the pangs of hunger they forgot the plights of their poor brethrens. In the interview Kamble exposed the scheme of Brahmins:

> ...Chambhar, Dhor, Koshti and others...were all Shudras...even the Marathas were Shudras. But the Brahmins were so clever, they took all the castes inside the village according to their own needs and very systematically built a hierarchy amongst them. And the bravest caste of the Mahars, who were the original

> inhabitants of this land, was yoked to their cart... they also created a sense of hierarchy amongst us. The Chambhars used to scorn us. We considered the Dhors to be beneath us...(Kamble, 151).

The schemes were as evident in the way 'yeskars' were treated. A yeskar was the Mahar man who would visit the village to beg for the stale food. This food would then be brought to the chawdi and distributed amongst the families according to their share. The yeskar Mahar had to carry a stick with a bell fitted at one end. The man who was the hero of the Maharwada for earning food that day stood with his back bent and saluting the upper caste men, women and children. The bell would warn the upper caste against pollution and leftover food be thrown in his blanket. He was chosen for the lowly jobs like cleaning the pandals at marriage or delivering news of the dead. He might or might not get leftover food at the end of the day. Under the scheme, upper castes would pose as if the yeskar stick was something utterly auspicious and to be proud of. The frustration of men in the village would then be equalled by their beating their wives.

Kamble's autobiography has more than often been tagged as the protest literature. The very act of a Dalit woman writing an autobiography elevates to the status of protest. Kamble's personal life though remains hidden more than often because she considered her community the 'self' and any expression of her personal life would be demeaning. In her interview she confesses that she would have to suffer the beatings from her husband but then it was normal for a man to hit and demean a woman and she did not find anything provocating in it. Kamble's work skips the depiction of sexual molestations and she focuses on her attempt to uplift her community as a whole rather than fragments of gender. *The Prisons We Broke* is not merely a protest but a documentary that introduced modernism. It broke the prejudices and demanded dignity for the people who ate pus oosing infected dead animals. It is a true saga of oppression and real face of resistance.

Works Cited

Chakravarti, Uma: "Conceptualising Brahminical Patriarchy in Early India: Gender, Caste, Class and State." *Economic and Political Weekly*. 1993. Print.

Devy, G. *The G.N. Devy Reader*. Hyderabad: Orient Longman, 1992. Print.

Ganguly, D. "Dalit life stories". *The Cambridge Companion to Modern Indian Culture* (Eds) V. Dalmia and Sadana. New Delhi: Cambridge University Press, 2012. 124-141. Print.

Guru, G. "Dalit Women Talk Differently". *Gender and Caste*. Ed. A. Rao. New Delhi : Women Unlimited, 2003. 80-85. Print.

Kamble, Baby. *The Prisons We Broke*. Trans. Maya Pandit. Hyderabad: Orient Blackswan, 2008. Print.

Narayankar Tejaswini, P., *Dalit Autobiography: An Evolution of Individual Self*. http://www.researchfront.in. Accessed on 12/08/2015. 2.2.(2014). Web.

Ramanathan S. *Situating Dalit Literature in Indian writing in English*. http://www.languageinindia.com. Accessed on 12/08/2015. 14. (2014) Web.

Rege, S. "A Dalit Feminist Standpoint". *Gender and Caste*. New Delhi: Women Unlimited, 2003. 90-101. Print.

Sathe, Putul. *Ethnography of the Marginalised Self: Reading of Dalit Women's Autobiographies*. Women's Link. 19.4. (2013). Print.

8

A Doubly Oppressed Voice in Urmila Pawar's *The Weave of My Life: A Dalit Woman's Memoir*

Suruchi Sharma

What the writer writes about is social reality, and not his/her individual life.

—(*The Weave of My Life*, 342)

Urmila Pawar is a famous Indian woman Dalit writer who writes in the Marathi language. Urmila Pawar was born in May 1945 at Adgaon village of Ratnagiri District in Konkan Region of Maharashtra, India. She was born in a Hindu Mahar family that generally weaves baskets from bamboos. Her memoir *Aaydan* was published in 2003 and it was later translated by Dr Maya Pandit as *The Weave of My Life: A Dalit Woman's Memoir*'. She has portrayed the sufferings of Dalits in her autobiography *The Weave of My Life: A Dalit Woman's Memoir.* Urmila Pawar is generally known for her short-stories in Marathi language. Urmila is the youngest child among seven siblings. When she was in the third standard her father passed away. Her father had taken education upto sixth class and he was a primary school teacher. It was a big blow to her family. There was no other source of income in her family that's why her mother tried to run the family somehow. As she was illiterate she started weaving cane baskets and sold them to run the family. Even Urmila, her brothers and sisters had to sell the baskets from door-to-door. These were very bad days for them.

The Weave of My Life has been written in realistic mode and has the authentic records of her life. Like other Dalit writers, Urmila Pawar has used earthly language that is generally used by the Mahars. She has used the daily vocabulary of the Mahars, how women use language when they quarrel, criticise or curse each other. There is an open discussion of bodily functions, the raunchy l and the rough language that they use. Male Dalit writers have also used such kind of language to give a realistic touch in their writing.

Although Urmila's father was not much educated yet he wanted to educate all his children, that's why after her father's death her mother had sent all her children to study in school and even in college. In spite of caste-based discrimination and poverty Urmila's brother and sisters were good in their studies and scored well in their school and college examinations. Urmila had to face some difficulties in her studies but despite of all she passed out her matriculation in 1964. She got married to Harish Chandra in 1966. She joined Public Work Department in Maharashtra. She has two daughters. She kept studying even after marriage. Her husband did not allow her for her M.A. in Marathi as he did not like 'more educated wife' than he was. After her masters she tried to do her doctorate on the topic of "Dalit Women's Participation in the Ambedkar Movement" but she could not complete her thesis as Bombay University declined her research proposal saying that she does not have a sociology degree and without it she cannot take such a research project. In utter frustration she kept continuing on that project in collaboration with Dalit woman activist, Meenakshi Moon, wife of Vasant Moon and published later as a book under the title *Amhihi Itihasa Ghadawala* or *We also Made History* under Zubaan, a Delhi-based publication house. Urmila started writing about dalit women's sufferings caused by men. Her writings were objected by men and they warned her not to write about men of her community, "You write, but write about how the upper castes misbehave with us. But it is not nice to point out the shortcomings of our men" (24).

'Aaydan' generally means weaving of cane baskets. Aaydan is also used for the utensils they use in their daily life. The concept of 'weaving' plays a very important role in this autobiography. As weaving the bamboo basket was the profession of the protagonist's mother, it shows that they lived in the utter poverty, hunger and destitute. The economic condition of Urmila Pawar's family was so poor that she used to have only two dresses for school which she wore alternatively for three or four days. When she was in the fourth class she got a scholarship of twelve rupees. Urmila Pawar has not seen twelve rupees in her life. Her teacher, Diwalker played an important role in her life and he told her the importance of cleanliness, hygiene and cleanliness. He told her to buy two new frocks from the money she got from her scholarship. Urmila Pawar's mother usually kept herself busy in weaving the baskets. When Urmila told her about the scholarship her face beamed with smile:

> Aye was weaving her baskets as usual. She did not see me when I crossed her and entered the house. Her face looked worried. She was engrossed in her own thoughts and her fingers flew over the basket. Going to her, I told her about the scholarship and held the twelve rupees before her. Suddenly her face lit up with a sunny smile and eyes sparkled. (Pawar, 91)

The theme of caste discrimination and untouchability has been portrayed in this autobiography. Urmila Pawar belonged to a very poor Mahar family and after the death of her father she had to bunk her school for many days so that she might be able to help her mother financially. She had to feel much humiliated when the other girls from the upper caste in her school brought nice dishes in their tiffins. Urmila knew her helplessness in this matter that's why she never even thought to mention these things in her home as she knew her family condition very well. Urmila recollects an incidence of her life when she was in the school. One day her classmates planned to cook food in the school; so every girl was to bring one or the other eatable like rice, lentils etc. When she asked from her classmates they told her to bring money "You must bring some money" (107) instead of bringing any material just because she belonged to an untouchable Dalit family. Sharmila Rege observes about dalit memoirs, "Memoirs of humiliation and resistance delineate the reproduction of caste as a form of modern inequality both in the village and the city" (336). On that day upper caste girls prepared rice, dal and vegetables and they did not allow her to touch any dish while preparing as she belonged to a Dalit caste. Though they sat to eat it together yet they were noticing how much she was eating and they whispered about her eating in the groups. For some days the girls whispered in the groups how much she ate that day:

> They did not allow me to touch anything. However, we all ate together. I really enjoyed the meal. The next day I was horrified to hear that my eating had become the hottest topic for juicy gossip. Girls were whispering in groups about 'how much I had eaten" (110).

Urmila was poor in English and her English teacher reprimanded and abused her for her poor command over English. He scolded her saying, "This is English, the milk of tigress; it is not easy, like acting in plays" (160). It was her school and her family environment that inspired her to improve their financial condition and social status. Whenever a person is not satisfied with the present conditions of a society or religion he tries to devise a new path like, Guru Nanak Dev, the founder of Sikh religion who worked against Hindu *Varna* system and established new religion in Punjab. He said, "I am not Hindu, I am not a Muslim, I am a Sikh, a new religion which is full of virtues and qualities derived from Hindu and Muslim religion" (Mense, 9)

The exploitation of women is one of the major themes in the autobiography. It is mentioned in it that men got comparatively better food while women were not given equal food to eat. The daughter-in-laws were exploited to the maximum level. The girls also lived in wretched hunger that they failed to control them at the sight of food. Urmila Pawar describes an incident when she went to a wedding at her sister-in-law's place with her two niece. They bounced at the food like gluttons and when they ask for rice repeatedly the cook got angry and called them monster. Urmila could not digest this word and she refused for more food.

> However, when we three spout girls set down to eat and begun asking rice repeatedly, the cook got angry, 'Whose daughters are these anyway? 'He burst out. 'They are eating like monsters' then someone answered 'they are from our" Sushi's family! Daughters of Arjun master!' On hearing this, the host came forward. 'Oh! Are they? All right, all right let them eat as much as they want! Serve them well!' The cook returned with more rice but being called monster was not easy to digest and we politely declined.(117)

Urmila was married in a poor home and she describes her first night openly in her autobiography like Kamala Das has written her personal moments also to her readers. The depiction of the room and bed shows the impoverished condition of her husband's home:

> The tiny room with its peeling walls, the single iron bed with its creaking iron strips, the smelly, moldy mattress with hard lumps of cotton, the dirty, stained, old

> bedspread, the flat hard pillow smelling like a naphthalene bag.....the sharp yellow strip of light from the bulb piercing the eye (18).

Apparently, Urmila was financially independent serving in a government job but she has to give her salary to her husband. She was not independent in this matter. When she was a girl she gave the money to her mother and after marriage she has to give money to her husband, Harishchandra:

> When I got my first salary, I could not believe that all that money was mine; that I could spend it the way I liked. Before my marriage, I used to hand over my salary to my mother; now I started handling it over to my husband. If this is not like deliberately offering head for the butcher's knife, what else is it?" (208)

Urmila Pawar is a bold woman who kicked out the problems coming on the way of her career and life. She continued her studies and research despite of the objectional attitude her husband. She kept writing also. When her first storybook *Sixth Finger* was published her husband felt proud of her success as a writer:

> His attitude towards me was full of contradictions. On the one hand, he was proud of my writing, he admitted to his friends and relatives. However, on the other, he immensely resented my being recognised as a writer, my speaking in public programmes and my emerging as a figure in the public domain. (246)

There is a depiction of conversion of people. The people embraced Buddhism due to many reasons. It was an easy way for them to come out of the Dalitism and to achieve the level of equality where nobody criticised them for their caste. People converted into Buddhism under the influence of Ambedkarite movement and after conversion they left their previous rituals and adopted the new rituals of this religion. This change could be easily seen in their rituals of birth, marriage and death: "The older rituals to mark birth, marriage and death were given up and new ones gradually came to be finalised, according to Buddhist religion." (111)

Urmila Pawar has written a custom prevalent in Maharashtra. At the death ceremony of a man, his wife has to break her 'Mangalsutra' and her bangles. She has to remove all the signs of a 'Suhagan' or wifehood. She has to remove her *kumkum* from her forehead with the left toe of the husband. Urmila disliked this death ceremony and she raised voice against this ritual. In the words of Sonali Rode, "Urmila Pawar's *Aaydan* describes her long journey from Kokan to Mumbai bringing the struggle of three generations for a Dalit modernity about which readers have hitherto heard so little." (*International Research Journal*, Vols. 3 and 4, 2008)

Baby Kamble's autobiography *The Prison We Broke* also tells the same conditions of the Mahar women. Like Urmila's mother the Mahar women have to do all the household chores and have to sell the wood to run the family. After that hard work they have to collect the left-over to feed their family. At any religious function their works automatically gets double. Kamble tells that the girls in Mahar family get married at the age of eight or nine and get pregnant and face problem in their delivery at the tender age.

If a girl fails to do the household duty properly, she is scolded by her in-laws. Reviewing Pawar's *Aaydan* Nilanjana Bhattacharya writes, "Maya Pandit's English translation of Baby Kamble's *Jina Amucha*, (1982) and Urmila Pawar's *Aaydan*, (2003) locating the establishment of a Dalit feminist stand point within the canon of feminism."

Since ancient time, the gender discrimination has been prevalent in our society. If it is a Dalit community then she is doubly discriminated. In Shantabai's autobiography *The Kaleidoscopic Story of My Life* she describes the situation how her father, Sakharam was on the verge to kill her at her birth when he came to know that another girl was born. He says, "All bloody girls. Granny, hand over that girl. And give me the pick and the shovel. I'll go (and) bury her" (93). Kumud Pawde also tells her story that she got a job in the university as a Sanskrit professor due to her husband's high caste surname otherwise she could not get this job. She writes, "I hear that a woman's surname changes to match her husband's -and so does her caste. That's why I say that the credit of being a professor of Sanskrit is that of the presumed higher caste status of Mrs Kumud Pawde. The caste of her maiden status remained deprived." (106)

Urmila Pawar has to live her life under very bad circumstances but due to them she became an iron woman and found her path herself. She rejected the traditional set of rules designed by the patriarchal social set up and raised her voice for the emancipation of Dalit women. Her hardships have not only made her strong but she determined to liberate the other Dalit women also. She has written in the concluding paragraphs of her autobiography:

> Life has taught me many things, showed me so such. It has also lashed it me till I bled, I don't know how much longer I am going to live, nor do I know in what form life is going to confront me let it came in any form; I am ready to face it stoically. This is what my life has taught me. This is my life and that is me. (320)

Thus, Dalit women have to struggle more in their life to crave a place for them. They are on one side economically weak, on the other side they are dalits. Moreover, their husbands put pressure on them and try to keep them under their control. Thus, they are under the control of those people who are already controlled by the high caste people. There is a dire need to examine their history on the basis of caste etc issues as Ruchi Tomar contents:

> There is a need to examine and evaluate Dalit women's historical experiences from the perspective of caste,

economic class, politics, and patriarchal angles, aimed towards the transformation in work, wages, and family life. Not only patriarchy and caste but also class divides Dalit women by bringing the embourgeoisment and Sanskritisation. Dalit feminism must respond to the complexity of salience of class and the differences create by the caste-ridden society. (Tomar, 2)

Works Cited

Mense, Krushna. *Shri Basweswar te Shri Dyneswar Ek Chintan.* Mumbai: Lokwangmay Gruh, 2009. Print.

Narayankar, Tejaswini P. "Dalit Autobiography: An Evolution of Individual Self." Vol. 2, Issue 2, Apr - Jun. 2014. Web. www.researchfront.in

Pawar, Urmila. *Aaydan.* Tran. by Dr Maya Pandit as *The Weave of My Life: A Dalit Woman's Memoir.* Katha, 2007. Print.

Rege Sharmila: *Writing Caste/Writing Gender, Narrating Dalit Women's Testimonios.* Zuban: New Delhi, 2006. Print.

Rode, Sonali. "Dalit Feminism: A Transformation of Rejection into Resistance." *International Research Journal.* Vol. 3 and 4. 2008.

Tomar, Ruchi. "Dalit Feminism: A Transformation of Rejection into Resistance." *The Criterion: An International Journal in English.* Issue 12, February 2013. pp. 1-10.

9

A Reading of Subjugation of Dalit Women in Baby Kondiba Kamble's *The Prisons We Broke*

Kusum Kanger

The Prisons We Broke (2008) is Baby Kamble's autobiography that was originally published in Marathi as *Jina Amacha* (1986) but was later translated into English by Dr Maya Pandit. This autobiography is an authentic document of the pains and sufferings of the Mahar Dalit men and women in Veergaon, Baby Kamble's village in Maharashtra. This autobiography foregrounds the hegemonised state of the Dalit women who make up leeway for their liberty but in vain. They don't have better life than animals. She describes that Mahars are those animals who don't have a tail. The text provides a true picture of the oppression of the upper caste people and the patriarchal set up of the Indian society. The Mahar women have to live in suppression and they don't feel safe even in their own homes.

Bâby Kamble was a very bold woman and she raised her voice against the patriarchal setup, exploitation and suppression of women. She embraces Buddhism to fight aghast the discrimination on the basis of caste. Baby Kamble herself was a victim of this caste system and she writes this autobiography not for herself but for the whole Dalit community. She uses the word 'we' instead of 'I' at many places in this autobiography. She has written the experiences of her community. She writes: "I wrote about what my community experience. The sufferings of my people became my own suffering. Their experiences became mine. So I really find it very difficult to think of myself outside my community" (136).

Whether it is a male or female autobiography, geographical location of Dalit people plays an important role. Omprakash Valmiki's *Joothan*, Bama's *Karukku* and Kamble's *The Prison We Broke* — all these autobiographies open with this geographical difference that dalits live in a separate place away from the high caste people and they are not allowed to take part in the social activities like other people. In *Joothan: A Dalit's Life* dalits live in a separate place in the village in Gaya District in Bihar. Omprakash Valmiki writes, "Our house was adjacent to Chandrabhan Taga's gher or cowshed. Next to it lived the families of Muslim weavers. Right in front of Chandrabhan Taga's gher was a little johri, a pond which was created as a partition of between the Chuhra's dwellings and the Village" (Valmiki, 1). Baby Kamble also describes the same segregation of dalits that they lived away from the other high caste people. She writes:

> Come to think of it what kind of life did this people really lead? What was their worth living for? Generation after generation wasted away in senseless worship of stones, in utter misery. Generation after generation perished. (11)

She describes that since their birth the ditch of caste is in front of them and this difference of dalits and non-dalits is told to them. They are told by their own caste people that they are untouchables in the eyes of the upper caste people.

Even the high caste people know about it. She gives an instance in the text:

> He (the upper caste shopkeeper) would give the innocent children lesions in social behaviour, "Chabu, hey you, can't you see the dirty Mahar woman standing there? Now don't you touch her. Keep your distance". Immediately a Mahar woman gathering her rags around her tightly so as not to pollute the child would say, "take care little master, please keep a distance. Don't come to close you might touch and get polluted" (14).

Baby Kamble's autobiography has very deep concerns regarding the discrimination on the basis of caste. She gives some instances that make us feel about the seriousness of the cancer of caste. She says that on one side dalits are untouchable but on the other all the works of the upper caste people are done by the dalits. Then why upper caste people don't do all their works themselves and why the dalits people are forced to do all inferior works. Do the dalits not touch their eatables when they grow them or do they not touch their palace when they build them? The text is written in the style of self-assertion:

> When the Mahar woman labour in the field, the corn gets wet with their sweat. The same corn goes to make your pure rich dishes. And you feast on them with such evident relish! Your palaces are built with the sweat and blood of Mahars. But does it rot your skin? You drink their blood and sleep comfortably on the bed of their misery. Doesn't it pollute you then? ... and you have been flogging us with the whip of pollution. This is all that your selfish religion has given to us. But now we have learnt how utterly worthless your religion is… (56).

The Prison We Broke is a narrative of pain, trauma and exploitation. Nayar says: While severely restricted and oppressed-rendered into victims, one might say because of their social contexts, their very acts of writing, articulation and construction of affective moral-webs with other victims within their narratives shift their identity from mere victims to something else. This shift takes them outside the identity of a victim into a self-conscious subject who, in the act of narrating his/her own story and also that of others, constructs a whole new subjectivity. (Nayar 1) Baby Kamble raises the question of caste in this autobiography. She questions, "They have two legs, two hands, two eyes and two ears and unchanged blood colour, red. How one can different by birth? May be he/she can dissimilar by skin, behaviour or looking but not by birth, caste and class. No one can answer Kamble's questions regarding his or her (Dalits) existence, "We never rebelled against you, did we? We did not perform *namaj* when you worshipped, did you? You considered the cow holy; we never insulted her, did we/we obeyed every diktat of your Hindu religion, we followed all your tradition-why did you single us out for your contempt? (38)

Baby Kamble's *The Prisons We Broke* is a rich document of Dalit victimisation. Kamble was born to an industrial father. She knows very well the patriarchal set up of the society. The condition of the Mahar women was very bad. Kamble narrates about 'maharwada' women who live in the utter poverty conditions. They had to sell firewood to the high caste people to meet both ends meet. They were not allowed to go on the same road on which high caste people frequently tread. But they could enter that area only when they sell the firewood. If they see high caste people coming to them, they have to bow them politely and they utter the words to them, "The humble Mahar women fall at your feet master" (52). There were separate lane for dalits and the upper caste people:

> There were separate colonies for the Mahar community members and also to the lower communities and Mahars were allowed to travel by the roads to these colonies only. The lanes were known as Dhangar Lane, Vinkar Lane, Mali Lane, Teli Lane and so on (54).

The same kind of treatment is done to even a high caste child. Kamble narrates if sometimes newly-wedded women don't bow to the high caste people, then they are cursed for this act. Their in-laws criticise and abuse them for it. Thus, they are considered like the servants of the upper caste. The Mahar women had to wear ragged saris. They cannot wear new saris and if they wear then also they will have to wear them differently. They cannot wear their saris like the women belonging to the high castes. They had to tuck the pleats of the sari in such a way that their borders may not been seen by the other people.

The marriage ceremony of the Mahar community has also been described by Baby Kamble in her autobiography. The bride's family had to perform all the rituals very humbly and they had to bear all the expenses of the ceremony. The ritual of the bath has been described very funny. Both the bride and the groom sat on a wooden board in the courtyard and two huge pots were placed in both sides. After that the bride was rolled around in the muddy water until she was fully besmeared with mud. After it, the bride and groom did not walk for five days. This ceremony was performed by a Brahmin priest and he came there just for money. He kept himself at a safe distance so that he may not get polluted.

Another main issue of child marriage has been raised in this autobiography. The girls were married at raw age before they attain the age of puberty. Baby Kamble herself was the victim of this institution of marriage and faced the worst fate. She was married at the age of thirteen. The life for the newly-wedded married girls was very bad. They were married at the age of eight or nine when it was the time to play with dolls. They were sent to their in-laws' home to start their new life. It was the age when they didn't know anything what really is a husband. They had to go through various types of suppression and violence. They had to pass from many ordeals in their new home. They had to prepare two baskets full of bhakris for the family. At the age of eight or nine as a bride they had to sit to prepare them but they would not cook them properly. Then their mother-in-laws would call the other women and told them like this:

> Attyabai, come and see what happening here is. Didn't you think that I'd brought the daughter of a good woman into my house? Look at the bhakris this slut has prepared. She cannot even make a few bhakris properly. Oh, well, what can one expect of this daughter of a dunce? (94)

They were expected to do all the household chores very silently without any complaints. Their mothers-in-law abused them if they did not do their work properly. "What's your aai really? Tell me! Is she a good married woman at all? Or does she know only how to run after the pot-maker donkeys? Didn't she teach you anything? I pamper you... my own sasu was spitfire. A burning coal! Holding a burning coal in one's palm was easier than living with her!" (95). They had to suffer all this and they could not tell this to their home. If they returned their parental home their parents scolded them and send them again to their in-laws' home.

The women's condition was very miserable. They suffered from mal-nutrition and especially after delivery they suffered from anemia just because they did not get a nutritional diet. The midwives conducted their delivery without professional skills and they were forced to eat only gruel after delivery. The Mahar people were dominated by the upper castes so they were looking for someone on whom they may dominate. They ruled over their newly-entered brides. Kamble writes about their new way to dominate on them:

> The other world had bound us with the chains of slavery. But we too were human beings. And we too desired to dominate, to wield power. But who would let us do that? So we made our own arrangements to find slaves — our every own daughters-in-laws! If nobody else, then we could at least enslave them. (87)

Thus, their life was not better than animals. Under such circumstances the dream of Ramrajya cannot be fulfilled. Gail Omvedt opines in this context:

> Reinterpretation and debates concerning the traditions of Gandhi and Nehru, as well as those of Ambedkar, Phule, and Periyar will go on, but so different is the situation from the colonial period that Ram raj is no longer a viable ideal in India today any more than Nehruvian socialism (Omvedt, 101).

Mahar people lived in the darkness of ignorance and they were not educated except a few people. They were not given any chance for their studies because high caste people thought that in this way Dalit people will get good jobs and they will be financially independent. They won't take any loan from them and they will live their life independently. The influence of the upper caste people will not be so dominant in this way. They were the blind followers of the pundits and the Brahminic hegemony. They believed in the Hindu gods and goddesses. They never dared to challenge them as they considered themselves weak and feeble. They didn't have any courage to flow against the tide. When B.R. Ambedkar started a movement, then he changed the lives of many people. Ambedkar told them the importance of education. He told the people to kick away ignorance and superstition from their home. He told dalits to live and eat hygienically. He told them, "My poor dear brothers and sisters do not eat carcasses any more" (65). Jyotiba Phule also worked for the dalits. Thus, under the guidance of these two people and a few other people the lives of dalits improved. Sharmila Rege also holds this view, "Both Phule and Ambedkar underlined the historical character of caste-based exploitation, rejected the *varna* order and suggested annihilation of caste as the only path to an egalitarian society" (Writing Caste, Writing Gender 37). B.R. Ambedkar has done unimaginable work to show path to dalits. He told them:

> From now onwards you have to follow a different path. You must educate your children. Divorce your children from god. Teach them good things. Send them to schools. The result will be there for you to see. When your children begin to be educated, your conditions will start improving. Your family, your life will improve. Your children will bring you out of this hell. We are humans. We, too, have the right to live as human beings. Your children will make you aware of this (65).

Baby Kamble describes caste discrimination in her school. The high caste girls remained away from the low caste girls because they had the fear of polluting by their touch. At the sight of a low girl, the high caste girls would cover their nose and mutter *chee, chee*. They would be away from that place. Caste was the hot discussion amongst the high class girls. They would take bath after reaching home as their parents would not allow them to enter the house as they knew that Mahar girls also sit in their class. The girls would start criticising the low caste girls even at a very small age. They criticised Ambedkar also who worked for Dalits' upliftment, "That Ambedkar has educated himself, that's why these dirty Mahars are showing off! That filthy Mahar Ambedkar, eats dead animals but look at the airs he gives himself! (109)

Untouchablity is a dominant theme in this autobiography. One day Baby Kamble enters a temple with some of her classmates. They had fear that the god Rama may punish them. They screamed and told the Brahmin priest that, "We are Mahar girls and the god has sent demons after us because we have polluted him" (131). Kamble describes that one day a Mahar boy touched the idol of Viththal and this incidence became a hot matter everywhere. Even the priest of the temple announced that:

> The Mahars had polluted the temple. They also declared that god Viththal's face had become contorted and that

> tears were flowing from goddess Rukmayi's eyes. Soon the news of the Mahars having polluted the divine couple Viththal and Rukhmayi spread all over Phaltan. In fact, it reached all the eighty-four villages in the state of Phaltan. Priest organised the chanting of scriptures and purificatory rituals to wash away the pollution with milk and *gomutra*. Finally, after one and a half months of incessant chanting, ceaseless worship, and of course substantial grants from the king, the Brahmin priest managed to cleanse the gods of the pollution, restored the original expression lord Viththal's face and stemmed the flow of tears from Rukhmayi's eyes (127).

Thus, *The Prisons We Broke* is a very important Dalit autobiography by a woman writer, Baby Kamble. She has beautifully depicted the dilemma and sufferings of Mahar community. She has narrated how Dalit women are forced to live a life in utter poverty and they have to live under pressure even at their own home and their new home after marriage. The theme of untouchability and castiest mentality plays a very important role in this autobiography. Thus, Baby Kamble has successfully narrated the potable plight of her community thorough her autobiography.

Works Cited

Kamble, Baby. *The Prisons We Broke*. Translated by Maya Pandit. New Delhi: Orient BlackSwan, 2008. Print.

Nayar, Promod K. "Bama's *Karukku*: Dalit Autobiography as Testimonio", in *The Journal of Commonwealth Literature*. Vol. 41. 2. (2006): 83-100.

Omvedt, Gail. *Dalit Visions*. New Delhi: Orient BlackSwan, 1995. Print.

Rajput, Deepa. Dalit among Dalits: Dalit Women with Special Reference to Baby Kamble's *The Prisons We Broke*. *Galaxy International Interdisciplinary Research Journal*. 2.2. (2014): 139-143.

Singh, Jaspal; Khanna, Parveen Kaur and Khanna, Arvind. "The Critical Analysis of the Mahar Dalit Situation in Baby Kamble's *The Prisons We Broke.*" *Journal of International Academic Research For Multidisciplinary.* 2.11. (2014): 391-96.

Singh, Shikha. The Enigma of Survival: Narrating Victimisation in Baby Kamble's *The Prison We Broke* and Bama's *Karukku.* 3.4. (2015): 171-76.

Valmiki Omprakash. *Joothan.* Trans. Mukherjee, Arun Prabha. Kolkata: Samya, 2007. Print.

10

Bama's *Karukku*: (Re)-reading Dalit History in South India and (Re)-interpreting the Identity of a Dalit (Wo)-man

Ramanuj Mahato

> I don't know when my wings will heal and gain enough strength so that I too will be able to fly again. Just as people through sticks and stones to wound a wingless bird, many people have wounded me with their words and deeds. Yet I know I'm moving forward slowly, step by step.
>
> — Bama, *Karukku* (122:2015)

As if criticising the hypocrisy of Indian society Bama expresses her all indignities towards Indian mainstream voices who subjugate the marginalised in extreme. Her relevant anger is erupted through her words that challenge the dominant Indian caste system and prevailing privileges enjoyed by upper-caste communities. Substantiating the role of dalit-woman, many dalit-women writers have approached to express their experience of oppression like Kumud Pawde, Urmila Pawar, Mukta Sarvagod, Santabai Krishnaji Kamble etc. are prominent figures who have really contributed a lot to portray the actual picture of dalit-woman in Indian context. Somewhat disconcertingly Bama portrays the oppressed lives of dalit community and more specifically dalit-women whose voices are silenced by a labyrinth of Indian mainstream communities. Drawing the analogy with *Daedalus* and *Icarus* myth, Bama's fight is tantamount to Daedalus and Icarus's flight that is symbolic of desire for freedom and complete emancipation from the claustrophobic maze of caste hegemonic society. In fact, in the labyrinth of mainstream culture, a Dalit loses his words, own culture, and identity but Bama's works are strong evidence of Daedalian as well as Icarian flight that resolves and shows essential paths of redemption from this *labyrinth* of oppression in spite of so many limitations.

Bama was born in Roman Catholic family in 1958 in a small village of Wathirayiruppu in Tamil Nadu and her real name is Faustina Mary Fathima. Her ancestors were converted from Hinduism to Christian family; and in this way she inherits her marginalised identity as a Dalit Christian girl. Bama works as high school teacher of Mathematics in Uthirramerur, a small in Kancgeepuram district. She stands as voice of dalit-woman's identity and her traumatic and claustrophobic life becomes a part of Dalit sufferings and marginalisation. Her inherited social identity is emblematic and symbolic representation of oppressed dalit society in India that lacks apt voice to protest against the mainstream Indian culture. Actually her voice is divergent and polyphonic that not only challenges the upper-caste communities in India but also criticises the role of mainstream Christian culture and upper-hand male dogmatism even inherent within the same dalit community. Thus, she has published her three critically well acclaimed full-length works of prose; the first one is *Karukku* (1992) and two significant novels, *Sangati* (1994) and *Vanmam* (2002) and three major collections of short stories, *Kisumbukkaran* (1996), *Oru Thatbavum Erumayum* (2003), and *Kondattam* (2009); and in finally her full length work, a novel, *Manushi* (2012) appeared. Among these works his first work *Karukku* is an autobiographical work that represents, according to Laxmi Holmström, the English translator of this work, "... a specific experience, the experience of a Tamil Dalit Christian woman" (xiv). Here Bama brings all those marginalised identities—TAMIL-DALIT-CHRISTIAN-WOMAN—under single canopy with synonymous understanding which challenges the mainstream aesthetic and reveals the real sufferings of a self as well as community; and in this context Holmström also adds, "it (*Karukku*) has a universality at its core which questions all oppressions, disturbs all complacencies, and, reaching out, empowers all those who have suffered different oppressions. It is precisely because it tells the story of Bama's personal struggle to find her identity that *Karukku* also argues so powerfully against patriarchy and caste oppression" (xiv). Therefore it is a story of universal oppression where Bama stands a voice of defiance that unveils the paths for social political and cultural freedom and recognition of each and every dalit individual from the labyrinth of Indian caste-struggle.

Corroborating her self-discovery, Bama in her autobiography *Karukku* brilliantly excavates her identity as a marginalised soul and also endeavours to project a subversive history of Dalit culture and it can aptly be called as *dalitography*, a real documentation of dalit history and it invariably echoes *'dalit ecriture'* which is already said in my another essay "Kumud Pawade's Antasphot : A Dalit can Speak" as "... a new identity of dalit writing that is unique in representing the true voice of dalit movement." (137:2015) And in this way, *dalitography* better justifies *dalit ecriture* that challenges the mainstream voices and culture and recognises dalit's own history, own culture, own utterances and own feelings and give voices to their own story of untouchability, humiliations and exploitations. As Bama herself writes:

> When I was studying in the third class, I hadn't yet heard people speak openly of untouchability. But I had already seen, felt, experienced and been humiliated by what it is. (13)

As Bama represents dalit Paraya community, her individual experiences are very well-connected with typical marginalised position of this dalit caste and its oppressed identity. But the important thing in this work is final resolutions and suggestions on the part of the author at the end of every chapter make this autobiography a complete *dalitography* recounting the ways how caste-discrimination can be resolved from this society and dalit (wo)-man can enjoy social political and cultural recognition in society. Bama's use of certain Tamil nomenclature like 'Nari paara', 'Vatttala Vitthaam paara' (01), and some other names of ponds like 'Taamara Kulam' (lotus pond), 'Baathrang kulam' (named for the priests or podagar who lived nearby), 'Jeevaneri kamma' (the lake of life), 'Aiyar kulam' (pond of the Aiyars), 'Periya kulam' (the big pond) (02), names of few fields like Mandavak kaadu, Otthaalu kaadu, Chadayaalu kaadu, (06) and and some streets names like Thevar, Chettiyaar, Aasaari, and Nadar and Naicker streets (07) strongly confirm her innate intimation with Tamil marginalised society. And Bama has pointed out, "It was only after this that I began to understand, little by little, that in that order, Tamil people were looked upon as a lower caste. And then, among Tamils, Parayar were a separate category." (24) About Parayar community Bama writes as "...the poorest of poor, struggling for daily survival, doesn't need spelling out." (79) In fact, all these consciousness of Bama, makes her an indigenous dalit soul who seeks her own alternative identity in the crowd of mainstream culture. Here Bama also portrays the tension between Naicker and Paraya community. She reminds that her both grandmothers worked as servants for Niacker families and even little children of Naicker families would not pay any respect to them in spite of being aged because Naicker was superior caste than Parayar and in Bama's words, "They (Naickers) belonged to a higher caste. They had the money." (53) Caste-conflict emerged as a significant phenomenon in the research of south Indian caste history. Another anecdote Bama refers highlighting the trap of exploitation for a innocent being caused by caste battle; the story shows the battle between Parayar and Chaaliyar caste and how headmaster of the school who belonged to Chaaliyar caste punished the author by giving wrong and false charges for one reason that she belonged to Parayar caste. There are so many references about the battle between Chaaliyar and Parayar community that echo the picture of caste conflict of that time and which were inevitable, irresistible events of caste oppressions. Another inter-caste conflict is seen between Pallar and Parayar community that is emblematic of maladjustment within the same oppressed communities. Her strong proclaiming about the humiliation transcends this individual story into universal level by combing self and history having a tremulous effect upon the society and in G. N. Devy's words "the subversive historiographic path of personalising history." (272:1992)

Except the caste conflict among various existing communities, Bama focuses how dalit people are even oppressed on religious ground. Hence, Bama mentions the dominant role of upper-caste Christians who are also pillar of mainstream aesthetic in society:

> It is only the upper-caste Christians who enjoy the benefits and comforts of the church. Even amongst the priests and nuns, it is the upper castes who hold all the high positions, show off their authority, and through their weight about. And if Dalits become priests and nuns, they are pushed aside and marginalised first of all, before the rest go about their business. (80)

Upper-caste Christian community swindles dalit people by many orthodox practices and Church affairs. Actually, the those upper-castes were busy enjoying their comforts and customs which were not for low-caste people; and the low-caste dalit people only have to give their share of money for flourishing their religious hypocrisies. Bama also unveils the reality about the convent school where nothing good is taught but only preaching of rituals what Bama says as a place where there is "no love for the poor and the humble." (106) In this context, Bama overlaps the Marxist ideology of 'class-conflict' with 'caste-conflict' and strives to seek the interpretation of Marxist relationship between base and superstructure which is very straightforward and represents "an oppressive base produces oppressive culture, in which only a few individuals – people who deliberately struggle to produce art that resists the aesthetic consensus of the age – are able to transcend." (22:2001) In fact, each form of all luxuries, benefits, facilities were available for only few upper-caste Christian children and the exploitation would occur to those marginalised communities who lived in the caste-hegemonic marginalised society and lacked the daring to protest. As Bama expresses her concern:

> When we went to school or to church we had to walk some distance, past several streets. The church, the school, the convent and the priests' bungalow were all in places where the upper-caste communities lived. Most of the children attending the school were from our streets. All the same, all these children had to walk the distance there in order to study. There were only few upper-caste Christian children. For them, the church, the school, the convent and the priests' house were all close at hand. There was no necessity for them to walk. (88)

It makes scared Bama when she thinks about the future of this strategic dalit exploitation by Christian well off community, "I don't know when such atrocities will end. It is likely that he who finds his comfort by exploiting us will ever change, or ever allow the system to change?" (80)

Another significant perspective regarding the marginality is the existence of dalit woman. Challenging the mainstream patriarchal rule Bama shows how dalit-woman is twice marginalised – firstly, by other women from upper-caste community who never feel sympathetic to dalit-girl's oppression and sufferings; secondly, by dalit-male within the same community. Bama here draws another picture of dalit-woman oppression through the belief of untouchability among upper-caste women towards dalit-woman/girl. The shameful incident as portrayed by Bama:

> The Naicker women would pour out the water from a height of four feet, while Paatti and the others received and drank it with cupped hands held to their mouths. I always felt terrible when I watched this. (16)

The author also shows how dalit-male instead of supporting the position of dalit-girl criticises her daring temperament and outlook in Bama's words, "If a woman so much as stands alone and by herself somewhere, all sorts of men gather around her showing their teeth." (119) Thus, dalit-girls are "forced to suffer pain and humiliation" (27) and it gets reflected through the symbolic implication of 'Uudan' myth; that the 'Uudan', a blower was permitted to beat her wife implies horrible aspect of dalit social dogmatism. Somewhat frustratingly due to poverty dalit-girl children are even discriminated and marginalised by dalit-male chauvinism and spend their life "collecting firewood, looking after the house, caring for the babies and doing household chores."(79); consequently, their life becomes full of burden and labour.

Bama has not only shared her personal anguish over caste discrimination but also challenges the mainstream hierarchy that believes that a dalit is born to be enslaved and oppressed. And here she also draws out her journey from childhood to adolescence which covers up her school days, family life and finally the working phase of her life as a teacher/nun. Bama believes that dalit-children would face many troubles and tortures accepting their lot; however, she keeps protesting against this type of hypocrisy practiced in the society where dalits are seen as a tool of exploitation and oppression and that would inspire her "to become a nun, but to be different" (103):

> And mainly because of this, those children seemed to accept everything as their fate. From dawn to dusk, they toiled away in the convent. As I saw all this, I became very troubled at heart. I was angry; I thought to myself, what sort of nuns are these, they claim that they are helping the poor and the needy, yet this is how they are. At times I confronted them and argued with them. (103)

Finally her dream turned into reality when she became a nun and she felt immeasurable happiness by teaching those hapless and distressed dalit-children. But her entire journey for becoming nun is based on the realisation of truth. Here, the story regarding the next phase of her life when she would work as a nun expresses the entrapped condition from which she constantly tried to escape but failed. She was imprisoned both physically and psychologically because she had to teach dalit-children but she had to stay their others' control and she had no choices left to serve freely there. Her job as a nun in a convent school was a primarily a voluntary choice but later it turned into a mandatory one. She found no opportunity to escape from this maze. In this book, the 'Postscript' episode narrates her personal experiences felt as a convent nun. It focuses how she felt helpless working there and thought for resigning the job due to the power politics manipulated by the convent authority. She was transferred from her native land to Kashmir and she was absolutely alienated there by the Mother Superior, as Bama herself depicts her hellish condition there:

> Each day I spent there was as if I was standing in the midst of a fire. The Sisters there wouldn't even talk to me. They would only talk amongst themselves. They took no notice of me, whatever. The Mother Superior there would only tell me what my task were, nothing else. I didn't want to waste my life any longer. I began to feel that I should leave the place, come what may. (126)

Though she decided to leave the convent but she was convinced that she could not leave the place out of her whim and there were so many tricks practiced by the authority to confine her and threw a challenge to her flight. Her indomitable will to fly away from the cage of this convent ultimately becomes successful; as Sister Sangeetha — who also strived to escape but failed and remained house arrested — like Icarus started her flight but her wings of freedom got melted away by the hellish fire of mainstream convent authority. In fact, Bama becomes metaphorically a soul of Daedalus who reached her destination by her courage and controlled and constant fight.

Most interestingly analysing all the chapters of *Karukku*, a maze is found in each chapter discussing the serious problems of dalit marginalisation but at the end of each chapter, Bama also tactfully endeavours to break the labyrinth of mainstream voices by her rational approaches and worthy remedies. She strives to challenge the mainstream Indian voices controlled by patriarchy, upper-caste domination, intra-dalit politics and religious hypocritical authority and has suggested plausible views regarding the change in society and her deep concern over dalit people gets expressed in various expressions but with same emotion — "Can we change this?" (17), "If not what can I do about it?" (24), "...what will happen to all these men in the end?" (47), "How can they afford to study, when it is such a struggle even to fill their bellies? (55) She has also suggested consequently the effective remedies that can be accepted as possible resolutions

— at first, dalit people should erase away the prejudices from their mind; secondly, they should also forget intra-dalit conflicts or skirmishes; thirdly, they should be supported by appeasing their hunger so that they can become eligible to have to "smell of knowledge or learning" (55); fourthly, catering knowledge and sense through cinema and plays; fifthly, recognition of dalit identity in various major post or positions; sixthly, dalit's own social awareness about the social reality; and last but not least, strong inner will to fight back against difficulties as well as adversities. Through her positive suggestions, Bama not only has shared her personal experiences but also has universalised the theme of dalit (wo)-man oppression in dalit marginalised perspective. Her protesting attitude reinforces 'mainstream writes back' that creates a scope for a new dalit identity proclaiming their equal rights and dignity in society and *dalitisation* of history through confirming *dalitography* and by marking a new history which is subversive as well as challenging:

> Are Dalits not human beings? Do they not have common sense? Do they not have such attributes as a sense of honour and self-respect? Are they without any wisdom, beauty, dignity? What do we lack? They treat us in whatever way they choose, as if we are slaves who don't even possess human dignity. (27)

In Greek legend, the Labyrinth was a huge maze constructed by Daedalus at Knossus (also Cnossos or Cnossus) in Crete for King Minos. It was designed like a home for the Minotaur, a creature with a man's body and a bull's head. The Labyrinth was such a complex network of passages and chambers that it was thought no one could escape from it. The term can be applied to any intricate or complicated arrangement. When Minos later refused to allow him to leave Crete, he escaped by making wings for himself and his son, Icarus. Although Daedalus escaped and flew to safety, Icarus flew too high and the sun melted the wax holding his wings together, so that he plunged to his death.

Daedalus, symbolic for flight, can be alluded to as a clever craftsman or maker of clever or complicated devices.

Work Cited

Bama, *Karukku*. trans. Lakshmi Holmström, New Delhi: The Oxford University Press, 2015. Print.

Devy, G. *The G.N. Devy Reader*. Hyderabad: Orient Longman, 1992. Print.

Gilmore, Leigh. *Autobiographies: A Feminist Theory of Women's Self-representation*. Ithaca and London: Cornell University Press, 1994. Print.

Jelinek, Estelle C. *The Tradition of Women's Autobiography: From Antiquity to the Present*. Boston: Twayne Publishers, 1986. Print.

Olney, James. *Studies in Autobiography*, New York: Oxford University Press, 1988. Print.

Pawde, Kumud. *Antasphot* (Marathi). Aurangabad: Anand Prakashan, 1981. Print.

Limbale, Sharankumar. *Towards an Aesthetic of Dalit Literature: History, Controversies and Considerations*. Trans. Alok Mukherjee. New Delhi: Orient Longman, 2004. Print.

Robert, Adam. *Fredric Jameson*. New York and London: Routledge Publication, 2001. (E-text)

Singh, Bijender. (ed.) *Indian Dalit Autobiographies: Marginalized Voices*. New Delhi: Authorspress, 2015. Print.

11

Little-Narrative of Infinite Pain: C. K. Janu's *Mother Forest* and Socio-economic Deprivation

Saikat Guha

C. K. Janu is a well-known "insurgent" figure of Kerala *aadivasi* movement for land, human rights, and preservation of forest. Hailed from the forest region of Chekkote in Wayanad district, Janu belongs to the landless tribal community called the Adiyar. She has withstood numerous sociopolitical upheavals in her short life surrounding the Malabar hills. Her "autobiography," actually transcribed by Bhaskaran, and translated from Malayalam into English by N. Ravi Shanker, is called *Mother Forest* which is an honest record of the inhuman oppression and exploitation of her community by the upper-class landowners. The silence of the tribals and dalits in the heart of India is devised by a wicked hegemony of those in political power who exclude the former from socioeconomic accessibility.

The flourish of women's autobiography since the 1960s, observes Linda Anderson, has been grounded in frankness about intimate feminine experiences, poststructural debates over subjectivity and rhetorical flourish. There is dissent over women's autobiography within the ambit of feminism itself as to what extent autobiography can be reflective of real-life experiences and objective representation of subjective temperament. Autobiography can rather be taken as what Diane Elam says, "strategic necessity at a particular time, rather than an end in itself" (qtd. in Anderson, 120). Although C. K. Janu is "uneducated" in the formal sense and uninformed of the philosophical developments surrounding feminism, her struggle and political aim may well be taken as "strategic necessity" of the present time. *Mother Forest* is an intensely personal record which is again problematised by political intervention acting on the site of the subject. Her struggle over the rights of the downtrodden people of her community is an ongoing agenda and far from closure. It is an "unfinished story" in both denotative and connotative senses.

The social, economic and political deprivation of the dalits and the tribals has been portrayed in recent times in a number of fictional works and autobiographies. Dalit autobiography is not simply the narrative of incessant unfurling of memories that join one's past with the present but also politically charged with rebellious and/or negotiating episteme. Along with C. K. Janu's *Mother Forest*, plebeian Indian women's autobiographies, for example, Bama's *Karukku* and Baby Kamble's *The Prison We Broke*, bear witness to the dalits' (and women's) victimisation ensuing from multiplicity of oppression and repression. Such autobiographies also question the relevance in India of the dominant Western feminist theories which, as Chandra Mohanty argues, erroneously homogenise the experiences of diverse groups and classes of women who flock in the Third World countries. Indian dalit and tribal women's autobiographies address the plurality that lie in the diverse ways lower-class women experience oppression and exploitation.

Apart from reflecting on the gatherings of sinned experiences of everyday, these autobiographies honestly portray socioeconomic dispossession and political repression of the dalits and tribals. Janu walks down the memory lane to reminisce how her community people had been exploited during her childhood. The elders used to toil in the agricultural fields throughout the day and the children used to stay at home or wander in the forest in search of fruits. The "mother" forest had been their only benefactor which provided them the means of life. But the forest and its adjacent fields were possessed by "migrant" elites who seized the area by depriving the tribals. The tribals have always been labourers without any land of their own, as Janu says:

> When our ancestors cleared the woods, burnt the undergrowth, sowed *thina* [a kind of millet] and converted the earth into fields, the *jenmi* [the feudal landlord] and the migrants of that time would make an appearance. They would befriend our men, give them *arrack* [alcohol made of rice and vegetables] or a small sum of money and transfer the land in their names. Our people, who had never had to keep records and documents for their lands, would once again have to work in those same lands as labourers and grow crops for the *jenmi*. At a wage that could not even keep hunger away. (Janu, 31-32)

As Janu's father left her mother with five children, the poor girl was sent to work as babysitter at the house of a school teacher in Vellamunda when she was barely eight or nine years old. However, it was perhaps the best years of her life as she used to live in the furnished house which was vastly dissimilar to their rural habitation. She saw with wonder electric light, furniture, radio and bus for the first time. Her marvel at the discovery of a world unlike their own is suggestive of the deprivation of the tribals. A large section of them are still living in backward places, excluded from the minimal requirements of life.

Janu's return to the forest region following the transfer of the teacher led her back to the village where she had to toil in the agriculture field at a low wage. Here she got entangled in a series of political turmoil. The literacy programme in the area was started by the communist party with the proclaimed intent to make people aware of their rights, but in actuality the party wanted the people remain uneducated so that they would not realise their shrewd politics. The education campaign ran irregular as the teacher did not visit them often. Moreover, after the whole day's drudgery the tired people used to feel sleepy and lacked interest in study. The landlords utilised the benefit of these people's illiteracy and innocence to exploit them.

The reinvigorated dalit movements since the 1970s incorporated the poverty-ridden, oppressed and exploited tribals within the scope of their movements as both the ex-untouchables, *Shudras*, tribals and labour classes suffer from societal segregation and economic dispossession. Tribalism is a subtly different from dalitism – while the former is concerned with the plight of the "native" (non-Hindu/non-Aryan) and largely uncontaminated people, the latter studies the so-called "lower caste" and formerly "untouchable" people who are placed at the bottom of the Hindu religious hierarchy. Unlike the dalits, the tribals might not have caste-consciousness, but they undeniably have class consciousness. Writers like Mahasweta Devi, who has argued in favour of the dalit and tribal rights throughout her career, says in an interview that both the communities should be located at the same footing because of their similarity with regard to their poor, subjugated and marginal existence in society. The new radical dalit political groups, like the Dalit Panther and Dalit-Bahujan, have included the former untouchables, "other backward classes" (OBC), tribals, peasants and lower-class women within its sphere to expose and resist the hegemony of "Hinduism" which permeates Indian sociopolitical scenario. Gail Omvedt argues that the dalit movement, "based on ex-untouchables and widening to include non-Brahmin castes of many southern and peripheral areas," has in recent times brought forward most strongly the ideological challenges by proclaiming "a new politics of a radically transformed non-Hindu identity, and in contrast to reformist Hindu identities *they define 'Hinduism' itself as an oppressive class/caste/patriarchal force*" (xi). Janu observes how the people of her community has recently started hanging calendars with pictures of national leaders and Hindu gods as a result of their contact with "civilised" people which manifests their "interpellation" into dominant Hindu nationalist ideology.

These lower class people, or the "proletariats" in a Marxist sense, only serve the upper-class and higher-caste people at a low wage, and suffer from humiliation. Most of them are landless and bound to starve so often, as Janu says, "Our problems mostly relate to our work, our lands and our hunger" (34). They are endangered classes living at the margin of society. They are voiceless in the sociopolitical discourse of India because the country's "mainstream" is flocked by upper-class people or elites who are distinctly upper-caste Hindu in most cases. Apart from the common fate of socioeconomic dispossession, the *Shudra* people (who now form the large demographic section called "dalits") and the tribal people are similar also in regard to religious habits. The tribals are nature-worshipper and pagan while the gods of the dalits, as Kancha Ilaiah writes, are also distinct from the upper-caste Hindu gods found in the Mythologies. Similar to Ilaiah, Janu talks of the Adiyar people's worshipping of a stone in memory of their forefathers: "In our community there are no gods or goddesses like among Hindus [...] when we were young there used to be a big tree near our hut in Thrissileri and a stone placed underneath it. We used to worship that, our forefathers rested there [...]" (19). But the ritual ground was snatched away from them because the land was bought by another feudal lord. The ownership of land shifts from one landlord to another while the Adiyar people remain landless labourers without any share in the transaction of lands.

In fact, the lot of these subordinated people was drastically exacerbated during the British rule whose interest was to exploit the colonised people, all and sundry. This furthered the tragedy of the people belonging to lower stratum of society who were pushed more to the verge of economic insecurity. But what is most ironic is that the Independence of India failed to accommodate the necessities of these people. The making of "nation" India was fabricated on the ideals of the neo-elite (Western-educated, upper-class and upper-caste leaders) who acquired and continued the British policy of exploitation and repression. The voice of the deprived and exploited classes remained muted in the national dialogue. Janu's *Mother Forest* is a resistance narrative which manifests the voice of protest from a brave tribal lady who leads a campaign against the ongoing wrongs on them. Her autobiography is a "little narrative" as opposed to "metanarrative" of the dominant national discourse. In the post-modern period, a sense of incredulity to metanarratives has been perceived. The ubiquitous dominance of the metanarratives attempted to choke the voice of the marginal people which needs to be retrieved. The little narrative of Janu illustrates the wretched plight of the socially excluded and oppressed people of the Malabar and thus puts into question the currency of the metanarratives of mainland India whose promise of equal development for all and societal justice is proved to be futile and illusory.

It is ironic that the life of the Adiyar people as depicted in the beginning of Janu's autobiography is quite different from their life towards the end of *Mother Forest* – at the time lapse of just about three decades. The elders used to work in the fields of the *jenmi* while the little ones took the landlord's cattle for grasing or used to roam in the forest eating fruits. Fruits were ample in the forest in the earlier days; in the words of Janu "in the forest one never knew what hunger was" (2). But the situation began to change with the coming of the elite "outsiders" who cleared the forest and started agriculture in modern technologies or established leisure houses. With the coming of the new owners, the tribals felt the greatest threat of extinction because of their uprooting from their territory and deprivation from agricultural works. The intervention of the political parties and other interest groups only aggravated the situation of the poor people who became prey to their avarice for power and money.

The party-system which has been depicted in Janu's autobiography honestly illustrates the disconcerting reality of ugly politics. The Communist Party with which Janu and her group were engaged was proved to be nothing but power-hungry deceiver. The party was only interested in vote-bank and not the genuine welfare of the tribal people. It appeared in the scene with the promise of popular welfare and to argue their rights: "someone described the Party to us as something that will get us more wages" (21). The party at first fought to ensure more wages for the poor people but gradually its real motive came into light. The party called the uneducated people to join their rallies and conferences just to fulfill its own selfish intent to win elections. Janu says,

> Problems specifically related to our people were not discussed much in the Party or the Union. The Party saw us as a vote-bank only. Therefore, issues related to our agricultural lands or better conditions of life for us hardly found their way into Party circles. The speeches made in the Party classes were not what we could easily understand. They were full of strange words with hidden traps. They tried their best not to let us speak. (34)

Nevertheless, Janu kept herself attached to the Party for a long time with the hope for the betterment of her community. Out of her profound discontent and sense of deception, Janu left the party and built a group with her own community members who were evicted from their own lands. They settled a habitation in the hills of Appootti near Mananthavaadi sometime in 1994 although the new landowners and police invaded the region with the result that the helpless people were again uprooted from their new settlement. Janu, along with her community people, was assaulted and arrested. This incident, however, reached to the world outside the unknown region and controversy followed regarding the tribal rights. Writers and social activists like Arundhati Roy supported the cause of the exploited people who were evicted time and again from their dwellings. As a result, the Kerala Government revised its Land Acts and tribal policy especially with regard to the Wayanad district.

Janu is acutely sensible to the fast changing time to which her community people are exposed. With the passing of the old feudal lords, the new owners of the land settle their leisure-houses, parks and so on. They are no longer interested in agriculture or the preservation of the mother forest because these are no longer deemed profitable. The new bourgeoisie equates everything with material profit. Let alone the tribal rights on land and forest, they don't even care for employing the tribals as workers.

Again, with the lop-sided development of the area, various new settlements, like school and market were founded. As the usage of land changed, the tribals lost their work in agriculture fields. At the same time, with the destruction of forest, they were unable to collect their food and other resources from the forest anymore. They were bound to buy everything from the market but their impoverished status made their sustenance uncertain in the new system. As a result, the tribals found themselves at the jeopardy of existence, and hunger became their common fate. Janu also brings out the hypocrisy of those in power by highlighting the fact that highways and markets were built by the government but no measure was taken for the improvement of the tribals. As a result, the tribals were rendered uncivilised, primitive and unworthy of civilised contact by the power grid. *Mother Forest* honestly depicts the conspiracy of the government to keep them subservient and deprived.

Like any woman's autobiography, Janu also criticises the men of her community for a number of reasons. The women are the chief bread-earners of family while the men remain aloof to their family and children. Janu's promiscuous father left her mother when Janu was a little child: "I was born of my father's first marriage, my father married twice after that [...] During my father's time all the men of our community used to drink toddy and arrack, as a result, we had to struggle a lot in childhood" (6). However, unlike the higher-caste Hindu society, there is no sharp distinction between man and woman in the tribal community. In the Adiyar community, women enjoy relatively more freedom. But they are burdened with household tasks and other duties. Janu expresses her resentment against the men of her community who sold their lands and crops on exchange of a bottle of arrack or a bit of tobacco, and thus brought unimaginable hardship to the entire household. The women are the prime keepers of family, as Janu says:

> In our community women always take up more responsibilities than men. [...] Women go to work in the fields. Digging, sowing, preparing the fields and any kind of work on land. Also, taking care of the little ones in the hut. But men are not like that. They spend a lot of time just doing nothing or wandering about in the forest. These days they waste their time on shop verandahs. They will just go on squatting there. They have become very lazy with easy access to toddy and arrack. Interference from outsiders has caused all this. [...] Most of them lost their lands for a pinch of tobacco or a glass of tea or some arrack. (46)

C. K. Janu's autobiography is a "little narrative" that registers infinity of pain of the "postcolonial subaltern" (dalit or tribal classes) in the pastoral setting of the Malabar. It fully exposes the sham of the postcolonial nation which is based on some fragile ideals. Pramod Nayar cites in this regard: "mainstream postcolonial society marginalises, oppresses and in some cases decimates certain sections, cultures and ways of life. The 'unity in diversity' myth or the illusion of the world's greatest democracy often conceals sharp iniquities, oppressions and injustices" (102). Nayar goes on to explicate the asymmetry of democratic structure in India which "ensures that the benefits of democracy or development accrue to metropolitan, able-bodied people of particular castes and classes" (*ibid*). Such observation is particularly relevant in the present context of Janu's faithful account of the pitiable tribal life. The "criminalisation" of Janu and her protest group, who were demanding justice, by the State jurisdiction showcases the fault-line in the democratic system of India.

Works Cited

Anderson, Linda. "Autobiography and the Feminist Subject." *The Cambridge Companion to Feminist Literary Theory*. Ed. Ellen Rooney. Cambridge: Cambridge UP, 2006. Print.

Ilaiah, Kancha. *Why I Am Not a Hindu: A Sudra Critique of Hindutva Philosophy, Culture and Political Economy*. 1996. Calcutta: Samya, 2003. Print.

Janu, C. K. *Mother Forest: The Unfinished Story of C. K. Janu*. New Delhi: Kali for Women, 2004. Print.

Mahasweta Devi. "Telling History." Interview by Gayatri Chakravorty Spivak. *Chotti Munda and His Arrow*. Oxford: Blackwell, 2003. ix-xxiii. Print.

Mohanty, Chandra Talpade. "Under Western Eyes: Feminist Scholarship and Colonial Discourses." *Feminist Review* 30 (1988): 61-88. *JSTOR*. Web. 25 Aug. 2014.

Nayar, Pramod K. *Postcolonial Literature: An Introduction*. 2008. Hyderabad: Pearson, 2013. Print.

Omvedt, Gail. *Understanding Caste: From Buddha to Ambedkar and Beyond*. 2nd ed. Hyderabad: Orient Black Swan Publishers, 2011. Print.

12

Multiple Facets of Dalit Patriarchy in P. Sivakami's *The Grip of Change*

Dwaipayan Mitra

The emergence of life writing by the Dalits has come as bombshell upon the ensconced domain of Hindu caste hierarchy. It offers a counter-discourse that challenges the age-old legitimacy of the *Varna*-Hindu society. From ancient time Indian civilisation has evinced its inclusive nature by welcoming people from different parts of the world. This moral ethos of India has been highlighted time and again by numerous thinkers and philosophers in order to forge a pan-Indian consciousness. In spite of numerous foreign attacks and invasions Indian civilisation did not relinquish its humanitarian principles and has continued to propel its inclusive ideals. Unfortunately, this country, however attractive the outward manifestation might be, is inwardly torn asunder by various dividing lines of caste, class, religion and gender. This harbouring of certain evils has stigmatised the outward glory of India. The most nefarious offspring of these evils is the sustenance of caste hierarchy. Raj Kumar writes:

> As a result, the caste system- with its myriad variations of super ordination and subordination, its confusions and contradictions- is able to sustain itself across different regions of India in varying degrees of rigidity. (2010:115)

In the face of several exploitations thinkers such as Ambedkar, Phule, Narayan Guru and Periyar have done a vital task in unifying the Dalits by infusing them with courage and support. Dalit movement also got its impetus from the movement launched by Dalit Panthers who, like the Black Protestants in America, advocated radical counter-canon to dismantle the caste system which climaxed with the emergence of Dalit autobiographies.

Dalit autobiographies provide a panoramic picture of the caste-stratified society and expose the ideology of the upper caste people as a mere fallacy. An exploitative system not only depends on overt coercion but also backs it up with some ideology. Louis Althusser points out in his essay "Ideology and Ideological State Apparatuses" that state machinery works not only through coercive powers but also through soft powers that operate, firstly, by ideology and then, by coercion. Dalit exploitative system premises itself upon the ideology enunciated in religious texts which actually safeguard the naked reality of unrelenting exploitation. These autobiographies have exposed the cracks inherent in this system and offer a subversive move that calls for a social change. These autobiographies such as Narendra Jadhav's *Outcaste: A memoir*, Omprakash Valmiki's *Joothan: A Dalit's Life*, Aravind Malagatti's *Government Brahmana* are not mere documentations of everyday lives but are archives of relentless exploitations principled on the notion of purity and pollution. These tales resonate with the voices of dissent against injustice and are marked by rhetoric of anger. They vindicate a journey towards empowerment following the path chalked out by Ambedkar, the hierophant of Dalit literature. What Toni Morrison once remarked about the motto of Black literature in her essay "The Site of Memory" is also applicable to the aesthetics of Dalit literature:

> Whatever the style and circumstances of these narratives, they were written to say primarily two things, One: "This is my historical life-my singular, special example that is personal, but that also represents the race". Two: "I write this text to persuade other people- you, the reader, who is probably not black that we are human beings worthy of God's grace and the immediate abandonment of slavery." (1987:104-105)

However, it would be wrong to essentialise Dalit autobiographies under an umbrella term negating heterogeneity. It has been pointed out by some critics that Dalit memoirs reiterate the same emotion of misery and pain and lack dialogic quality. Probing deeply we find such a criticism lacks deep scholarship. We find that among the Dalit memoirs there exists certain degree of politics and dominations. For example, women Dalit discourse is inflected by gender issues as well as caste issues which make it further problematic for grouping under a common head. They are Dalits among the Dalits. As a result, Dalit women are haunted by a different kind of complex unlike Dalit men. The tripartite marginalisation of being a subaltern, a Dalit and a woman imbue the female Dalit autobiographies with a different colour. Dalit autobiographies by male writers seldom portray the domestic violence. It is also worth noticing in this context that while a plethora of Dalit memoirs by male writers has been published and translated into English, female Dalit memoirs are quite few in number. The lack of education and the lack of agency to support them are two of the important factors for the paucity of publications by Dalit women.

In *The Grip of Change* P. Sivakami has eked out an identity for Dalit women through the semi-autobiographical narration. The novel was published in Tamil in 1989 and translated into English in 2006 by the author herself. K. A. Geetha opines:

> *Pazhaiyana Kazhithalum* evokes a great deal of discussion because it was critical of both the Dalit movement and of Dalit Patriarchy. The novel articulates the longing of young Dalit women, eager to be liberated from the shackles of caste gender oppression. (2014:109)

Since its publication the novel has sparked off severe brainstorming as to the relation between gender and caste. The opening line of the preface shows that Sivakami attempts to chalk out the narration of the novel in her own way, "I am one of the many exploring the inexhaustible mysteries of caste; of course, in my own way." (2006: vii)

If we judge the novel it gets crystal clear to us that Sivakami foregrounds the Dalit women's issues which are quite different from Dalit men's issues. Gopal Guru in his article "Dalit Women Talk Differently" articulates the need for a foundation of the independent and autonomous organisation of Dalit women for a number of reasons. Apart from charting the external factors of caste, Guru tells the internal constraints within Dalit patriarchy that poses serious problems for them. He categorically writes:

> In the post-Ambedkar period, Dalit leaders have always subordinated, and at times suppressed, an independent political expression of dalit women. This political marginalisation has been openly condemned by dalit women at the regional conferences of Dalit women and at the Delhi meet. (1995: 2549)

Gopal Guru goes on to argue that Dalit men are replicating the same tools to dominate the Dalit women by which they are dominated by the upper caste people. All such factors led Guru to urge for a local resistance within Dalits by the Dalit women that will safeguard the identity of Dalit women. By giving centre-stage to the women

Sivakami attempts to trace the different voice of Dalit women with a penetrating vision.

Right from the beginning of the novel we come to terms with the plight of Thangam, a Dalit woman. Thangam means gold and her name becomes ironical as she is accorded no value by people. After the death of her husband, Thangam is denied the right to property by her brothers-in-law as she did not have children. She also overcomes the amorous advances of her brothers-in-law as she tells Kathamuthu:

> My husband's brothers tried to force me, but I never gave in. They wouldn't give me my husband's land, but wanted me to be a whore for them! I wouldn't give in. Each time one of them came near me I brandished the broom. After that none of them came anywhere near me. (2006:7)

Thangam's rejection of the proposal of her brothers-in-law shows her grit in the teeth of teeming problems that try to denude her of dignity. To make both ends meet and carve out a respectable identity for herself she joins as a labourer in the farm of Paranjothi Udayar. But the wheel of misfortune does not come to a halt for her as she is sexually harassed by Udayar and also thrashed by her brothers-in-law though she committed no crime. This also points towards a close linkage between caste and economy. Suruchi Sharma acutely observes in her article on *The Grip of Change*:

> It is a bitter truth in the society that dalits are considered untouchable and impious and so is the case of dalit women. If dalits women are not worth touching how and why they can be sexually harassed by the upper caste people who enjoy having sex with them. (2015:102)

We see that it is the body of a Dalit woman that becomes the locus of the novel. It is the violation of the body of a Dalit woman that triggers off a series of incidents leading to a caste war. Meena Kandasamy in her analysis of the novel aptly observes:

> The rare beauty and honesty of the narrative arises from its body-centricity. Thangam's body bears testimony to the difficulties faced by Dalit Women. On a closer reading, it looks like a major, defining part of the novel was entirely played out on the Dalit woman Thangam's body... Even her struggle for land is likened to her body and her fertility. (2006:194)

However, by inscribing the body into the texture of the novel Sivakami is applying, what Helene Hélène Cixous terms as, 'ecriture feminine'. Cixous writes in her essay 'The Laugh of Medusa' that female body has been silenced by discourses from ancient time. She refers to the ancient time of Plato who set great store by the metaphysical world negating the physical world. That is why in order to foreground repressed elements Cixous urges feminist writers to deploy a language that will situate the desires of the body and subvert the masculine language, 'Write your Self. Your body must be heard' (1983:284). In writing with the body Sivakami has achieved a fusion of Feminist and Dalit issues and evolved an elliptical, non-linear style.

It has been pointed out by critics that there has been a dalitisation of the female body. They categorically point out that various Dalit movements pioneered by Dalit leader ended up creating a masculinisation of the female Dalit body. Moreover, in her essay "A Dalit Feminist Standpoint" Sharmila Rege argues that some women liberation movements merged the issue of caste and class by overlooking the real issue. This kind of misdirected politics can be seen in the way Kathamuthu, a local Dalit leader, deploys the case of Thangam to wage a battle against the upper castes. He also changes the real incidents to his advantage silencing the pivotal issue. Kathamuthu changes the whole incident of Thangam being raped by Udayar to that of Thangam getting thrashed by Udayar for having walked on the streets restricted for the Dalits and gives to the whole issue a different hue. Thangam becomes a mere pawn in the hands of Kathamuthu for his vested interests. Arunima Ray writes:

> The focus now shifts from Thangam to the clash between the two castes. The irony of the whole situation is that the series of incidents that get unleashed starts due to the fact Thangam's body gets violated. But the way Kathamuthu deals with the case, the main issue gets totally sidelined. (2011:205)

That Kathamuthu merely takes advantage of the caste issue is made clear when he himself tells the police inspector:

> But you know, my own people couldn't bear to see me successful. Otherwise, I would have been a member of the legislative assembly. They only vote for those who pay... (2006:22)

Hence, the question of deliverance becomes a will-o'-the-wisp for Dalit women. It is true that through negotiation with Paranjothi Udayar he helps Thangam getting a compensation of ten thousand rupees. But when the meeting ends, he himself pockets the money. Even after winning the court case regarding the possession of the land the misery of Thangam does not come to a stop. She now falls victim to the sexual lust of Kathamuthu who exploits her when she was in a haze of intoxication. The reaction of Gowri, Kathamuthu's daughter, when she comes across this scene sums up everything: 'Dogs! Dogs in this house! Shameless as dogs!' Gowri shouted, she went back to her room and locked the door, weeping. (2006: 93)

It seems that Kathamuthu uses the discursive Dalit body of a woman to tilt the scale of sympathy in his favour. The *modus operandi* of Dalit patriarchy is evinced not only in the documentation of the plight of Thangam but also through some snapshots of the life of Kangavalli and Nagamani who are the wives of Kathamuthu. Time and again it is suggested by the writer that they are under constant domination of Kathamuthu. In the opening section of the novel we see Kathamuthu yelling at Kangavalli for having intervened in the discussion, 'Are you here to pass judgement early in the morning? Go inside and get some coffee. Now' (2006:7). Even Kathamuthu turns a deaf ear to the advice of them. Even they are mum about the polygamy of their husband. Amidst these doleful snapshots of the operation of Dalit patriarchy one ray of hope is the emergence of young Dalit women who are impervious to the coercions of Dalit patriarchy. Gowri, Kathamuthu's daughter, represents the prototype of an empowered Dalit woman who is capable of withstanding the onslaughts by Dalit as well as upper caste patriarchy. Gowri wages an uphill battle against various atrocities attempting to conform her to normative path for a Dalit woman. She protests against her early marriage and boldly asserts her desire to carry on education. Her admission to college marks a serious attempt towards an emancipation of the Dalit women from the clutches of patriarchy. Gowri also tries to educate her mother and Nagamani so that they unite to launch a crusade against the authority of Kathamuthu:

> Gowri constantly goaded Kangavalli and Nagamani with talks of women's liberation. However, both women were used to bending to Kathamuthu's demands. They were happy for Gowri, but felt it was too late for them. (2006:125)

She imbibes a different political viewpoint than her father and gives him a tough challenge in the political field as well.

That the semi-autobiographical novel is not only a mere critique of Dalit patriarchy but also a vindication of the way this patriarchy can be annihilated is evinced in 'Author's Notes' where the author takes a deconstructive position to point out the gap between fact and fiction. Here Sivakami appears as a fierce critic of her own text imbued with an empathetic perspective so that she can rise above the watertight compartmentalisation. She herself writes in the preface:

> I wrote the Tamil novel, *Pazhaiyana Kazhithalum,* when I was twenty-six. But when I read it later, I found that my expressions were limited to that of a seventeen-

year-old girl. Perhaps due to the fact that I could not stretch myself to the distant past with ease and fluency, and the present proved to be tough meat to chew. (2006: vii)

The way Sivakami reduces the dominance of the author is commendable. Critical thinkers such as Roland Barthes and Michel Foucault have observed that the conception of author is tied to the notion of authority which delimits the participation of the reader. The conception of author as demi-God or the function of the author whittles away at the proliferation of meaning. To put it in a deconstructive parlance, the notion of the author functions like a transcendental signified that stops the free play of meanings and impedes the polysemy of interpretations. In the 'Author's Notes' Sivakami does off the mantle of a severe critic of Dalit patriarchy and observes the good qualities inherent in the character of Kathamuthu. That is why she confesses frankly:

> Some facts about Kathamuthu had been selectively omitted. Even when her father had been well off and did not have to engage in physical labour, he had worked on his farm with enthusiasm. (2006:148)

She also points to the way authorial function limits the perspective:

> The author of *The Grip of Change* had constructed an effigy of her father and burned him in the novel. It was the author's perspective rather than the whole truth. (2006:148)

The revision of the story from an objective point of view veers towards a possibility of dissolving Dalit patriarchy. Kancha Ilaiah earlier gave us a hint of the possibility of eliminating Dalit patriarchy by his references to the non-possession of material property by the Dalits which compel everyone, male or female, to work that signifies an egalitarian move. Here, Sivakami offers us another possibility by urging us to steer clear of the prevalent stereotypes and imbibe an inclusive approach. This possibility can be seen in the way Thangam gets a place in the house of Kathamuthu and earns, to some extent, a respectability hitherto assigned to her. In this way Sivakami scrutinises the loopholes as well as signals strengths of Dalit leadership. It is better to round off the discussion with the observation made by Meena Kandasamy:

> Sivakami criticises the Dalit movement and exposes the cruel face of Dalit patriarchy through feminist eyes, and yet, clearly veers away from becoming, a 'caste traitor' because of her engagements with the search for solutions. (2006: 195)

Works Cited

Cixous, Hélène. "The Laugh of Medusa." *The Signs Reader: Women, Gender and Scholarship*. Ed. Elizabeth Abel and Emily K. Abel. Chicago: University of Chicago Press, 1983. Print.

Geetha, K.A. *Contesting Categories, Remapping Boundaries: Literary Interventions by Tamil Dalits*. UK: Cambridge Scholars Publishing, 2014. Print.

Guru, Gopal. "Dalit Women Talk Differently". *Economic and Political Weekly*, Vol. 30, No. 41/42 (Oct. 14-21, 1995): pp. 2548-2550. Print.

Kandasamy, Meena. "And One Shall Live in Two". *The Grip of Change*. P. Sivakami. Chennai: Orient BlackSwan, 2006. Print.

Kumar, Raj. Dalit *Personal Narratives: Reading Caste, Nation, and Identity*. New Delhi: Orient Blackswan, 2010. Print.

Morrison, Toni. "The Site of Memory". *Inventing the Truth: The Art and Craft of Memoir*. Boston: Houghton, 1987. Print.

Ray, Arunima. "Gender in Dalit Discourse: Reading Sivakami's *The Grip of Change*." *The Postcolonial Woman Question*. Ed. G.N. Ray and Jaydip Sarkar, 2011. Print.

Sharma, Suruchi. "Dalit Marginalisation to Resurrection in P. Sivakami's The Grip of Change." *Indian Dalit Autobiographies: Marginalized Voices*. Ed. Singh, Bijender. New Delhi: Authors press, 2015, Print.

Sivakami, P. *The Grip of Change*. Translated by the author herself (from Tamil). Chennai: Orient BlackSwan, 2006. Print.

13

Bama's *Sangati*: The Autobiography of a Dalit Community

Mohd. Anwar Husain Khan

> In our time, direct colonialism has largely ended; imperialism, as we shall see, lingers where it has always been, in a kind of general cultural sphere as well as in specific political, ideological, economic, and social practices.
>
> — (Said, *Culture and Imperialism*, 8)

Bama is renowned Tamil Dalit writer who has *Karukku* (1992), *Sangati* (1994), *Kusumbukkaran* (1996), *Vanmam* (2002), *Oru Tattvum Erumaiyum* (2003) under her name. *Karukku* is arguably the first Dalit women autobiography. It has been translated into several languages including English and French, and won her the Crossword Book Award. It is the story of a Dalit community. It narrates their lifestyle, culture, rituals, their struggle and problems. Her second novel, *Sangati* also has similar theme and in a way, wider in its scope because it focuses on the whole community instead of an individual's story, as Lakshmi Holmström puts:

> The tension throughout *Karukku* is between the self and the community: the narrator leaves one community (of religious women) in order to join another (as Dalit woman). *Sangati* moves from the story of individual struggle to the perception of a community of *paraiya* women, a neighbourhood group of friends and relations and their joint struggle. In a sense, *Sangati* is perhaps the autobiography of a community. (xv)

Sangati is rather a collection of autobiographical stories which are arranged in the form of a novel. Bama talks about the novel:

> My mind is crowded with many anecdotes: stories not only about the sorrows and tears of Dalit women, but also about their lively and rebellious culture, their eagerness not to let life crush or shatter them, but to swim vigorously against the tide; about the self-confidence and self-respect that enables them to leap over threatening adversities by laughing at and ridiculing them; about their passion to live life with vitality, truth, and enjoyment; about their hard labour. I wanted to shout out these stories. (ix)

These anecdotes range from the birth to the death and honestly portray the sensitive issues of Dalit feminism, namely, eternal poverty, child labour, right to education, early marriages, inequality on social and economic level, domestic violence, justice and liberation. Tone of the author is rebellious, as Bama admits in an interview. Her style of writing does not let her work to fall under a certain category, as "most Dalit writing in Tamil has tended to be fiction or poetry. Bama is among the few who bridge autobiography, fiction, polemics, and also a call for action" (xxi).

When Bama states to Sarangi that "the life of a Dalit woman is totally different from a non-Dalit woman," one is posed before the double-question of how the life of a Dalit woman is different from that of a Dalit man and at the same time from a non-Dalit woman. From the novel, we come to know that a Dalit woman has to work as hard as a Dalit man in the fields or factories, and in most cases, even harder than men. The difference starts from that very time because the salary of woman is reasonably low than that of a man, given that the job is same. Besides, when the couple come home, man either takes rest or goes to his friends but the woman prepares meals and feeds the children. This is not the end; she also has to face a sexual assault from her husband on daily basis, "Neither their bodies nor their minds felt rested when they woke up. Promptly they vented their irritation by quarrelling with everyone they met. And then after this bout of useless wrangling, they had to run to their work" (Bama, 67). Quarrelling and abusing becomes the habit of a Dalit woman. It worsens the situation because hearing those bitter words husband start to flog her and in Dalit communities no one can save a woman from her husband. We witness some instances in the novel when the uncle of narrator kills his wife; a pregnant woman is pulled from hair publicly and several women are flogged by their husbands or fathers. When it comes to justice, it seems that people and authorities favour the men. Eventually, "the stronger ones somehow manage to survive all this. The ones who don't have the mental strength are totally oppressed; they succumb to mental ill-health and act as if they are possessed by peys [spirits]" (Bama, 59). It is to be noted that peys possess only females — they are scared of men, according to the tradition. One can imagine the amount of violence committed against the female.

Bama studies the reason for this domestic violence as the complex of Dalit men who are totally oppressed by the landlords and employers. Their false pride results in "all that violence was because there was nowhere else for them to exert their male pride or to show off their authority. All that suppressed anger was vented when they came home and beat up their wives to a pulp" (65). She is not a bit hesitant to analogise a Dalit man with a dog.

The irritation caused by dissonant marital life makes their tongue bitter. Often they use sexual derogatory terms in their gossips which rises above the extent when there is a quarrel. Even the simple backbiting includes obscenities like "whore," "slut," "sister-in-law," etc. Bama examines the language and comes to the result that "they have neither pleasure nor fulfilment in their own sexual lives, they derive a sort of bitter comfort by using these terms of abuse which are actually names of their body parts." (68)

The discrimination of females in the Dalit community starts from the day they born, as "many women have died because they have their babies at home, without proper care. But they don't have the means to pay for hospital care. And neither nurses nor doctors will come into our streets as willingly as they go to others" (90). If the mother is dead, the surviving children have to be ready for toiling. Their childhood is skipped and killed by eternal poverty as the major duty falls on a girl child because for them females are meant to do domestic chores. They have to work in the fields or factories before they come of age. Even if the mothers are alive, there are limited sources of income — most of times they have not stomach full of food. If this happens (and it happens mostly) female children are the ones who suffer the most. It has become a tradition that the male child is fed at the first place. Then the adult ones and at last comes the turn of girl children. Nobody bothers about their hunger. If they argue, their mothers bitterly credit it to the social norms.

This is not the all. The girl children are also not free to play games. Their entertainment and laughter is forbidden. They have to do domestic chores with their mothers. The situation worsens if the mother happens to be pregnant.

Then it is the female child who manages the domestic duties and in addition to it, brings up the new sibling. In certain cases, the children have to labour to meet the both ends. New discriminations come with it. Apart from discriminations the adult Dalits face at work, the children are also prone to be physically abused. And this abuse does not come singularly from the employer, parents also hurt them by snatching their salary. The novel portrays a similar incident where a poor girl has been beaten by contractor and by her father.

There is no culture of education. Most of the females are not sent to schools. Even if some girls manage to go schools, they complete only five forms. So, at about ten years of age, they leave the school. Because of this, they are all married near the age of puberty. When the schooling was forbidden, they were married even before ten. But recently (considering the time in novel, that is, 1970s) the appropriate age for marriage is puberty. In fact, when a girl reaches puberty, it is celebrated and rituals are performed. The girl has to remain at home for sixteen days. She is not given any work and family makes sure she bathes every day. It is to be noted that the cleanliness is not a habit of the Dalit community. They occasionally bathe when they have to go to church for weekly communion. It seems that the traditional ceremony of coming of age is to make sure the hygiene in the periods. After the ceremony, the search for proper groom starts. Most of the girls are married in a few months. There is left no reason to defend the girl from being married because in Dalit community, they already have no childhood.

Conversion does not change the fate of a Dalit. A Dalit remains a Dalit forever. Even the Christian religion does not believe in the caste system but the Dalits are continued to be disrespected. They are persistently given menial jobs like sweeping the church, in the name of salvation. Even the situation gets worse in the case of women. Hindu religion allows married women to marry second time even if the first husband has not died. But in Christian religion such privilege is not there. Woman has to live with the first husband until he dies. Taking the Dalit domestic violence in mind, on certain occasions, it becomes too difficult to live with husband. Christianity has no solution of it. So, conversion can sometimes only add to the problems.

Bama traces the reason for conversion of her community Paraiyas, "when my mother and Perimma were little children, the Christian priests came to our village. When they promised that if our people joined their faith, their children would get a free education, it seems that all the Paraiyas became Christians" (5). The promises appear to be unfulfilled and the aid from government cease to come "because they did so at that time; now it works out that they get no concessions from the government whatsoever" (5). So, everything seems to be political and the authorities are not a bit concerned with the situation of Dalits.

All that happens to Dalit women is not necessarily the grimiest in comparison with upper-caste women. In fact, there are a few traditions which are commendable in Dalit community. One such tradition is the cut off of evil dowry system. It is known that dowry system has become a lavishing ritual in Indian marriage ceremonies - people spend more than their capacities to maintain their false pride. Bama talks about marriage traditions in the upper-castes:

> It's only on the surface that they look so good, really. It isn't that easy for them to get their daughters settled. They have to cover the girls' necks with jewellery, give them cash in their hands, and write off property and land in their names. Even after all this do you think the girls are happy in their new homes? Their in-laws keep on complaining that this and that is not enough, and they torment the girls. (112)

That is why the girl children are killed before they can see the world. But in the Dalit community there is no tradition of dowry and consequently, no evil of female foeticide. On the contrary, it is the groom who has to pay some gifts to the family of bride in order to get married.

Due to the economic reasons, Dalit women do not develop idolatry to the traditions – they are not bound to follow the marital ornamental cultures of the upper-caste women. They don't have any time for these petty rituals. In upper-castes, there is a tradition to wear certain jewels when a girl marries. She has to follow the same tradition until her husband's death. If her husband dies, she is forbidden to wear any jewel and has to wear white clothes. This cessation of jewellery after husband's death also has no significance in the Dalit community. Bama states:

> If a man dies, there is no rule that says his wife must immediately go into white saris nor that she must behave in such and such manner. She will carry on in her usual way. And this is because, even when her husband is alive, it isn't compulsory that a woman must wear a pottu on her forehead, nor bangles and other jewellery about her person, nor smear herself with turmeric. Where does she have the jewellery in the first place? And where does she have the time to smear herself with turmeric, have a bath, and dress herself up with pottu and flowers? She runs to work at dawn and comes home after sunset. So whether her husband is alive or dead, she will follow the same routine. She might, perhaps, remove her tali. On the other hand, some women never wear a tali, though they marry and live with their husbands. Talis are not that important among us. (90)

Hence, a woman of upper-caste practices a colourless life after the death of her husband. In addition to it, she is forbidden to marry second time. But there is no such restriction in the Dalit community; a widow can marry again. "Some women marry a second time after the death of a husband," Bama talks about the Dalit Christian community, "that is quite normal among us. On the other hand, among the other [upper-caste] communities of our village, you can see straight away the indignities suffered by widows. In our street though, everyone is held the same; widows are not treated differently" (90).

There is a prevalent difference in the second marriage rules between the various Dalit communities. The Dalit communities those belong to Hindu religion allow a woman to marry second time even if the first husband is alive. But that is not the case in Christian Dalit communities because Christianity allows a woman to remarry only after the death of first husband. Taking the domestic violence into consideration, it becomes difficult to live with a man in most cases. Hence, it is the Christian Dalit woman who suffers. So, religion does play part even the both categories are Dalit. It is to be noted that the rules are meant for women only - men of both religions are free to keep women.

With the passage of time, Dalits have an increasing access to education. As a result of it, they are becoming more aware of their rights. But the identity of being a Dalit disturbs them. Bama states:

> Among the more educated, nowadays, all this [ornamental culture] is changing. These people for some reason, want to copy the upper castes. It's becoming a real problem having to make so many jewels for the bride and giving a lump some worth so much, on top of that...Such people can change themselves into a different caste only in these superficial matters, though. Because, whatever we do, whatever rituals we copy from other castes they, for their part, always rate us as beneath them. So what is the point of trying to copy them? Why should we lose all the better customs that are ours, and end up as neither one thing nor the other? (89)

So, distancing from the identity is not the solution of the problem. Bama advises all Dalits to be united. Justice is also male-centred and biased. A Dalit panchayat [communion] is assigned to do it whose working does not seem free from any politics. The judgement can be figured out from the fact that only men are allowed to sit there; women have to stand backside. In the procession, the authority does not allow the alleged to speak, as if all the proceedings have already been decided. If someone resists and speaks to defend oneself, the punishment becomes more intense. For instance, when the upper-caste landlord molests a girl, he comes to the panchayat before the girl can do anything and narrates a false story. The panchayat believes his version of the story and bothers not about the evidences. It seems that the Dalit justice is under the mercy of upper-caste. They do not question the upper-caste, even the evidences contradict them. The reason being, they have to go for work in their fields – if the landlord is enraged, how will they feed their families?

Similar patriarchy can be seen in the norms of inter-caste marriage. In case, a man chooses a woman from other community, it does not harm the Dalit culture but if the same is done by a female, she is first of all embarrassed before the village communion. Then her father and brothers will flog her to death. The community allows this violence as pretty reasonable.

In some cases, even if the man kills his wife, there is no askance of justice from the woman's house because they know the panchayat will not deliver the justice and the other institutions of justice are inaccessible to them.

The account of voting day is humorous, and at the same time evokes sympathy. Bama shows how the leaders and the party members respect the Dalit people at the day of voting but when the sun sets the nights and days remain the same for five years. Leaders from all parties choose some Dalits to promote themselves. If some tension happens between the parties, it is these Dalits who get hurt - nothing happens to the leaders. Women in the novel talk about a murder of a Dalit boy in similar manner. In fact, voting is the day when the poor people have a chance to ride in the vehicles which are meant to transport them to polling booth. The poor people do not miss the ride even they do not properly know how to vote. Apart from this, the voting day proves to be another blow on the people as they do not get any work for it is being a holiday. Without work, they hearths do not burn and they sleep without food most of the times.

Holmström reads Raj Gauthaman's exploration that "there are no models for Dalit writing. Sequence, chronology, perceptions of time, form, and language must all be reconstructed in Dalit writing as it evolves. His primary examples of such reconstruction are Barma's *Karukku* and *Sangati*" (xv). *Sangati* follows a typical pattern in its chapters. First of all, the incident is portrayed in a relatively simpler mode. Then the narrator asks an explanation from her grandmother whose explanations befit the submissive tradition. After that, narrator asks the same from her mother who is on a bit revolutionary side. Her thoughts depart from the received norms. At last, narrator herself gives an explanation which is even more revolutionary. Most of the times her explanations present solutions to the problems but in a few cases, they fail to ensue any result. Similar is the case of denying marriage. If she means it as a solution, it does not seem a solid one. It can help on an individual scale but on the community level the goal must be harmonising the marital relationship, not to overthrow the relationship. The Dalit men should be educated accordingly. It does not mean that an unmarried woman should be on the receiving end. It is pathetic that the way our patriarchal society disrespect such woman. The conception is satirised as "they seem to think that once a woman is married and has a tali her neck, she is also signed, sealed, and delivered over to one man. They assume that otherwise she is the common property of many fellows, and they will leer at her suggestively" (121).

It is not only the men who molest a single woman; even the women persistently annoy her. Being a single woman, Bama shares her own predicament as, "women gossip just as much if not more. Even women teachers who are my colleagues find my lifestyle unbearable. They keep a sharp watch on whatever I do, and spread tales in no time, embroidering and adding whatever they like to imagine" (121). So, for a Dalit woman, she has to face upper-caste patriarchy, Dalit men and even, the women.

The emancipation from class and gender oppression of the African women, Christine N. Quanta states, "will come about through the critical examination of all political, economic, religious, educational and cultural institutions... (15). In order to achieve it energies of both men and women are needed to be harnessed. But it is pertinent that even if a nominal liberation is allocated to the oppressed communities, only men access it – women's plight remains intact. Similarly, the government policies for Dalits do not make a change because the domestic oppression of females plays a significant part in barring the female emancipation. The patriarchal tendencies, Quanta continues, "must be fought at all levels, and I believe this confrontation should take the form of consultation, co-operation and criticism" (15).

Sangati shows us how the plight of a Dalit woman is different from that of a Dalit man. From the birth as a female child to the death she witnesses a variety of blows to her physical and emotional health. Her lives start with malnutrition. Her childhood is buried under hard work. No one cares about the law of child labour because no government representative is willing to visit the area. The novel discusses no childhood dream at all because circumstances do not let them have any. The girls are married before they get to adulthood — a few of them have no idea of sex. Some die giving birth as the hospitals are inaccessible. They don't have any wild guess of basics needs like "shit-rooms," electricity, etc. This discloses the ground realities of so-called progressive schemes.

The situation of Dalit woman worsens by domestic violence. As we see in the novel, not a single time the problem is shared with the police. This could result in an affirmation to the government records that no violence has been committed in a Dalit community. Perhaps they know the truth, but the ignorance of Dalits becomes an excuse for them. If we examine a campaign named "Bell Bajao" to rule out the domestic violence, we would come to a result that the campaign does not really fit to these Dalit communities because most of them don't even have any bell on their doors. That shows the limited scope of the campaign. On the contrary, the Dalit men are assaulting their wives publicly outside their homes. So, we witness how the government policies succumb before they reach these sensitive areas. A lot of work is to be done.

Works Cited

Bama. *Sangati: Events*. Trans. Lakshmi Holmström. New Delhi: Oxford UP, 2015. Print.

"Bell Bajao." Web. 28 August 2015. http://www.bellbajao.org/home/men-for-bell-bajao/

Holmström, Lakshmi. Introduction. Bama xi-xxiii.

Qunta, Christine N. ed. *Women in Southern Africa*. London: Allison and Busby, 1987. Print.

Sarangi, Jaydeep. "Bama Faustina : Conversation with Jaydeep Sarangi." *Muse India* 62: Jul-Aug 2015. Web. 28 August 2015. http://www.museindia.com/regularcontent.asp?issid=45&id=3636

Said, Edward W. *Culture and Imperialism*. London: Vintage, 1994, Print.

14

Powerful Clamp of Caste in Kumudtai Pawde's *Antaspot: Thoughtful Outburst*

Himanshu Sharma

'What comes by birth but can't be cast off by dying — that is caste.'

(Dangle, *A Corpse in the Well*, 25)

This above statement by Pawde beautifully describes real anguish of her heart. Caste has been like an incurable disease for dalits that always follows them wherever they go. To get rid of this, the dalits as tormented souls started getting education and then wrote their own experiences in their autobiographies. Only writing the autobiography does not solve the problems, there are other concepts like exploitation, suppression, dissonant voices, atrocities, untouchability and feminist approach also which are generally found dominant in almost all Dalit autobiographies.

Generally autobiographies narrate the writers' own experiences of life during childhood, youth, job, career, achievements and other main incidences of life whereas Dalit autobiographies have the themes of oppression, resistance, pain, exploitation, subjugation, untouchablity, hardships, poverty etc. Their life has been described not better than animals in the autobiographies. Either they have to feed on them or they have to compete with them for their survival. They are forced to eat the carcasses in their utter poverty. Their habitation has been described at a segregated place on or nearby dunghills or the human excreta. One or more such topics are easily found in almost each Dalit autobiography.

Kumud Pawde was born in a Mahar family in Nagpur in 1938 as Kumud Somkuvar. She married with Motiram Pawde who was a social worker. She has got Pawde surname from her husband. She is a renowned author, scholar and a Sanskrit professor. She has been the president of All India Progressive Woman's Organisation. Thus, organisation was established in Nagpur in 1974.

The word '*Antaspot*' literally means 'outburst' but Kumud Pawde clearly mentions in the second edition of her book that this word must not be confused with an emotional outburst rather it is a very thoughtful outburst of feelings. Kumud Pawde has tried to explore her community very dexterously. During the analysis of people both the joys and pains can be expected. She has explored that the women in the Dalit communities are doubly exploited. She writes "Because of this, I began to feel as if my brain will burst and when this state expresses itself in words — the thoughtful outburst happens. This is my position at Antaspot" (Pawde, 4). Kumud Pawde explains that *Antaspot* is not an autobiography but critical narrative of her experiences and all Dalit life stories are critical narratives and not autobiographies (Rege, 4).

Kumud has depicted the memories of her childhood in her autobiography. She has, like other Dalit autobiographers, used 'we' instead of 'I' at many places to represent her community. Shweta Singh observes this point, 'The subject in Dalit women's autobiographies is thus not "I" but "we"' (Singh, 45). Kumudtai depicts that Hindus attacked on Nagpur in 1946. Since then she was a mere child and she did not know who the Hindus were. She wanted to know about the Mahars also. Her mother explains to her that they are also Hindus but they are from the lower caste, the Hindus she was talking about were from the upper caste. She was born in a low Mahar caste but she is praised for her knowledge of Sanskrit and for her ability to learn and teach it. The point is not new as there may be many people who have learnt Sanskrit and taught it also but the strange thing was that the caste which she belonged to was the lowest of the low and Sanskrit is considered for the upper caste people only. That's why all praised Kumud Pawde for her knowledge of Sanskrit. Kumud Pawde had to face many problems in her struggle to learn Sanskrit and even after being a professor she had to face many problems. She describes her pain when she writes:

> 'In what former life have I committed a sin that I should have to learn Sanskrit even from you?' 'All our sacred scriptures have been polluted.' Some despair is also conveyed by their facial expressions. It is all over. *Kaliyug* has dawned' (Dangle, 25)

Kumud Pawde tells an incidence of 1971 at the auspicious occasion of the Vijaya Dashami. The Maharashtra State Government has arranged a felicitation meeting in Nagpur to honour of the scholars of the Vedas. Sh. Madhukarrao Chaudhary was the ex-education minister and he wished that Kumud may introduce these scholars in Sanskrit. Her heart was thumping as it was a challenging task for her. Many people were against this act that a Dalit girl may introduce the Vedic scholars. Shudras and women were not allowed to learn Sanskrit. She also got objection even from her caste. 'Why did you need to make the introductions in this manner? To humiliate us?' (Dangle, 26-27) Kumud Pawde feels proud for this wonderful opportunity she has got in her life. But the culture and environment was still preventing her to do so:

> Whereas our traditional books have forbidden the study of Sanskrit by women and Shudras, a woman from those very Shudras, from the lowest caste among them, will today, in Sanskrit, introduce these scholars. This is the beginning of a progressive way of thinking in independent India (Pawde, 26).

She narrates the problem of untouchability in her childhood. When she was a student in her school, the other girls in her school were from the Brahmin or the upper caste. She remained very neat and clean and always wore better dresses than the upper caste girls. She did not like the bad odour of *shikakai* from the upper caste girls and she herself left sweet fragrance and she always bathed with Pears shop. Her house was well-plastered with mud than the other girls' houses. Still she was not allowed to play with them. The mothers of the upper caste girls would prevent them to have her company as she was a Mahar girl. They would warn their daughters if they found them anywhere, 'Be careful! Don't touch her. Stay away from her. And don't play with her. Or I won't let you into the house again' (Dangle, 27).

She describes an incidence of her life. She tells that once there was a thread ceremony of one of her friend's brother from the high caste. She was not invited in the ceremony just because she belonged to a low-caste family. But Kumud could not stop herself and out of the curiosity she also reached there. She was looking at the activities, the sacrificial fire and the incantations of the Vedic hymns with full concentration. Suddenly her concentration was broken up by a woman who spoke to her, 'Hey, girl! What are you staring at? Can you make head or tail of it? Here take a *laddo* — and be off! (Dangle, 28) She was looking at her with the disgusting eyes. But Kumud did not listen to her silently. She also refuted immediately, "What do you take me for — a beggar? Giving me a *ladoo*! Can you see injuries on anyone just because I watched them? (28) After it she did not stayed there and immediately left that place but the biting words regarding her caste still followed her. Someone was saying from behind, 'These Mahars have really got above than themselves. '(28) The Dalit girls and women have to live a very painful life and society is more or less responsible for it. Tapan Basu writes in this concern, "There is no girl in our cheri who has not been coerced or raped by the dominant caste men when they go to the fields to fetch water or for work". (Basu, 124)

Kumud felt much wounded after this incidence of thread ceremony. Then she went home and asked her father about the language of the Vedic mantras. Her father told her that these mantras were in Sanskrit. He told her that Sanskrit was a difficult language and she could learn it if she tried. Her father told her that he also knew Gayatri Mantra and in this way he started enchanting the Gayatri Mantra. She got inspired from her father and determined that she would learn Sanskrit and prove her worth. But learning Sanskrit to a Mahar girl was a big challenge as Sanskrit was considered the language of the Brahmins and the upper caste people and Mahars did not learn that language due to their caste.

When she entered in high school she chose Sanskrit in the ninth class as an elective subject. No any teacher was happy to give her Sanskrit as an elective subject. She asked her teacher, Hatekar about her decision. He suggested her to takes Maths and Science also alongwith Sanskrit as by choosing these subjects she could become a doctor but she denied taking Maths and Science. She told him that she did not want to become a doctor. And ultimately she did not listen to anybody. She was firm in her decision and took Sanskrit as an elective subject and completed her matriculation though with some difficulties. After that she decided to do

M.A. in Sanskrit but other people laughed at her decision. They told her that it was easy to pass matriculation but it is not so easy to complete M.A. in Sanskrit. She was discouraged now especially by the people of her caste. But she didn't say anything to them. They wanted to prove it by her actions. She admitted in Morris College and worked hard on her studies.

Even in the college also caste did not spare her. The high caste Hindus taunted her. They said, 'Even these wretched outcastes are giving themselves airs these days — studying in colleges' (31) but she turned a deaf ear to their words and concentrated on her studies. She worked hard and got scholarship. The college staff from the peons to senior officers similarly did not like her to study in the college. They were feeling jealous of her as she was having fun and was enjoying with the money of her scholarship. They criticised her and said, 'She's having fun and games at the expense of a scholarship. Just bloated with the government money!' (Dangle, 31)

She completed her graduation with good marks and ultimately joined postgraduate department of the university. Very renowned and erudite scholars were as the faculty members in the department of Sanskrit in the university. The head of the department of the university was a person of all-India repute. He did not like her learning Sanskrit and his venomous language explicitly expressed his disapproval. He was not traditional man and but his way of teaching was very good. She faced some difficulties but ultimately she completed her M.A. with distinction.

Now after completion of her M.A. she started dreaming of becoming a Sanskrit lecturer. During post-graduation in Sanskrit, it was a big achievement for her as she was the only girl from the scheduled caste who has did her M.A. in Sanskrit. She faced many difficulties after her M.A. and she did not get any job even after two years. The people commented on her when she went in search of the job, 'So now even these people are to teach Sanskrit! (33)

Kumud was feeling very bad when she was still unemployed even after two years of her M.A. but she did not succumb against the odd circumstances. She took a bold step and put her case in writing to the Cabinet Minister, Sh. Jagjivan Ram. He placed the letter to Pandit Nehru who was very astonished to read her letter. He sent a reward of two hundred and fifty rupees to her and told her to meet the Chief Minister of Maharashtra. Yeshvantrao Chavan was the chief minister at that time. He sent a telegram to her to meet him. But the Chief Minister also did nothing and just consoled her saying, 'We'll definitely make efforts for you but you won't get a job in minutes; it'll take us some time. We'll have to give thought to it, have to hunt out something' (Dangle, 34)

Next year Kumud Somkuvar took admission in M.A. in English literature to keep her occupied and the same year she was married. It was an inter-caste marriage and her husband belonged to an upper caste. Only after two months of her marriage she got a job as an assistant lectureship not due to her own knowledge of Sanskrit but because of the high caste surname of her husband. The interview board members gave her job to see her surname Kumud 'Pawde' an upper caste surname. In this regard she writes, 'That's why I say that the credit of being a professor of Sanskrit is that of the presumed higher caste status of Mrs Kumud Pawde. The caste of her maiden status remained deprived (Dangle, 34). Ruchi Tomar opines that:

> There is a need to examine and evaluate Dalit women's historical experiences from the perspective of caste, economic class, politics, and patriarchal angles, aimed towards the transformation in work, wages, and family life. Not only patriarchy and caste but also class divides Dalit women by bringing the embourgeoisment and

Sanskritisation. Dalit feminism must respond to the complexity of salience of class and the differences create by the caste-ridden society. They should make an attempt to emphasise the unity of caste, class, and gender and rejects the efforts to bifurcate their identities. (Tomar, 2)

Kumudtai describes that dalits were unnecessary harasses and exploited by the public. She tells an incident of her life that her aunt was harassed by the police because her son had eloped with an upper caste girl. Her aunt also came to know that they had married in a local Buddha Vihar. The girl's family told them that it was the case of abduction of a girl. Kumudtai brought the couple back and the girl accepted in the police station that she had eloped herself and nobody forced her while her parents kept instigating her to speak against the boy, 'Baby, did any one force you into this decision?' (Rege, 248)

Thus, Kumud Pawde's *Antaspot* is a lifelong struggle of her life. She has to face many problems and hurdles to get his education and job as a Sanskrit lecturer. The autobiography beautifully depicts the patriarchal hegemony even within the Dalit community. This is not the only autobiography that has the voice of protest but almost all Dalit autobiographies deal with the same butt. Dr Tejaswini P. Narayankar postulates that "Dalit women's autobiographies portray the conditions that tore dalit women's lives to pieces brutally" (Narayankar, 6).

Works Cited

Basu, Tapan. *Translating Caste*. New Delhi: Gyan Books, 2002. Print.

Dangle, Arjun (ed). *A Corpse in the Well* (1992). Hyderabad: Disha Books, 1994. Print.

Narayankar, Tejaswini P. "Dalit Autobiography: An Evolution of Individual Self." *Research Front*. Vol. 2, Issue 2, Apr - Jun. 2014. 1-6.

Pawde, Kumud. *Antaspot.* (Marathi). Aurangabad: Anand Prakashan, 1995. Print.

Pawade Kumud: 'The Life of Dalit Woman,' *Dalit Women in India: Issues and Perspectives*, New Delhi, 1995. Print.

Rege, Sharmila. *Writing Caste/Writing Gender: Narrating Dalit Women's Testimonies.* New Delhi: Zuban, 2006. Print.

Shweta, Singh. "Representation of Dalit Women in Dalit Men's and Women's Autobiographies." *The Delhi University Journal of the Humanities and the Social Sciences* Volume 1: 2014. 39-48.

Tomar, Ruchi. "Dalit Feminism: A Transformation of Rejection into Resistance." *The Criterion: An International Journal in English.* Issue 12, February 2013. 1-8.

15

Demystifying the Curse: Reading Kausalya Baisantri's *Dohra Abhishaap* as a Journey of an Untouchable Woman

Guni Vats

> The dalits have limited themselves and are not left with the enthusiasm to grow.
>
> —(Baisantri, 121)

When the greatest minds of the world deliberated upon the most important issues that bound society in hierarchical orders, they apparently forgot to consult a woman, and the darkness in which the lower castes were eventually cornered to, women faced the worse. They had to accept and amend as per the laws laid by the mighty wise men and then had to carve a society which would eventually dominate them. Kausalya Baisantri's autobiography *Dohra Abhishaap* (Twice Accursed) does not complaint and crib about the discrimination but she takes a self-introspective journey; a journey that brings out the hypocrisy of every section of society and the irony that pains her. Her autobiography is the innocent memoir of a girl who learns her caste and its place in the society and struggles to establish a respectable place for herself. She questions the established norms and fights the obstacles with the vigour that ultimately earns her a social standing and importance.

Twentieth century changed the face of Indian literature with a new sensibility of the modern. The modern aspect could precisely be witnessed in Baisantri's autobiography. The ease with which she describes the filth and the use of colloquial language explains the intention of her writing; she wrote for the common man and not for the few who were embarrassed of their existence. Dalit literature was often accused of an attempt to portray the filth of the dalit community and thus expect pity from the society. Baisantri's autobiography changed this general perception. She was not writing as a spokesperson of her community against the higher castes but a social narrative that brings out the reality of existence of a dalit woman. Born in the second decade of the twentieth century, when Indian was in a political tumult, Kausalya witnessed and wrote about the marginalisation of the weaker sex of the untouchable section of society. Her *Dohara Abhishaap* seems like an understatement to what dalit women were subjected to.

Kausalya sets a platter where she serves what she received without any ornamentation. With the innocent narrative, she connects the community through self. She does not spare any phoneme of the lyrics of society she witnessed. She serves reality with all its filth. The very few chapters would witness the food habits that glorify the blood stained unhygienic conditions that these dalits adopted. They would bring blood dripping chunks of cow's meat in a piece of cloth with flies hovering around the blood stained cloth, leaving blood all through the road. As a sort of confession, Kausalya discloses her being an *asprishya* in the very beginning of the novel. She then takes the reader closer to her community by explaining the sort of work these people did; they would only get a chance to do the work which required physical exertion like chopping off woods and some menial work at the occasions of wedding. Since the first chapter she laments the lack of education in her community that led to the death of her grandfather, who lost his life to the lack of basic medical amenities and superstition. She sets the stage for the need of education she struggles to acquire later in the novel.

Kausalya's autobiography is not a chronological social narrative but an unprohibited string of events that find a place in the order she remembers them. The events brutally depict the reality of a patriarchal society which did loosen its strings for women but all in the interest of its men. Remarriage was not prohibited in the *asprishya* community, both widows and divorced women could remarry but then the official ceremony would be called *paat* instead of wedding though the rituals were more or less the same, the widows were adorned like a bride with all the necessary markers of a married woman but she would be taken to the groom's house at night when no one could see her. There was no loud music or gaudy celebrations though a feast was still arranged for the family of both sides. The divorced women would not be taken at night but her *paat* was same as that of a widow. The remarriages were merely a garb to cover the sexual urges of mortals because in any case they were not given any respectable position in the household:

> The widows were not supposed to take part in any auspicious occasion like wedding or *puja*. They were entitled to wear a pendant of the form of *savat* of either silver or gold so that everyone could identify her as the second woman. (17)

On the contrary however a widower need not go through these demeaning and insulting rituals, he could marry a virgin gallantly whereas a widow or a divorced woman could not even think of marrying a *kunwara* man. The hypocrisy of patriarchal society did not stop at the politics of marriage. The men would not stop at one wife, their manliness would suffice only if they had acquired at least two wives and given them a dozen children each to look after and cry at their deaths. Bigamy was popular and no one resisted it, if the first wife uttered something she would be beaten to pulp.

The hierarchy of caste did not only divide society into higher and lower castes but there existed sub-castes. As Kausalya states:

> There were twelve and half sub-castes in our Mahar caste. Kosre, Bavne, Ladvan, Aadhvan, Somvanshi, Barke, Jhaade Bavne etc. Each of them used to mingle but the affairs of wedding were restricted specifically to the sub-castes. (22)

The groom's side paid dowry to the bride's, much like the bride price. The rituals might differ but the ways and standard of living were more or less the same. Education held least importance and the illiteracy had taken over the better of these people. They had surrendered their lives to the superstitions of Hinduism, they would pray and chant if someone in their families fell ill but never look for scientific cures. They had accepted life and death as the fruits of God and had thus no sense of family planning, the women would bear children every year and more than half of them would die because of the ill conditions and lack of medical facilities. The women would be forced to suffer the grave pain of death of their children almost every successive year. The marriages took place at a very young age and in a few years the mother and daughter would be delivering children at the same time. Kausalya's mother and elder daughter had children of the same time. Parents would work and the elder siblings would be expected to take care of the little ones.

The curse of being a girl child was the gravest. She was expected to do the household chores, look after her younger siblings, and bring them up like a mother. The new born would be doped so that he sleeps longer, the overdose of which would prove fatal most of the times. The child would lie in the rags filled with urine for hours, waiting for the mother to return from work and clean him up. Sometimes they would accompany mothers to the work places where they would lie in a corner crying and unattended. The frustration of bearing so many children and the pain of losing them took its toll on the mothers. They would at times think of getting rid of her children by throwing them away in a garbage pit and at better times they would pray for their lives. The girl's destiny is determined by her father and then her husband, this was followed ominously. Kausalya was named Kachri at her birth which means garbage, to ward off the evil spirits and give her life. The proper name was then given by her husband. The lives of girls were dependent on the men but the condition of dalit women involved another level of discrimination. They were not just the poor, illiterate women but were the untouchable women.

The hegemony of caste was executed well by both the upper and lower castes. The upper castes would not let the untouchables procure a respectable job; they were forced to do the menial work:

> Men and women would roll *bidis*, women would sweep the homes of Anglo-Indian, cook food, take care of their children etc. the English would at times employ men as their butlers... (31)

The untouchables never thought of education or of bettering their lives. They would feast the day they got paid and would starve the rest of the days. If people amongst them would strive to better their position, they would only pull them back. The resistance of same caste is a concern Kausalya has dwelled on in all its perspectives. The people of her own *basti* would mock her for going to school on cycle, the brats would tease her, the epitome of illiterates would urinate at their walls but her mother lived through everything patiently and carried on teaching her children. Kausalya got most baffled when she saw women were against women and could not bear them to be successful. The elder women of her community would comment seeing Kausalya determined to study:

> "She has grown so already, her breasts are hanging down her chest, still not married, would she marry once she grows old?" Some would say: "Oh, let it be. Would she have remained a virgin till now? So many boys stop by, so would nothing have happened till now?" (75)

Baba Saheb Ambedkar had changed the face of Dalit in the pre- and post-independent India. He had given them a new ray of hope, he had handed the down the hope of education and had encouraged all women to study and teach their children. He brought a wave in the untouchables living in the filthiest corners of villages and hit them with a realisation that they were as much a part of this nation as the Brahmins were and deserved every but that has been taken away from them. Ambedkar shatters the piousness of Brahmanism and Hinduism that existed amongst the lower castes. He made them realise that they did not need to clean the filth of their homes and could carry on with their rituals without the 'holy' presence of a Brahmin. It was Ambedkar who changed the way dalits thought till now and as a result of his toil, Kausalya started her education and fought for it at every step. Dolas argues against Dalit literature in *Writing Caste/Writing Gender:*

> Dissatisfaction from life narratives stems from the fact that many dalit life narratives focus more on the pre-Ambedkarite era and thus do not adequately represent the history of history of agitation and progress. (12)

Kausalya offers whatever Dolas has pointed out. She emerges as a social worker and a political enthusiast and has written about the political movements in detail. May it be the student union or getting scholarships or demanding a due place of women in society, Kausalya has lived and written about it all. Her autobiography is the saga of a bold woman who bears the inferiority of an untouchable child bearing the scornful glares of all the other classmates who were all of superior castes and grows to becoming a woman who withdrew her chit fund group because they seemed uncomfortable with her caste. Her character displays all the qualities of a Bildungsroman, she grows in all aspects with life and learns to accepts her own self.

The teachers would pick on her in school and would make her do the household chores. She would be ashamed of her dirty school dress, her torn school bag, her lunch box, the very existence of her caste, the profession of her father but she never gave up. The discrimination and prejudice lead a blame of theft be forced on her once, it shattered her self confidence but she would always gather her and move forward. The society now seemed barbaric once she had acquired the basic education. She had started questioning the established superficial norms where it's always a woman which is blamed and punished. She keenly observed the relationships and found out how futile and vain they were. The husband would force his wife to be insulted amongst the entire *basti* only because another man was trying to take advantage of her. She failed to understand why it's always the fault of a woman when a marriage does not work out. The more she questioned, the worse she had to face.

Dohra Abhishaap is not a cry of a discriminated woman but the life of an intellectual woman. She minutely observes the crevices of relationship between the higher and lower castes. It's not only a condemnation of the superior caste. She mentions the Jaiswal *baniya* who owned the land on which her *basti* was made and who would never force the tenants to pay a certain amount. He was a genuine man who had awarded Kausalya for passing her matriculation exam. Then there were the women of upper castes who would wear old saris while buying bangles from Kausalya's mother, so they could bathe immediately after bearing contact with an untouchable. In the working of the administrative machinery, she discusses the class of petty bourgeoisie who had acquired a respectable position but would not do anything to uplift their community. Kausalya measures her acquaintances through their wisdom and not caste. This was the ultimate goal of Ambedkar's movement and Kausalya's efforts.

The curse of being a dalit woman got bitter with Kausalya growing young. The guys of the community would tease her but she being a bold woman would slap them and be done away with. Whatever endeavour she took on her, she had to suffer the lust of men who considered a poor untouchable girl some public property. The time she went to the civil hospital for her sister's check up, the watchman who was of the same caste duped her to a fifty years old man from which she wittily escaped. Then the bureaucrat who had promised her the installation of a tap tried to use her. The section that religiously exercised untouchability would not mind feeding on the untouchable girls. The upper caste men would have the lower caste women as their keeps. As she puts it:

> What face do these people put up! Under the garb of innocence hides the evil. Looking at women they get lusty and just want to feed on her. (91)

The argument of dalit literature goes back years. Translator and teacher Arun Prabha Mukherjee says, 'autobiographies are not sob stories but stories of anger against injustice' (10). Kausalya has not limited her anger to her autobiography but her personal life screams of it. She married Devendra Kumar Baisantri, a D. Phil. student and a social worker. Her autobiography does not hide 'self' but she reaches community through self. Her marriage was an inter-caste affair and a union of minds. Devendra was already married but her wife died and left him with no kids. The marriage was not what Kausalya had hoped. Despite of his education, Devendra was the 'Man of the house' and controlled the lives of everybody else. He treated everybody like his slave and would order Kausalya around. He would keep the groceries under lock and key and would supply only the amount he thought was appropriate. After a long battle he agreed to give an allowance of thirty rupees to his wife packed in the way he paid his servants. After a lifetime of insult, Kausalya finally stood up for herself and took a divorce.

From the insecure girl Kausalya grew up to be an independent woman. She learned to accept her community and her existence. She shows the filth of society without trying to cover or beautify any part of it. The description of the excretion place which would be smelly and crowded and people would defecate outside the designated cabins and in rains it would all just float on water and breed flies. Born in such a place, Kausalya reaches out to her community through her social work. She feels for her society and knows that in the progress of every self is hidden the progress of community. *Dohra Abhishaap* is not merely a testimony or historical document. It is the struggle of doubly marginalised soul who thrives to become better and walk along with every hand she can hold and change every life she can touch. All those who could not be affected by her person, this persona aims at inspiring them. It's not a sob story or a testimony of embarrassment; it's an open book which shows the filth of society without making any judgments. She questions the very foundation of this vain society, the society that claims that Mahar are meant for menial work and entertainment while Brahmins are meant to acquire all the respectable knowledge.

Works Cited

Baisantri, Kausalya. *Dohra Abhishaap* (Hindi). Delhi: Parmeshwari, 2015. Print.

Devy, G. *The G.N. Devy Reader*. Hyderabad: Orient Longman, 1992. Print.

Ganguly, D. "Dalit life stories". *The Cambridge Companion to Modern Indian Culture* (Eds.), V. Dalmia and Sadana. New Delhi: Cambridge University Press, 2012. 124-141. Print.

Guru, G. "Dalit Women Talk Differently". *Gender and Caste*. Ed. A. Rao. New Delhi: Women Unlimited, 2003. 80-85. Print.

Narayankar, Tejaswini P. *Dalit Autobiography: An Evolution of Individual Self*. http://www.researchfront.in. Accessed on 12/08/2015. Volume 2, Issue 2, April-June 2014. Web.

Ramanathan S. *Situating Dalit Literature in Indian writing in English*. Http://www.languageinindia.com. Accessed on 12/08/2015. Volume 14, 12 December 2014. Web.

Rege, Sharmila. 'A Dalit Feminist Standpoint' in Anupama Rao (ed.) *Gender and Caste*. New Delhi: Zubaan: An Imprint of Kali for Women, 2003. Print.

———. *Writing Caste/Writing Gender: Narrating Dalit Women's Testimonies*. New Delhi: Zubaan, 2006. Print.

Sathe, Putul. *Ethnography of the Marginalised Self: Reading of Dalit Women's Autobiographies*. Women's Link. Volume 19, Number 4, October-December, 2013. Print.

16

Poverty, Tyranny and Fear in *I, Phoolan Devi:* The Autobiography of India's Bandit Queen

Pradip Sarikhada

Dalits are the broken-down, depressed, oppressed and backward people. The definition of dalits has been written in a letter to Zelliot by Gangadhar Pantawane. In this citation Dalits and their positions have been beautifully explained, "To me, Dalit is not the caste. He is a man exploited by the social and economic traditions of this country. He does not believe in God, rebirth, soul, holy books teaching separatism, fate and heaven because they have made him a slave. He does believe in humanism. Dalit is a symbol of change and revolution" (qtd. in Pujari, 142). They have been under the suppression and oppression of the upper caste people since centuries. Many Dalit women have written their autobiographies so that other people also know their saga of sorrows. Phoolan Devi also has been an illiterate Dalit woman who could neither read nor write. Her autobiography *I, Phoolan Devi: The Autobiography of India's Bandit Queen* is a heart-rendering story of her life. She has to live her life in utter poverty. They were only two living sisters and she had no brothers. That's why her uncle usurps their property. He makes a big house and he wants that Phoolan Devi and her family may remain poor.

Phoolan Devi is known as the Bandit Queen of India. She was born on August 10, 1963 in a village Ghura Ka Purwa in Jalaun District in Uttar Pradesh. She was born in a lower caste called Mallah (boatmen). Her father, Devi Din and her mother Moola Devi were very poor. Phollan had three siblings but only one survived till adult age. Her family lived in astute poverty and they owned around one acre of farmland.

Poverty is one of the main themes of this autobiography. Phoolan Devi and her family were so poor that they did not have a good house to live in. It was a mere hut, "The walls of our house were coated with mud and the roof was made of straw" (6). There was no proper arrangement of clothing for the family members. Phoolan Devi writes, "I had only one dress. And no shoes. Nobody in our family owned any shoes" (8). The animals and the men lived together in her village just because there was the dearth of money.

It is the general concept of the society that girls are not welcomed in the homes when they are born. Especially the poor have problems with the birth of a girl child because they think girls extra burden to their poverty. In the novel *Inside the Haveli* when a girl is born to the poor servant Gangaram and he is very sad. At this the cook, Khyali consoles him saying, "Girls are a burden I admit but what can one do once they are born" (Mehta, 8). Thus, the poor think that they have to feed the girls till they are young and after that they have to give them dowry at the time of their marriage. Phoolan Devi's autobiography also focuses on this point:

> Four girls in a family was a great misfortune. In the village, they said it took four boys and one girl to make

a happy family. Sons brought rupees when they married, the dowry from the bride's family. Girls were just more mouth to feed. (27)

In the winter, Phoolan and her family slept inside. Her sister, Rukmini had a blanket but Phoolan shared her khat with her younger sister, Choti. They had to spread straw under them so that they might save themselves from the cold weather.

There was a great tyranny and fear of the Thakurs in her village and the strong persons in Phoolan's village. The Pradhan of their village was a wicked man. The girls of the low caste had to do the work told by the upper caste men. Phoolan also has to work in the Pradhan's house. One day the village Pradhan slapped her when she asked a piece of mango from her. She asked, 'Please can I have a little piece of mango?" (10) Phoolan Devi got a very fierce slap instead of getting any mango. She writes, "The slap was so fierce that I heard it resound in my head. I was stunned — I could not see clearly, everything was spinning around me, and I fell over" (10). Phoolan Devi went to her house and tells everything to her mother. When her mother came to know about it her eyes bulged with anger. She grabbed Phoolan by her arm and dragged her to the Pradhan's house. She said to Pradhan, "You think we bring children into the world just to be your slaves? Instead of hitting her like that you should have just killed her! Go on, kill her! Then she won't ask you for any more mangoes. Kill her if you want!"(11)

Phoolan's uncle Bihari had stolen their land and the family had to see very bad days in their lives. '...and my first dress had to be made from a piece of my mother's sari" (16). She was surprised how her real uncle could be so rich and they so poor, "I didn't believe him. How could someone so rich be my uncle? Someone with servants and a house with floors made of concrete? If he really was our uncle, surely he would try to help us, not beat us and insult us!

Bihari despised us" (16). Her uncle Bihari created problem three times in the marriage of her sister, Rukmani but the last time he could not break this marriage because the groom party told him if he tried to meddle with the affair he will be in trouble. In fact, her uncle Bihari had fear that this family was strong and after this marriage they will lose their power.

One day there is a fight between Phoolan and her sister, Choti. When they go to their home running, Choti tells her mother that Phoolan is beating her. To hear it, Phoolan's mother beats Phoolan very cruelly, "My mother grabbed me by the hair and beat me so hard on my behind with a stick the pain almost paralysed me" (42). She beats her so hard that two big weals are developed on her left buttock and next day one more weal develops like a mango. Phollan is in great pain due to her mother's beating and she tells her mother, "Amma, you hit me too hard, I cannot even sit down. It hurts too much" (42). The abscess grew bigger day by day and Phoolan was in the condition that she was not able to move from her *khat* even to relieve herself.

The village girls lived in the constant fear of the upper caste people. The Village Pradhan and his sons always lived in the lookout of the beautiful village girls or women. Many lessons were given by her mother to Phollan Devi and her sister. Her mother tells Phoolan, "A girl mustn't speak to any man apart from her father or her husband, Phoolan. If a man takes her without marrying her, then she is everybody's, and no husband would want her after that' (27). Such pieces of advice are easy to hear for her daily: "Don't speak to strangers, don't go near the Pradhan, don't do this, don't do that!" (39) Her Amma tells her:

> 'If you meet a man and he tries to touch you or if he tries to force you to go with him, don't let him! If a man offers you money, you mustn't speak to him. Run and tell me as fast as you can. Even if he says very ugly things, you must tell me. If you don't obey me I'll cut you into little pieces and throw you into the river!' (39)

The village Pradhan Kishna was a cruel man. Phoolan Devi has witnessed her tyranny at many times. Phoolan's friend, Ram Dhakeli's father was killed by him. Ram Dhakeli's mother was very beautiful and the village Pradhan was looking for the opportunity to molest her. One day her bullock bolted in Pradhan's fields. Pradhan seized this opportunity to molest her but she did not get ready to go with him. She told Pradhan's misbehaviour to her husband. Her husband was a blacksmith and he got angry and threatened the Pradhan for what he did to his wife. But Pradhan was a callous man and his men beat him with bamboo lathis. He was unable to move due to their beating and his family had to take him on the *khat* to his house. He died the next day due to excessive beatings. Thus, the life of the dalits is very tough and this autobiography is a story of tyranny and oppression of the upper caste or strong people.

If we discuss about Phoolan after reading her autobiography, she has been depicted as an innocent person throughout. But she is also accused that she did not use the decent language. According to the norms and rules of the society, only men have the right of the property and Phoolan had no brother to claim the property. She thinks that her brother, Maya Din is claiming to have the full rights on their land. She does not let down herself and starts scuffling with him. (Wikipedia)

When she was eleven years old, her marriage was settled with a man, named Putti Lal. She was married in that age as per social rules so that she may grow up in her in-law's house and learn all the rules and ritual of the new family. But she did not feel good there. She ran away to her parents' home. But her parents rebuked her for her childish habit and sent her back to her in-laws' home but this time also she raised hell in her in-laws' house and she again returned to her parents' home. Her parents again tried to send her back to her husband's home but her in-laws refused flatly to accept her until she gets maturity (Wikipedia).

During her stay in her parents' house, Phoolan could not tolerate the tyranny of her uncle, Bihari and her cousin, Maya Din. Phoolan Devi started her battle of life when her cousin confiscated their land illegally. She took the help of some local social workers. In fact, it was her grandfather's land taken was unlegally taken in his custody by her cousin, Maya Din. He was unhappy over her behaviour. He went to police and tells them that Phoolan Devi had stolen things from his house. She was kept in jail for three days. She was made naked in front of her father in the jail. They gave her a sound beating. The police beat her black and blue and tyrannised her. She was brought in front of the judge and she was forced to accept her crime of thievery. When she returned her village, all the villagers saw her with the eyes of contempt. The village women taunted her and asked her with how many men she slept in the jail. Their family was not allowed to take water from the common well and a sum of money was demanded from them to compensate the honour lost by Phoolan Devi in the jail.

After Phoolan was released from jail, her parents wanted to send her to her in-law's home. They approached to Phoolan's in-laws with the plea that she was now sixteen years of age and therefore old enough to begin cohabiting with her husband. However, Phoolan's in-laws had come to hear about all the happenings of the past two years, the fruitless court case against Maya Din, and Phoolan's jail experiences. They initially refused to accept Phoolan. However, Phoolan's in-laws were very poor, her husband was now twenty-eight years old, and they thought that he might not get another bride for him especially when his wife was still alive. Divorce was not possible in that condition. Phoolan's family sent Phoolan to her in-laws's home and they accepted her this time. Phoolan's parents performed the ceremony of *gauna* (after which a married woman begins to cohabit with her husband). But here also she could not get a good life for her. She was unhappy in her parents' home and here also she could not get a little bit comfort. Phoolan writes in the preface, "My husband has threatened to beat me" (Preface 1) especially when she was in more tender age.

She could not live with her husband as she was not feeling comfortable in the suffocating environment. Within a few months, Phoolan, this time no longer a virgin, again returned to her parents. Shortly afterwards, her in-laws returned the gifts that Phoolan's parents had given to them and sent word that they won't be able to accept her as a bride in that house. This incidence occured in 1979 and Phoolan was now sixteen years old. But a wife leaving her husband, or being abandoned by her husband, is considered a serious taboo in rural Indian society, and Phoolan was now in that category. She was taunted and insulted both at home and in the village for being a foul-tongued troublemaker unwanted by anyone.

After that she was kidnapped by the dacoits. Baboo Gujjar was the leader of dacoits and he wanted to molest her but Vickram Mallah was another dacoit who prevents Baboo for doing this heinous act. He says:

'I told you not to touch her she belongs to my community.'

'So what? Who cares? You even don't know her. She is not one of your family.'

'If you touch her I'll shoot you', said Vickram.

'If you shoot me, I'll shoot you, and then what? We aren't both going to die for this little hussy. She's the one we should shoot!' (240)

Vickram saved her and kills Baboo. He became the leader of the gang. He fell in love with Phoolan and marries with her but one night he and other mallah dacoits were killed by Shri Ram another dacoit who was a Thakur by caste. He put the blame of Vickram's murder on Phoolan Devi. He said, 'She killed Vickram the Mallah! The little whore, she killed him! But we caught her! Come and see! (369) Phoolan Devi was brutally raped for around three weeks. Tapan Basu writes about the rape of the girls, "There is no girl in our cheri who has not been coerced or raped by the dominant caste men when they go to the fields to fetch water or for work" (Basu, 124).

Phoolan was able to escape with the help of a Brahmin. She made her own gang and wanted to kill Shri Ram but he escaped somehow. To take her revenge Phoolan Devi ordered to kill around twenty Thakurs at Behmai. Her enemy Shri Ram was killed by another dacoit over the issue of a woman. Phoolan helped the poor girls and women. She gave money to the needy and finally surrenderred in 1983. She writes, "One day I heard on the radio that the Government of Uttar Pradesh had dropped the charges against me" (494) and came out of the jail in 1994. She started her political career by becoming the Member of Parliament. She was brutally murdered by Sher Singh Rana on 23 July, 2001 and eventually Rana got life imprisonment.

As a conclusion, it can be said that Phoolan Devi had to live her life in utter penury. She had to bear the tyranny of the caste as well as the tyranny of the patriarchy. The life of the Dalit poor has been depicted like a hell in this autobiography. Phoolan's autobiography narrates that dalit girls and women lived their lives under the constant shadow of fear in her village. But Phoolan Devi was a bold woman who did not succumb in front of the oddities of the circumstances and she took her revenge. She did not call it crime but justice, 'What others called a crime, I called justice.' (*I, Phoolan Devi*: Back Cover)

Works Cited

Basu, Tapan. *Translating Caste*. New Delhi: Delhi University, 2002. Print.

Beverley, John. "The Margin at the Centre: On Testimonio (Testimonial Narrative)", in Sidonie Smith and Julia Watson, eds. *De-colonising the Subject: The Politics of Gender in Women's Autobiography*. Minneapolis: University of Minneapolis, 1992. pp. 91-114.

Mehta, Rama. *Inside the Haveli*. New Delhi: Penguin, 1996. Print.

Devi, Phoolan, Cuny, Marie-Therese and Rambali, Paul. (1996). *I Phoolan Devi: The Autobiography of India's Bandit Queen*. London: Sphere, 2014. Print.

Guru, G. "Dalit Women Talk Differently." Gender and Caste Ed. A. Rao. New Delhi. Women Unlimited, 2003. 80-85.

Pujari, Veeresh B. "Semantical Change of the Term Dalit in the Present Context." *Research Spectrum*. Vol. 3, Issue 2, August, 2012, pp. 141-143.

Zelliot, E. *From Untouchable to Dalit: Essays on Ambedkar Movement*. New Delhi: Manohar Publishers and Distributors, 2001. Print.

https://en.wikipedia.org/wiki/Phoolan_Devi

17

An Exploited Serf and Patriarchal Chains: A Study of Viramma's *Viramma: Life of an Untouchable*

Dr Namita Panda

As dalits had to go through a very bad time, many Dalit people determined to get rid of the evil of the caste and they went for the higher education and changed their socio-economical positions. They created awareness among dalits and they also started writing about their sorrows and miseries. They wrote poetry, plays and autobiographies. Men started writing about their sufferings and even women also joined their soldiers with them. On one side there are autobiographies by the men Dalit writer, on the other there are many women Dalit autobiographies also. Om Prakash Valmiki's *Joothan,* Narendra Jadhav's *Untouchables,* Sharankumar Limbale's *The Outcaste: Akkarmasi,* Laxman Bapu Mane's *Upara: An Outsider,* Siddalingaiah's *Ooru Keri,* Mohandas Namisray's *Apne-Apne Pinjre,* Surajpal Chouhan's *Tiriskrit,* Daya Pawar's *Baluta,* Shyam Lal Jedia's *Untold Story of Bhangi Vice Chancellor,* Kancha Ilaiah's *Why I am not a*

Hindu?, Vasant Moon's *Vasti: Growing up Untouchable in India* etc. there are many autobiographies by men Dalit writers. Urmila Pawar's *The Weave of My Life*, Bama's *Karukku*, P. Sivakami's *The Grip of Change*, C.K. Janu's *Mother Forest*, Baby Kamble's, *The Prison We Broke*, Shantabai's *The Kaleidoscopic Story of My Life*, Bama's *Karukku*, Kumud Pawde's *Antaspot* etc. are women Dalit autobiographies. Out of these some are memoirs.

Dalits are those people who are socio-economically weak and those who are suppressed, oppressed and exploited by the upper caste or aristocratic people. These are not those who only belong to lower strata of society. The word *Dalit* does not refer only to Buddhists and Backward Class people, but also to all those who toil and are exploited and oppressed (Wankhade, 5). According to Murugkar, "Who are Dalits? All Scheduled Castes and Scheduled Tribes, neo Buddhists, labourers, landless and destitute peasants, women and all those who have been exploited politically and economically and in the name of religion are *Dalits*. (Murugkar, 4)

Viramma: Life of an Untouchable is a beautiful Dalit woman's autobiography. The incidences of her life are described to Josiane Racine who is basically from Tamil Nadu and she lives in France. She came to India in the nineteen eighties for a research project on ethnomusicology. Then she met Viramma. She found that Viramma is a multi-talented woman. She was a folk singer, a trained midwife, a sorceress, labourer. She could sing all kinds of songs herself. It took around ten years from 1980 to 1990 to speak about her life story to some cone. Her story was first published in French in 1995 and it was later published into English by Will Hobson in 1997. She belonged to the Parayar community and she had used the day-to-day conversation of this community and many words of this community could not be published to maintain the courtesy as such kind of words cannot be used by the decent people. She has used many words of swearing, slangs and sexually explicit language.

She safeguards herself by saying that the meaning of a particular word depends on the contexts and time on which it is spoken.

The first chapter of book describes Viramma's family background. The book opens with the background of her family that she belonged to a serf family. Both her paternal grandfather, Samikkannu and her father, Nadesan worked as serfs for Swara Reddi under the *jajmani* system. She tells that the serfs lived like slaves who worked hard and get very less in return still they were loyal to their masters:

> My paternal grandfather Samikkannu was a serf in Swara Reddi. He was a just man, a staunch worker and loyal to his masters. He was an agricultural labourer but he also practiced sorcery. He could cast spell and tame demons. Everyone feared him and respected him. He had five children by his first wife Kannima, the daughter of a carter from Karai. The demons took three of them: only my father and my aunt Adi survived. (1)

She described that their family lived in astute poverty. Their life was not good and they lived devoid of basic amenities of their life. They did not have bathrooms, toothpastes or nutrient food to eat. They got ready for their school very early with "a little water on the face, arms and feet and a little ash to brush out teeth. Then we'd swallow some rice in water and millet gruel. My little brothers went around naked" (4). When Viramma recollects her childhood she is filled with joy. She describes it using pleasant words as she has spend a very nice time in the company of her relatives and family members, "My childhood passed as if I was living in the kingdom of the gods on earth."(4)

Viramma faced many problems in her life but despite of all she enjoyed her childhood by playing, listening to her grandfather Munissami's interesting stories and spending some time with Rukkumani, Kitteri, and Nilamma's company. When she was in the age of going to school, she is not allowed to go to schools and in her community girls are not allowed to study in school located in *ur* where the Parayas were not allowed to get education. She had to take interest in the domestic chores. Through her experience, she comes to know about the caste hierarchy. She comes to know about the life of the two upper caste girls, Janaki and Minathi who never got a chance to come out of their homes and enjoy their life independently in the open environment. She feels much sorry for their restricted life style:

> "Always shut away in their big house, the poor things! Friendship, discovering nature, Grandfather Munissami's stories - they were forbidden all of that. That's the lot of high-born children!"(13)

The life of the children has also been depicted very tough. They were not allowed to play in their childhood. As soon as they grow little in age, their parents engage them in their family trade so that they may be able to help their parents earn some money and feed the other members of the family.

Viramma's grandfather and grandmother worked as serf and when Viramma gets married and goes to the new house she finds the same tradition in her new family also. She finds that her husband's family was working as serf under one Reddiar's family under the same *jajmani* system. It was not the only family; there was no any family who did not work under the *jajmani* system. Many families have to devote their labour, time and energy under the landlord's guidance. The landlords did not give them full wages but they had to work under them as there was no any job for these people and they were helpless in that situation.

They kept them in poverty so that they may be forced to work under them. Becoming a serf was a bit better for their life as they felt secure about their income in the form of wages. Moreover, in this way they were able to take loans from their landlords to run their family smoothly. But the landlords did not give them loan at the normal rate rather they charged exorbitantly high rate of interest. It was the reason that they could not pay it throughout their life. In this way this system of serfhood continued from one generation to another. The landlord was a patron for them and he gave them some piece of the land for cultivation. In this way they ran their families and earned some respect in the village also. But they had to keep their landlord happy. If he got angry he would give them punishment. He would either stop their wages or snatch the basic amenities so that their lives may become unbearable. Viramma's family was one of such serf's families and it also had to see very bad days without any respite.

Viramma narrated that the Parayas would never revolt against their landlords however they torture them. Their life was very miserable and they worked hard in their fields still they slept hungry. The landlords sometimes exploited them beyond their limit of toleration still they kept quiet. They were illiterate as well as landless that's why they bore all the pains of life silently. Their lives were depended on the labour and the wages they got after the hard work. They tried to keep themselves happy also by singing songs, stealing some grains, telling lies and taking rest during their working hours. These petty things gave them pleasure.

They tried to keep themselves happy and contented in all circumstances like a hungry dog who keeps shutting his eyes when his master is having meals. Their plight was like that dog who can just see but despite of being hungry cannot even look at the meals. Viramma criticised the male chauvinistic attitude of her society. She narrated that men don't behave with their wives in a decent manner. The life of the girls was also not good. They were considered a burden of their families. The birth of a girl in the family was considered bringing misfortune for the family. The birth of the boys was not criticised as they were considered earning members of the family. The parents also did not like the birth of girls in the family. The boys were considered the helpmate in their works at fields and homes while the girls were considered only as a member who can eat or cook. At the time of Viramma's birth her family got disappointed at the birth of a female. Her parents had three daughters and Viramma was the fourth so her family was disappointed at her birth. Her family said when she was born, "Here's another little bitch been born" (3) but this incidence was easily forgotten by the family as such kinds of indecencies are the parts of their lives. So they had to forget such events of their life. Eventually the clouds of disappointment of her birth scattered and she was accepted as an accepted member of the family. Viramma writes, "We can't live if we brood on them the whole time. So the disappointment of my birth was quickly forgotten and I was welcomed into the household very well" (4). Viramma was a Dalit and above all a girl child that's was why she had to accept her fate as a silent sufferer. In the words of Gayatri Spivak, "The Subaltern cannot speak. There is no virtue in global laundry lists with 'woman' as pious item. Representation has not withered away" (Spivak, 4). Viramma narrates that there were many castes in Karani and caste discrimination was the major problem for them. She writes, "But Karani has definitely got caste! (158). Reddiar, Mudaliar, Udaiyar, Tulukkam, Vaniyan, Ambattan, Komurri, Vannan, Koravan, Sakkili etc. castes have been described by her at Karani and Ceri. Thus, the life under these different identities was not so smooth for the dalit people and they had to live under pressure.

In conclusive remarks, it can be said that Dalit autobiographies depict the dehumanised conditions and very bad experiences of the Dalit writers and add a new chapter in Indian literature as Showkat Ahmad Naik observes, "Dalit Autobiography, a recent offshoot, introduces a new world of experience in Indian literature. It widens the range of expressions and makes use of the Dalits who have been excluded from the mainstream Indian society and discriminated, exploited, humiliated and marginalised on the basis of low caste status. (Naik, 278) Viramma's autobiography also beautifully narrates the subjugated pictures of women and degraded positions of the serfs under *jajmani* system and thus, they lose their own identity in the search of a morsel of food.

Works Cited

Murugkar, Lata. *Dalit Panthers Movement in Maharashtra: A Sociological Appraisal.* Bombay: Popular Prakashan, 1991. Print.

Naik, Showkat Ahmad. "Contradicting Monologue: Dalit Autobiographies as a Counter Discourse." *Research Journal of English Language and Literature (RJELAL) A Peer Reviewed (Refereed) International Journal.* Vol. 3.3.2015 (July-Sep). 278-282 http://www.rjelal.com

Spivak, Gayatri Chakravorty.*"Can the Subaltern Speak? Marxism and the Interpretation of Culture"*. Chicago: Illinois University Press, 1988. Print.

Viramma; Racine, Josiane and Racine, Jean-Luc. *Viramma: Life of an Untouchable.* London and New York: Verso, 1997. Print.

Wankhade, N. M. *Presidential Speech at First Dalit Sahitya Sammelan,* Nagpur: 1976: 5.

18

Reflection of Dampening Down of Persona in Urmila Pawar's *The Weave of My Life*

Dr Sumitra Singh

Urmila Pawar, a genuine Dalit writer talks about her experiences as a female born in a male's world. She has to undergo many trials and tribulations in her life. She has grown up in circumstances offering a myriad world of experiences and challenges. Her frank and direct style of writing reflects inner difficulties and projects expositions of the effects of the outer world on her. The text depicts the oppressions suffered by the Dalit community and also brings forth the moral question that becomes answerable for the conventional streams of mediocrity in an ever changing world. Urmila Pawar unravels the various threads of her life presenting various shades of her personality.

The Weave of My Life is the English translation of her Marathi book, *Aaydaan*. Pawar says that her mother used to weave *aaydans* which are small things made from bamboo. Weaving includes putting the threads together. When threads are weaved together, a fabric is framed. Similarly when the threads are unravelled or unwoven, things really go apart and nothing concrete comes out of it. These things are somewhere linked with us humans. Pawar believes that her life has been a similar weave and unweave of pain, suffering and agony. Things that woven her life as a person and unwoven things making her painful. So, organically, her life resembled the weaving done by her mother for aaydans. Making an aaydan was the main economic activity of Pawar's village. This activity was obviously in the centre of the village so that the upper castes could take the advantage of those cane baskets for their sanitation purpose. Pawar writes, "My mother used to weave Aaydan and I was writing this book, both were activities of creation of thought and practical reality of life."(3)

There has been an isolation under which the Dalit community suffered a lot. The sufferings were of different kinds. Be it emotional or physical or psychological, this community had to bear the burden of humiliation and perform the most undesirable duties in the society. For many years, the Dalits were believed to be racially inferior and submissive and also polluted by nature and therefore quite segregated from others. Urmila Pawar represents the three generations that have suffered the stress. Her writings depict the scenario therein and how she evolved out of them.

Urmila Pawar grew up in Konkan coast near Mumbai in the Mahar Dalit community which was centred in the villages to completely segregate them from the rest of the society. This was done so that the upper caste could call upon the so-called 'inferior sect' any time and use them for their own purpose. Pawar writes, "The community grew up with a sense of perpetual insecurity, fearing that they could be attacked from all four sides in times of conflict. That is why there has always been a tendency in our people to shrink within ourselves like a tortoise and proceed at a snail's pace."(7)

In later times, Pawar went to Mumbai and literally started a Dalit literary movement and voiced her opinion. In the midst of all social and political changes, Pawar shared her experiences being a woman and an activist whose consciousness helped her in arousing and awakening herself and her community literally in the span of time.

Through the descriptions of her early family life, Urmila Pawar skillfully takes the reader through a rich archive of Dalit history. Remarkable in many ways, her autobiography demonstrates the deep fissures between the feminist movement and movements for the uplift of lower castes. Pawar's own experiences as a Dalit Buddhist female activist abound in the difficulties she faced while joining these different causes." — Rochona Majumdar, University of Chicago. (in an interview)

Pawar remembers that society in those times, when she was growing up had myriad influences. The society in some areas could see the change but many held a stagnant state of mind and had nothing much to see but to believe in their plight. Poverty, illiteracy, disease and the loom hauling over them continued. The influence of Ambedkar and Savarkar had been instrumental in awakening of the Dalits. Pawar mentions that Ambedkar used to organise Mahad Satyagraha and Savarkar used to organise inter-dining for various communities. Pawar as such never attended them but her father used to be a part of them. Many people participated in them.

Further are the instances where she mentions about the lives of her family members and neighbours and classmates, the stories of which are woven together in a subtle narrative that slowly unravels different aspects of their lives in manifold ways.

Urmila Pawar wrote at a later stage of her life, a time when a person has already lived a major part of his or her life. She recreates the magic in her writing when she writes about her childhood or describes her adolescence and adulthood. As a child her speech was unpolished and she herself was not so hygienic. She writes very clear about it. Slowly with age and experience, she matures into a fine lady with standard Marathi dialect a move towards wisdom and gaining more knowledge.

Pawar talks about her trauma and problems; issues related to caste, class and gender in the Indian context. There reflects a sense of rediscovery and identity crisis. Indian culture is showcased in terms of interpersonal and inter-communal relations, clashes and religious tolerance.

Pawar's father died when she was in third standard. So, her mother had to take the lead. She then started making those aaydans. She was not depended on anyone or any community for nurturing her children. She brought them up on her own. They lived in abject poverty. Pawar recalls that she had only two sets of clothes that she wore alternatively.

Pawar as a child considered herself to be ill-mannered as she had the habit of spitting around. That meant both ill-mannered and unhygienic. She thanked her teacher Diwalker who taught her good manners.

She was intelligent! She got the first scholarship of twelve rupees in the fourth standard; seeing the rupee notes for the first time (ten rupees and two one rupee notes), she was administered to buy two frocks by her teacher.

"Aye was weaving her baskets as usual. She did not see me when I crossed her and entered the house. Her face looked worried. She was engrossed in her own thoughts and her fingers flew over the basket. Going to her, I told her about the scholarship and held the twelve rupees before her. Suddenly her face lit up with a sunny smile and eyes sparkled." (237)

As a child, she was very conscious of her caste. She knew that she was born of a low caste and that she was not entitled for many things, including good food and clothes and other goodies. She remembers, "The upper caste girls always used words like 'Ladu', 'Modak', 'Karanjya', 'Puranpolya'. They brought such novel items in their tiffin boxes as well as at times we went on excursions. However, I never asked myself the stupid question, why we do not prepare such dishes at home? We were aware, without anybody telling us, that we were born in a particular caste and in poverty, and that we had to live accordingly."(3)

Not just that Urmila states the things happening at her place. Talking about women at home, she writes. "When the menfolk went out and women and girls remained at home, they dined at *kata*. A small quantity poured in water and cooked as a soup, with chili powder, salt and a piece of mango or maul. This was called *sagar*! Women ate their rice with the watery dish. The song we used to sing:"Hey what is that funny" dug noise, what is the foul smell spreading all over? Well, what they cooked was fish water! Someone has had a bellyful and how! She wears a short sarees, down to the feet now to hide what trickling down from her butt." (44)

This so-called Sagar was the main course meal for the daughter-in-laws. Religious faith was also undergoing changes those days. Many people got converted to Buddhism: "The older rituals to mark birth, marriage and death were given up and new ones gradually came to be finalised, according to Buddhist religion." (57) Much was because of good meals that was served at various religious inter-dining ceremonies. However, the plight with the girls and women remained the same. They were considered to be inferior and therefore the less privileged and the deprived.

Pawar narrates an incident stating, "Once, I went to attend wedding at my sister-in-law's place, along with two of my nieces. However, when we three spout girls set down to eat and begun asking rice repeatedly, the cook got angry, 'Whose daughters are these anyway?' He burst out, 'They are eating like monsters' then someone answered 'they are from our 'Sushi's family! Daughters of Arjun master!' On hearing this, the host came forward. 'Oh! Are they? All right, all right let them eat as much as they want! Serve them well!' The cook returned with more rice but being called monster was not easy to digest and we politely declined."(6) Adgaon was the native place of Urmila Pawar, but for her education purpose, her family was staying near Ratnagiri. Pawar recollects the school days memory. One day her classmates at school had decided to cook a meal. They had discussed what everyone should bring; rice, lentils, and so on. Pawar remembers the incident, "What should I bring? Nothing, they said.' You must bring some money" (5-7). They were going to girl's house called Tarlatan Savant as her parents were away. Girls cooked at a like Sushi Dhaka, Kamal Chaman and Sunland Bhopal cooked a simple but testy meal of rice, dal and vegetables. As Pawar writes this painful incident, "They did not allow me to touch anything. However, we all ate together. I really enjoyed the meal. The next day I was horrified to hear that my eating had become the hottest topic for juicy gossip. Girls were whispering in groups about 'how much I had eaten." (8)

The above shows humiliation in every breath, as if a thousand death undergone in a day. This also reflects issues related with cultural inheritance-that the poor was born to be remain poor and be humiliated. Further, religious faiths needed to be changed. All Indian gods and goddesses had to be replaced by Dr Ambedkar's photo and Lord Buddha's photo as blind faith, some with little understanding and some with no understanding at all.

As Urmila narrates, "We put all of them in a basket. In fact, the silver and the brass would have fetched a tidy amount if we had sold the stuff. However, we have firmly resolved to discard the gods with all the accompanying paraphernalia. Therefore, we went to the river with the other people, the young children in row. On the way, people chanted the same traditional invocation but with a completely different set of words: O ye Gods; Yes that's right, Maharaja, Go back to your own place. 'Yes that's right, Maharaja You never did well to us." (96) The community was having faith in the blind faith and unethical and inexperience medical assistance.

Women always had no say in the society. This includes her own family. Although, her father was a reformist, he never cared for her another daughter Sushi who got married early. She even died of pain and agony. Parvati, her sister-in-law also lived a life of misery. She neither lived her life her own way or eat her own way. Suffocation prevailed in every home. So, not that the Mahar community suffered from the so-called elite that time in the Indian society but that women suffered a great deal much from her own men in the community.

Suffering was at all levels, in school too. Urmila remembers as a child, her command over the English language was too bad. Her English teacher used to tell her, "This is English, the milk of tigress; it is not easy, like acting in plays." (10) Women were exploited sexually also. In the autobiography she writes, "My maternal uncle plays dolls with me and pretends to be my husband drags me into an alcove and presses me hard." (11)

It is a natural desire of humans to love and conform. Pawar needed and yearned for the same. Her love for Harishchandra was passionate indeed. She vividly describes her first night with her husband in a rickety room with a bagful of live clams. Urmila narrates, "Never mind! My husband's hands were groping all over my body. The tiny room with its peeling walls, the single iron bed with its creaking iron strips, the smelly, moldy mattress with hard lumps of cotton, the dirty, stained, old bedspread, the flat hard pillow smelling like a naphthalene bag.....the sharp yellow strip of light from the bulb piercing the eye..."(13)

If she wouldn't have been there, her husband might have suspected her virginity! So, she remained silent and submitted completely. Women were supposed to be dependent on their men. And that continued. Not just that when Urmila received her first salary she remarks:

> "When I got my first salary, I could not believe that all that money was mine; that I could spend it the way I liked. Before my marriage, I used to hand over my salary to my mother; now I started handling it over to my husband. If this is not like deliberately offering head for the butcher's knife, what else is it?" (14)

Urmila narrates various incidents of women beating and continuous harassment even when she started working. She recalls the natural surge of women of her community to have a male child. She remembers a woman stealing a male child just to please her husband lest he should leave her consciousness of class and caste prevailed then and now.

Both Urmila and her husband realised it in their lives. Urmila suffered the psychological trauma even from her husband who wanted her just to be a 'wife', taking care of him and his children and to be in the confines of the house.

It was Urmila's sense of having her own identity and esteem and continuous battles with herself and the immediate society that she emerged as a Dalit activist and as a decorated writer.

Works Cited

Pawar, Urmila. *Aaydan*. Tran. By Maya Pandit as *The Weave of My Life: A Dalit Woman's Memoir*. Katha, 2007. Print.

Bhattacharya, Neelanjana. Review of *The Prisons We Broke* by Baby Kamble and *The Weave of My Life: A Dalit Woman's Memoirs* by Urmila Pawar, in *Jadavpur Journal of Comparative Literature*. Vol. XLVI, 2008-2009, pp. 155-162.

Dharmarajan, Geeta (2004). Separate journeys: short stories by contemporary Indian women. *University of South Carolina Press*. p. 126.

Rege, Sharmila. (2 July 2006). *Writing Caste, Writing Gender: Reading Dalit Women's Testimonios*. New Delhi: Zubaan. pp. 256–265.

19

Selected Dalit Women Autobiographies: The Unheard Agonies

Dr M.B. Gaijan

"Dalit women writers have shown unique spirit to shatter the ideal image of women established in the society. Women have their sufferings and pains. In the marketing of women's bodies. Even today women are fighting against for their rights and triple exploitations — caste, gender and poverty. This struggle is the struggle of women's dignity. For the freedom of females, the voices of women must unite and make them the loudest." (Thorat, 151)

I

Woman, all over the world, since the barbaric era to the time of Bio-Tech-advancement remains the largest oppressed and exploited section of human world. In general patriarchal policy and practice exploit woman sometimes by flattery, fairy words, fictitious fantasy or factual reality. And, sometimes in a sweet ways, sometimes in a harsh way, unimaginable sophisticated cruelty and injustice heap on women. Patriarchal religions also support patriarchal policy and practice. And woman's bio-chemistry that causes their sensibility sometimes also become cause of their suffering.

India is the multi-castes, multi-cultural fast developing democracy. In every caste and culture woman remains the second sex, except, a few exceptions cases. By and large, still the fruits of safety, equality and liberty for women are far from them. Indian women's progress and status is closely connected with their caste. Upper castes' women may suffer less. But the women of the backward castes suffer more.

Among the backward castes' Dalit women remained doubled victims, at their huts, houses and by other caste people. Their story of suffering is unimaginably shocking. Their saga is nothing but the journey from zero to Hero. They were/are born and brought up in poverty, hate, untouchability and untouchability based injustice and crimes. They overtake all hurdles and emerge as the women of democratic India. As a visionary of modern India, Dr Ambedkar has always remained the lighthouse to this oppressed humanity at every stage. He remains the source of inspiration, actions for empowerment through education. In this paper selected Dalit women writers' autobiographies are evaluated.

II

Here, in this part, the First Generation of Dalit women autobiographies are considered. Under the influence of Jotiba Phule's mission to educate Dalit girls and empower them through education and Dr Babasaheb Ambedkar's vision, the first generation of educated Dalit women in India emerged from Maharashtra. They wrote their life-struggles. Their medium was their tongue, Marathi. Leading Dalit women autobiographers and their works are as thus; Shantabai Dani's *Ratra Din Aamha*, Mukta Sarvagod's *Mitleli Kavaade*, Shantabai Kamble's *Majya Jalmachi Chitrakatha*,

Baby Kondiba Kamble's *Jinne Ambuche,* Kumud Pawade's *Antasphot,* Urminal Pawar's *Aaydan,* Janabai Kachru Girhe's *Maran Kala,* Vimal Dadasaheb More's *Teen Dagada Chi Chul*[2] and others. All the autobiographies present facts of Dalit women's suffering, their struggle and at the last establishing their identity as human being.

Shantabai Dani's autobiography presents untold agonies. Shantabai Dani's *Ratra Din Aamha* is originally published in Marathi and translated into Hindi as *Dhup Chhava* represents Dalit woman's struggles. A few parts of her text are translated into English translation also available. She had actively taken part in Ambedkarite Movement and led the protest against the Pune Pact, she was arrested. Throughout her life she fought for the human rights of the downtrodden. Later on she became known social activist and political leader. Her life-story was full of struggles but her mother and teacher's help changed her life.

Poverty was/is the curse for Dalits. During the pre-independence time, they were born in starving families, where everybody was not getting a piece of loaf to pacify the hunger of their stomachs. Shantabai was the child of pre-independent India. Her childhood experiences translated and cited by Sharmila Rege;

> "The poor feel more hungry. The poor have healthy bodies – that is why they probably feel hungry.......We had to eat whatever had been cooked in the morning. In the evening as I would return from school, the *bhakari* kept in the basket at home would dance before my eyes. Just *bhakari,* chili powder, onion and salt that was like the special food for the poor...... I hung my school bag on the hook and opened the basket. It was empty. I lift the lid of the vessel. That was too empty. Not a drop of curry in it! I was very hungry......I was crying. As usual there was no one at home. The neighbour women asked for the sake of it;.....Why are you crying?.......What's the matter?......Can you give me just a quarter of a *bhakari.* (96-97)

Shantabai has been the witness of utter poverty of Dalits. She writes in her autobiography the pitiable plights of Dalits. Sharmila Rege postulates about Shantabai's experience of life how she was beaten by her aai at one occasion:

> Aai was poor but had a lot of self-respect. An educated daughter of mine is actually begging for food! She was angry. She went in, got a stick, and began to beat me up. I cried and cried until the evening and finally slept outside the hut on an empty stomach......Her anger calmed down. She woke me up at night embraced me and caressed me......She ran her fingers through my hair saying, "I am wicked woman beat my own daughter........Both of us were crying. I was feeding the snacks to my mother." (97)

This is neither fiction nor fantasy but the reality and agony faced by Dalits in the huts at the outskirts of villages of India. Lack of food was the major issue for major Dalits. In this sort of circumstances Shantabai continued her learning.

After completing her schooling when she left Nasik and joined her training college in Pune, she didn't get humanitarian response in the college but humiliation. There was no money with Shantabai's parents to buy new saris, blouses and ticket for Pune, so Shantabai came late to the college. Sharmila Rege cites Maya Pandit how Shantabai was asked when she went for hostel admission; "What's your name? Where have you come from? All right, all right...But there is no place in the college hostel now. All vacancies have been filled.......You should come earlier."(104-105) At last she was given a place in the verandah. Here also she faced humiliation and discrimination due to her caste. Sharmila further quotes about Shantabai's painful experience;

> "The training college was a government institute for women only..... She was served food in the verandah...The *bhakari* would be thrown down into her plate from a distance. The curry used to be served with serving spoon kept at a distance from my plate." (100)

To create hurdles and prevent the downtrodden from learning this remains the culture of orthodox Indian while the enlightened Indians have always helped them. Indian history tells that Shambuka and Ekalavya's learning was prevented. In Shantabai's autobiography she writes that her teacher had helped her while the traditional minded people made injustice to her. But from all adverse circumstances she had overcome and established her identity as a strong woman.

Kaushalya Baisantri's contribution remains unique in Indian women's voice against injustice and cruelty. Kaushalya Baisantri's autobiography *Dohara Abhshap* (*Dual Curse*) is considered as the first generation Dalit woman autobiography.

The author was highly motivated by Dr Ambedkar and his mission before independence. She was one of them who joined Ambedkarite movement at the early stage. She was the joint secretary of All India Dalit Women's Council. The council was formed in presence of Dr Ambedkar on 20th July 1942. She was also elected as the Joint Secretary of Scheduled Caste Students' Federation. She remained very active up to 1947 from Vidarbha, Madhya Pradesh. After her marriage with Devendra Baisantri her life got changes. (Thorat, 6-7)

In *Dohara Abhishaap* Kaushalya presents Dalit women's real condition, their suffering and struggle to survive in adverse circumstances. Dalit women are nothing in the eyes of orthodox. For a small cause Dalits are give great penalty. Dalit women's naked pared is shocking and shame but it is reported. The autobiography presents Sakharam's wife's naked pared. As the autobiography presents, the supervisor has teased Sakharam's wife but the orthodox gave penalty to victimised woman; and it was this:

> "After sometime they all have brought Sakharam's wife out. Only the blouse was on her body and this woman

has a small cloth to cover her body. On her forehead there was white *bindi* and in her neck the garland of footwear. She was sat on the back of donkey and held procession in whole colony. The people of the colony shouted at her." (72-72)

Even her husband Sakharam has not trusted or protected her, she had no cloth to cover her body so she remained at the outskirt of the village, at last jumped in the well and ends her life. After the short time of her death, the man got married again. On a large scale, Dalit women are crushed twice, at home by orthodox husbands and out of home by orthodox upper castes.

In the autobiography, Kaushalya boldly writes about her married life. Before their marriage, Devendra was a Dalit activist, Kaushalya knew him so she married with him. But after marriage Devendra became traditional Indian husband and Kaushalya's misery began. But as Ambedkarite activist she has declared what she felt:

> "Patriarchal society cannot accept women's liberal living. To show his superiority, husband goes to that level, he labels own wife as a licentious. Son, brother and husband all may unhappy. But I want freedom to express myself before people—society. Many more women have the same experiences as I have. But they are afraid to express them because of fear of and society family and suffocate throughout their livings. To open the eyes of orthodox these sorts of experiences must be brought before people."(7)

She has presented reality of Dalit families, even educated. Further she writes Devendra was not only insulting, neglecting her also abusing and beating her. As a traditional Indian husband, for him wife is nothing but the tool to pacify lust and maintain lineage. At the end, she writes, there was no change in her husband's dealing with her, she filed case in the court for justice, a little amount as the maintenance given to her. Thus, Kaushalya's story is the untold story of many India wives.

III

In the second generation of Dalit women's autobiographies the writers are considered are born after 1950. They are brought in democratic India but they also suffer. Dr Sushila Tankbhore's *Shikanje ka Dard* (Pain of Being Caught in the Clamps) is the celebrated Dalit woman's autobiography in Hindi. As the title of Dr Sushila suggests it is the life story of woman who is caught in the clamps, here *clamps* symbolise many social evils. Dr Sushila represents reality of *Valmiki* community among the Dalits. This caste is considered Dalit among the Dalits. So their colony remains away. Dr Sushila was born in the Dalit colony in Banapur, district Hoshangabad, M.P. Here Dalit colony was near to bus station/railway station. At the outskirt, without the facility of basic human life, it was inculcated in their minds, that girl-children should grow up and then get marriage and make their in-laws and husbands happy. People of this caste, even today, are living in the wretched condition. She bitterly criticised Hinduism because of inequality.

She writes about her married life with Sundarlal Tankbhore. He was elder than her in age and a school teacher. When she was in her second year B.A., according to the caste custom, their marriage was arranged. As a teacher he was neither smoking, nor drinking. He allowed Sushila to study further before their marriage. But after marriage, when she came to Nagpur, as usual Sundarlal Tankbhore becomes traditional Indian husband; he has started creating hurdles for Sushila. He deals with all family members with affection but not with Sushila.

After completing her graduation when she joined her B.Ed., here she becomes victim of teasing by Bengali girl Data. She teased Sushila; "Oye! Listen she is pregnant" (85). As a matter of fact Sushila was married but was not going to be a mother. But later on, after some time when there was talk about Sushila's married life, Data and Mrs. Trivedi, a school teacher and Sushila's classmates talk thus. At this Mrs Trivedi said smilingly, "Your husband love you too much so he tells to remove his shoes". But Bengali bold Data has strongly said; "This is nothing like love. He got maid without paying so play act. Don't do this sort of work, isn't any self-respect for you? (88)

Sushila writes about her pain in married life. On a small cause, her husband becomes serious and silent, speak nothing. He tells her; Beg pardon by touching your forehead to my feet, then I'll listen you" (88). She writes when there was a quarrel between husband and wife, he beats her. Her sister-in-law increases the volume of radio so other people cannot hear the cry or shouting. Sister-in-law also tells; "It is husband-wife's matter" (89). But she struggled hard to survive in adverse situation with spirit.

Bama's *Karukku* represents Dalit women's struggle from Tamil Nadu. The work is translated into English, German, French and regional languages. It represents social reality Dalits' condition. For the harmonious adjustment with the mainstream, Dalits may change their names, dress, food habits, cities even religion, inspite of that they remain Dalits in the eyes of orthodox. The orthodox wants no change in dealing with Dalits. This fact presented by Bama in her work *Karukku*.

Karukku presents reality of Dalits in rural Tamil Nadu, in some villages of India, Dalits suffer worst. Untouchability is still alive. It becomes hate and hate-related crimes and injustice to Dalits. Bama has artistically presented this fact before the readers. Her life journey begins from her village to convent, Madras to Jammu and back to Madurai.

Bama writes about untouchability in the village, even old women are treated thus:

> "The Naicker women would pour water from height of four feet, while Paatti and others received and drank it with cupped hands to their mouths........My other Paatti was the same. As soon as dawn broke, she would go to the Naicker houses, sweep out the cowshed, collect up the dung and dirt, and then bring home the left-over rice and curry from the previous evening.......One day I went with Paatti to the Naicker house. After she had finished all her filthy chores, Paatti placed the vessel that she had brought with her, by the side of drain. The Naicker lady came out with her leftover, leaned from some distance and tipped them into Paatti's vessel, and went away. Her vessel, it seemed, must not touch Paatti's; it would be polluted."(16)

She also writes about her tragic experience when they were playing coconut touching game. Later on the coconut fall down she was insulted. To come out from the environment of insult her brother advised her. Her brother's advice shape Bama's life. The brother who Master degree, advised her to empower herself by education and she followed. But Dalits have to suffer at every level, in the academic institutions and in public life, this fact is reflected in her life.

After completing her schooling when Bama has joined the convent, she also faced the same injustice. Later on she becomes a nun and worked as a teacher, but here also she faced the same thing. Her journey from Madras as a Mathematics teacher then Madurai, and then Jammu and Kashmir and again her journey back to Madurai, this indicates nothing but injustice because she is a Dalit woman. At the end a friend helps her in Madurai. Thus, text presents Dalits condition in rural Tamil Nadu and urban Tamil Nadu.

IV

Dalit women autobiographies, right from first generation to second generation, present unimaginable untold agonies.

The autobiographies represent the socio-cultural reality of India, rural as well as urban India. Women suffer a lot being women and they suffer more because of being Dalit women. But they do not frustrate of disappointed. They bravely face the condition created by the orthodox. Education empowered them. Make them stronger and confident. At the end, they establish identities as revolutionary Indian women.

Works Cited

Bama, *Karukku*. New Delhi: Oxford University Press, 2nd Edition. 2012. Print.

Rege, Sharmila. *Writing Caste/Writing Gender: Reading Dalit Women's Testimonios*. New Delhi: Zubaan, 2006. Print.

Tankbhore, Sushila. *Shikanje ka Dard,* Published in *Dalit Asmita*. IIDS Quarterly, Vol. 1. Oct-Dec. 2010. Print.

Thorat, Vimal. *"Asmitavadi Vimarsh me Stri Swara"* Key Note Address, in *Samajik-Sanskrutik Andolan Aur Asmitavadi Sahitya,* Report by Dilip Katheriya in *Dalit Asmita,* July-Dec. 2012. print.

Thorat, Vimal. *Rakha hi Jane hai Jalane ka Dard,* editorial, *Dalit Asmita,* IIDS Quarterly, April-June 2011, Vol. 3, pp. 6-7. Print.

20

Casteism, Classism and Sexism: (Re) Examining the Intergenerational Syllogism in Baisantri's *Dohra Abhishaap* *(Twice Accursed)*

Dr Aparna Lanjewar Bose

I

Dalit Literature grew out of Dalit socio-political consciousness and awareness of Dalit struggle for emancipation from inhumanity and inequality. It was a product of the inspiration of Dr Babasaheb Ambedkar—the one man army whose relentless tirade against caste Hinduism gave a dignified living to countless many. The word Dalit was popularised by the Dalit Panthers—the writers-cum-activists of Maharashtra. This literature which entails and emanates the emancipatory ideology of Ambedkar for an equitable and just social system and is written by a Dalit—a former untouchable who has borne the severe brunt of oppression, subjugation and marginalisation is considered as Dalit Literature. The Phule-Ambedkar-Buddha philosophy was/is at the centre stage of Dalit literary creation. The writings in Maharashtra in Marathi language began with this sole objective and expressed disgust, anger, revulsion and protest against ongoing perpetuation of inhumanities and cruelties on the Dalit community at large. The writers didn't write for social fashion neither did their writings steep to any essentialisms of sorts or even sweeping generalisations but voiced the concerns of the community vehemently. The definition of the word Dalit was broad and the parameters of Dalit writings were all very clear.

Later, when Dalit literatures came out from other languages and regions of the country few of the narratives were called as Dalit autobiographies solely on the ground that it was written by a former untouchable. These autobiographies did depict the pathos of the Dalit community, the humiliations and pains of the protagonist suffering on account of caste, class and sex. And narrated how these were overcome but what these narratives intrinsically lack is the Ambedkar ideology that serves as a backbone to the entire corpus of Dalit writing. Interestingly, these narratives swear by the Dalit writings of Maharashtra. Having said this further, the philosophy of Babasaheb Ambedkar was not restrictive or meant only for the Mahars or Backward castes and tribes of Maharashtra alone but was meant for one and all. Though it's a different matter that the Mahars were the elites amongst other Dalit communities (Nor were the Mahars the sole beneficiaries of Babasaheb's struggle for justice just because Babasaheb belonged to the Mahar Caste, as is infamously assumed by some half baked scholars). In fact, Ambedkar's ideology and philosophy had no linguistic, regional, national boundaries and was not tethered by any particular caste or region to be kept in safe custody for posterity. Therefore, when some Dalit narratives came out in other languages what was tangible was the metamorphic development of the protagonist; the narration of pain, suffering, humiliation, awareness and all but what they obviously lacked was its point of initiation and inspiration in Ambedkar's thought process. They seem to be self-inspired. Quite contrarily these narratives are strangely devoid of the great man's vision, ideals, philosophy or world view but have stormed the markets nevertheless for currency. They seem to be written with un/certain pose. I believe it's time to sit and reflect whether such narratives inwardly lacking in Ambedkarism or Ambedkarite thought and purpose, should be classed as Dalit narratives solely because they are written by former untouchables.

II

Leaving this debate aside and speaking about the Hindi Dalit narratorial scenario. At a time when the Dalit autobiographical scenario had a pronounced gender, Kausalya Baisantri's *Twice Accursed* (*Dohra Abhishaap*) comes not just breaking the male bastion, but expounding the gendered caste experience — a subject most carefully shunned by the Dalit male writers in their works. She becomes one of the foremost voices in the language of her choice in what is genuinely conceptualised as Dalit literature serving a definitive purpose.

She begins by giving a graphic description of routine life in a poor working class Dalit household of Empress Mill workers at Nagpur, of the kaleidoscopic Dalit Basti with different characteristic personae and their idiosyncrasies. Interesting historical facts, certain traditions, customs and cultural practices prevalent in the Dalit especially the Mahar community, highlights the rich Dalit cultural aspect. The importance of Jalsa and Dalit Rangbhoomi and the mammoth power that they wielded to educate the masses (p. 67) are rendered flawlessly.

She speaks of the post-conversion scenario to Buddhism by Ambedkar, its socio-political implications, of little women seemingly insignificant for history to remember but who contributed in their own ways towards social upliftment and emancipation. The example of Jhulabai — the Adivasi Gond woman or then Jai Bai Chaudhury the untouchable woman who started a school for girls that enabled girl students like her to study.

She records her own disgust at times for the lowly status accorded to her people, the sense of shame she herself felt as a school girl, the discrepancies, divides and the deprivations. Her narrative reflects the dichotomy in regard to food, shelter and clothing. She highlights on illiteracy, lack of awareness, lack of proper guidance, lack of proper family planning measures, sanitation, medical facilities in the untouchable society with all its sub-castes (not many writers speak about), the scheduled caste and schedule tribe divide, the pathetic situation of Dalit converts to Christianity, of penury afflicting the Dalit community and how these stands in the way of showcasing talent and opportunities, Her tryst with government offices to get home a water tap connection, the exposition of apathy, taboos, gender and caste biases and once in a while a kindly intervention by a kindred soul expostulates another facet that though as a nation we are out of colonial dominance yet the lingering dominating hierarchical mind set was of caste Hinduism that perpetrated power relations and power equations of socially superiors and socially inferiors, possibly even worse than the colonisers themselves. The attitude of postcolonial India was of denial—denial of dignity, basic amenities, rights privileges or even access to things predominantly accessed by the caste Hindus by birth.

The writer's defiance against her lowly status (p. 84), her active political participation, her role as Joint Secretary of Scheduled Caste students federation and later on of the CP and Berar Scheduled Caste students federation. The sexists attitude of some Dalit Leaders towards young women (pp. 90-91) her meeting with Mr Baisantri a promising Dalit

Youth from Bihar at the All India Scheduled Caste Federation, Her intercaste, interregional, interlingual marriage and the challenges faced by her within and without. Later how this marriage becomes a fractured dream brings to the forefront that a Dalit man may go ahead with Babasaheb's thoughts and ideals but after gaining material progress and position, buries those very thoughts and ideals somewhere on the way when it comes to oppressing his own woman. Also, woman battering, verbal and domestic violence are issues within the community that need to be readdressed but she has the sense enough not to make sweeping generalisations about Dalit men in general when she compares and contrasts her non-rational officer husband with her rational working class father. She highlights on the misogynistic public institutions which are rather more oppressive for Dalit women. On how some educated Dalit individuals after acquiring position are making a mockery of Babasaheb's ideology by indulging in idol worshipping and in futile competitions rather than competing in intelligence and knowledge. "To compete with Brahmins you don't need to have a Pooja room or place of worship in the house but by reading, writing and gaining knowledge like Babasaheb Ambedkar who later gave them a tough competition is what is required."

She reflects on the attitude of upper caste women towards low caste women (Haldi Kumkum Programme (p. 84), heinous attitude of the lower ranking people towards higher ranking Dalit officials, of how caste reaches anywhere before you do. And how instead of feeling ashamed of how the Maratha and Brahmin women behaved with her, giving them back a fitting reply enough to shame them. She shows the evils plaguing the present Dalit community at large and how it's getting brainwashed, befuddled; how openness and frankness of girl is considered baneful both by Dalit men and women. She reflects her agony on the fact that Dalit issues are not prioritised, that some Dalits are not interested or enthusiastic about changing things for themselves and the sullen attitudes harboured by some Dalit males themselves (pp. 120-121). She graphically describes the aftermath of the Mandal implementation, the flames of hatred directed towards the Dalits by the so-called educated middle class.

Dohra Abhishaap (*Twice Accursed*) is about the narrator taking control of herself and her life, of fighting the barriers of caste, class and sex, of showing the potential to bring about a meaningful change in other peoples' lives, and of casting outcaste itself. Says Baisantri, "I do not consider my caste low nor do I consider others high. I do not believe in casteism. One of my sons married an Iyengar Brahmin girl. second son married a Bengali Kayastha and third one married a girl from Madhya Pradesh. My daughter married in Sikh Religion, while my own took place with a man from Bihar. We have long given up caste." The narrative ends with her vehement assertion "we need to stand up, to build the power within us for our own progress without being dependant on others."

III

Dalit women narratives give us a collective womanist perspective and consciousness. Dalit woman was twice deceived first by the Dalit male himself in whom she reposed the trust that he being the "oppressed other" would give her cause a just representation. However, the Dalit man in narrating his experience seemed all over the narrative and even if women were represented then it would be in a certain mould that the Dalit man would want to fit them in. Secondly, in the post-independence period when women clamoured for equal rights, the Dalit woman's experience, subjugation and multiple marginalisation's were looked upon as homogenised category or then generalisations of all "women are Dalit as all women are oppressed" were made. The quintessentially Dalit woman and her cause was missing and ignored. The fact that the Dalit women experiences were different and needed to be addressed differently, rather than the homogenising tendency under the broad category of women, was not felt. As a result of this her voice remained largely unheard and at best subdued. It was then that she realised that her presence in these women groups comprising largely of the upper class and caste elites would only amount to tokenism. That she needed to take the mantle of her liberation in her own hands to voice herself fearlessly. Similar to the Black women in America, the Dalit women oppression continued under casteism, classism and sexism in India.

Patriarchy is so deeply entrenched in the Dalit male psyche that the same "oppressed" turns the "oppressor" when it comes to his women and disallows her participation in both public and private spheres. The negative internalisations of his inferiority and incapability, imposed by caste did make him assert for his rights as human but all along the line it became much more a movement to get rid of casteism and not sexism and to a large extent served only the Dalit male interest.

On the other hand, re-examining the Dalit women participation in movements it can be conceded it was mammoth and not as is assumed that she didn't come forward because of Dalit patriarchy, or due to her own lack of interest. Right from the pre-conversion period to the post-conversion to Buddhism, women were aware that the Dalit liberation struggle had a gender, and that sexism was there within and without but also felt somewhere that they would be accorded space after the larger Dalit cause was served. But when disillusionment came from all sides she took the mantle once again this time to lash out against sexism both within and without, to speak about her live, living, growth, development and consciousness. Dalit Women narratives began to appear during the 1990's first in Marathi and later in other languages. Women writers like Shantabai Kamble and Baby Tai Kamble were those earliest writers who moved out of their villages gained education and worked for the welfare of the community at large. These writers have cherished and nurtured the ideals and values of Ambedkarite thinking.

To say that our lives were like cats and dogs and so it's a Dalit narrative or that we were born in a certain community so it's a Dalit narrative, would be inappropriate. It's important to see how deeply entrenched the Ambedkarite values are in these narratives atleast the Maharashtra Dalit Sahitya movement from whence other regions draws heavily, works on this one important and integral ideal. Kausalya Baisantri's autobiography is truly a Dalit autobiography in that sense.

To the question whether this huge corpus of writings be termed testimonies, narratives autobiographies, memoirs etc. I believe one should not get into that debate, as what is prima facie important in them, is the exposition of the self that suffered (and continues to do so) from the vantage point of the self that feels the urgency to document that suffering and therefore Dalit narratives not just talk "differently" they emote, aspire, exhibit and serve differently. These narratives disallow the "deliberate" official forgetting of history of untouchability, of monstrous inhuman caste practice, and highlight the resilience shown by women, in their struggle for emancipation. They attempt to make constant reminders for a generation that needs to be in sync with the past in order to understand their present in a better way.

The Dalit woman who is absent both in women and men narratorial content not just challenges but contests her absence and surprisingly, through her own personal narratives renders voice to voiceless beyond all caste categories. She becomes the society's everywoman and everyman.

IV

Kausalya Baisantri's autobiography is a study of three generations of women represented by her maternal grandmother, her mother and the writer herself. The narrative of the grandmother is through the viewpoint of the mother/daughter, the mother's narrative is through the viewpoint of the daughter and the daughter/writer's narrative is through the viewpoint of a Kausalya Baisantri who in the process of life and living has lost her "self" somewhere and who now collects the remaining threads of her life to weave such a tapestry of a woman who has the potential to accept, any challenge and while doing so the numerous problems encountered, situations she braves, the inferences she draws and the analysis she makes of the same. The narratorial strategy interfuses in a way, giving us a peep into the three worlds of these women and their multiple viewpoints.

Her autobiography is three dimensional which shows how each of these women deals with the challenges posed by their respective circumstances, how they rebelled against casteism and women oppression in their own way. Firstly, the oppression because you are born in a particular caste, the oppression because you are born poor, the oppression because you are born a woman and in that too oppression because you are a woman born in an untouchable community, thus unravels the multiple levels of oppression and the sum totality of all these is *Dohra Abhishaap*.

It traverses three periods of Indian history the pre-independence, post-independence and the present times it includes the period of pre-conversion and post-conversion to Buddhism by Ambedkar and his followers and its aftermath in all its dimensions. It bears an interesting testimony to the Dalit reformatory movements and the British colonialism. It is a fascinating link to three generation of women and their struggles against casteism, sexism and poverty and their individualistic ways of dealing with the same.

Their times and circumstances may be different but the commonality lies in their experiences as Dalit and as women, in their Dalitism, their lies an inherent urge to better themselves. The fact remains that each women rationalises her situations quite individualistically and devices her own methodologies, and alternatives to purge themselves from the "twin curses" of caste and gender. They seek ways for their own salvation with grace and dignity instead of making compromises and give back in handfuls to the society with greater returns. No doubt the path chosen by them is wrought with multiple challenges due to these twin disabilities and the third one which is "class" but they are able to surmount and survive. The intersectionality of caste, class, gender is brought to the forefront.

Starting with the grandmother's narrative, as retold by the daughter to her daughters; her early marriage and the disastrous almost unforeseen consequences of the same when she is pronounced as a child widow do agonisingly raise pertinent social issues. And then later when she is remarried again, this time to a haughty, self-obsessed much married man for security reasons. Till the time when finally, one fine day to save herself from his tyrannies and the children from his uncalled for tempers, the perilous journey she undertakes to freedom; without giving a damn to the societal conventions her leaving her house permanently with her children. The tragic episode of one of her child dying on the way due to fever and the grief-stricken mother's makeshift burial for the child and eventually landing into the city to begin afresh. Slogging her bones day and night to give a better life to the only remaining living daughter would seem surreal and out of some story book to the reader but it's a narrative and its real and that is what matters. Till her very end by the roadside where she is found, along with little saved money, enough for her burial to be conducted with dignity, she embodies not just her zeal to accept death her way as she had accepted life but epitomises an emancipated vision that transcends all boundaries.

Later her daughter who is Baisantri's mother with the help of her working class husband starts her own loving world of sharing and caring, she works together with him as a mill worker and dreams of a new social system free of biases for her and her daughters. The manner in which she resists the superstitions and orthodoxical practices, casteism, sexism around her is best exemplified by the daughter Kausalya Baisantri through the Haldi Kumkum ceremony that included a gathering of women from different upper castes and their predictable treatment of the Dalit women joining them. Later this same mother takes headlong the backwardness of other backward communities and without caring much for the people and a social setup where sub-castes menace was overtly visible solemnises the intercaste marriage of her educated daughter Kausalya to a man from Bihar.

And further Baisantri's own cultural shock post-marriage. The humiliations and denials faced as a woman, her spectatorship to the backwardness of her educated Dalit husband from Bihar — A man who had actively volunteered in the neo-Buddhist movement of Dr Ambedkar could treat his own woman at home with contempt is the greatest contradiction she brings forth and yet the stoicism shown by her in continuing with the marriage because it was of her making to the time she strongly feels the need to move out, to reorganise and mobilise the un/educated and educated Dalit women and also draw the so-called educated out of their complacency which had set in, once they were safely perched in salaried government jobs. The writers eventual relocation to Delhi, getting active with women's groups and finally disassociating herself from the man called "husband" whom she married for his intelligence and dedication for the Dalit cause but who post-marriage remained detached not just from her but also from the society.

The narrator seems to be making pertinent pointers to the Dalit community at large who after acquiring white collared positions due to the greatness of Ambedkar do not feel the need to introspect and treat their own women with indignity. Dalit women too like them were partakers of that endless struggle for a dignified living and a struggle which they have borne more multiply and vehemently than their male counterparts. Their only generous acknowledgement would be non-confinement of their own women inside the four walls and providing those women adequate means for an outlet for expression of an experience which is essentially the Dalit female experience. This is explicitly exampled by Baisantri in an anecdote on how educated Dalit men behave and confine their women from being part of public platforms, their preposterous hesitancy and the convincing she had to do to disable this mindset.

Lack of awareness and inaccessibility to knowledge resulting in bigger households, larger family setup, callousness and tendency to shirk from responsibilities on the part of men, wife battering, domestic violence, psychological traumas and oppression within educated Dalit homes, the humiliations faced by the Dalit women, the violence, distrust and the patriarchal hold on her, by not giving her adequate dues to the various multitasking and roles manifested by her both inside and outside is I believe yet another way for the Dalit man to vent his frustration. The three generational saga here quite effectively renders this.

V

Analysing this frustration further, it is the frustration of not being able to adequately guard and protect her in the face of ongoing social onslaught on her dignity and of not having the same vantage position of smooth acquisition of multiple avenues meant for socio-economic cultural betterment enjoyed by the non-Dalit male members at large. This frustration comes partly from himself, partly from the socio-economic positioning, paraphernalia, partly for being rendered helpless almost impotent in the wake of continued crimes committed against his women. These proactive outside sources are actively usurping the Dalit man's bed when his women are raped. These outer sources are the non-Dalit entities, the socially higher-ups who by their mean gestures show that they can have what they want and get away with it; that the Dalit man's bed in vulnerable enough to be invaded. This has hampered their own progress towards attainment and fulfillment of gender roles. The dehumanising effect of rape and molestations can thus be underscored here. The Dalit female being socially and economically on the lowest receiving end, the infamous mis/conception harboured by the male community at large is that she is easily available to satisfy and gratify their perverse hunger and their native grudge against the Dalit community. By using sex as a subordinating tool it also incites a challenge to the Dalit man's masculinity.

Yet the dichotomy needs to be mentioned here that poverty for non-Dalit women might have been bone-breaking but at least they were free from the oppression under casteism. Sexist slurs might have been part of their lives too, but their exposure was never that frontal and direct as was the case with Dalit women who were leered at, lusted at, by men outside and treated inhumanely inside. The best example to bring forth from the book is of the Dalit woman who worked on daily wages to run her family, and who is constantly shamed by her upper caste contractor, and when she complained to her husband, he contrarily accuses her of being immoral, seductive and characterless, she is denigrated by the entire Basti area stripped and paraded on a donkey with her face blackened. And she ultimately ends her life. The husband brings home another wife (p. 71). This episode becomes just one of those countless attempts made to subordinate and suppress the dignity of the Dalit woman, a way of claiming power and authority over the "weaker sex."

Today, even if advocators of "untouchablity does not exist in India" or "caste does not exist" may snub this as a remote incident of the past or may even sit to blame the Dalit man very conveniently for such mishaps. Yet the fact remains that such incidents of public shaming still occur today in "Global India shinning India" and the news bulletins are not silent about these. Therefore, such incidents cannot be isolated as stray/remote or be downplayed as incidents happening in the past nor can the Dalit man be blamed entirely without analysing the psychological, physiological causes and assessing the role of the social hegemonic structures that also create such Dalit mind sets.

Other glaring social issue is of the women to women oppression visible in all generations. Each deals differently Baisantri's mother was taunted, humiliated because she decided to educate her daughters and as an act of hatred and jealousy some use to deliberately defecate at her doorstep. Her policy was to protect her daughters, ignore and carry on with her work for she knew the importance of education. The other example is of Ramkuwar a woman who has no right over the money she earns and equally no right to love another man she falls for when her own husband disowns her. She is constantly abused and humiliated in the Basti by her paramour's wife. Baisantri's assertive intervention when she tells this woman to mind her husband first and beat him as he is also equally involved in the game of love, further warning her against coming to the Basti and creating noisy scenes (pp. 71-72) shows Baisantri taking the bull by the horns. Similarly, the infamous incident of Sakharam's wife getting paraded also exposes the insensitive attitude of women towards women. Incidentally what arrested my attention was Baisantri's mother, who being so conscious of the rights and honours of her daughters doesn't speaks out against this public shaming and disallows her daughters from witnessing it. Was she protecting her daughters from patriarchal insensitivity, insensate pride of other women or then does she like the others represents the general fears of a society that can barely manage to live on subsistence level with pride and honour to actually stand up for or venture out to protect someone else honour. Does she foresee the repercussions of all this for her own grown up daughters.

On the other side, it may be neatly contented that Dalit women in the first place has to set out to work because of the tendency of the Dalit man to shirk or run away from responsibility or keeping financial control under him and rendering insufficient support to the woman but also so that he can (mis)utilise the finances he wants by boosing and gambling away his frustrations. But then this can be contested as not being the only reason why the Dalit women have to set out to work. Primarily, being laborious she wants to shoulder the financial burden of the family and contribute in the attempt to give a better living for her children. The example is Baisantri's mother who sets out to work so that the money contributes to the family and she can ultimately save some bit for her daughters and their education. She was lucky unlike her mother and daughter to have an understanding partner in her working class husband.

It is erratically assumed and argued that what else is there in Dalit autobiographies apart from sameness, pain, anguish, humiliation. Well these are one-sided and un-thought of statements issued in Dalit narratorial honour. Instead of making one decipher its multi-layeredness. It diverts and compels to look at it only in a certain pose or anticipates a singularly biased vision of these narratives. These blatant statement givers should stop making irresponsible statements. Because the thrust of these narratives is to show how we lived and experienced; how different that living and experiencing was from others; how we have survived and borne it the way we did and not how others did; how we have out of social obligation spoken out and will continue doing so.

Interestingly, in Baisantri's case she doesn't make any claims of being a writer or litterateur then why should she write? To answer this I believe is the urge to say something as a Dalit, as a woman, the necessity to show/reflect the psychological trauma of untouchability and being born untouchable that leaves an indelible imprint on any Dalit mind. And above all the "mothering Dalitness" in her, that sums it all. Her narrative is no longer hers but of the marginalised Dalits irrespective of what sub-castes they belong to. In her growth, resilience and identity lies the growth, resilience and identity of the community. So it cannot be singular in account or approach or for that matter individual.

I rate *Dohra Abhishaap* (*Twice Accursed*) as a true Dalit autobiography that lashes out at the anathema of casteism, sexism and classicism. The three generational women not just become the building blocks and pillars, cementing women to women bonding, but also education and awareness in the community that till date is a hapless victim of nepotism, jabber and deceit of the caste Hinduism. This clearly indicates the equation of dominated and dominator. These narratives pose challenges for students of historiography to look at Dalit history and documentation in fresh light and solicit to interrogate the unwritten part of history that is ignored or bypassed to serve vested interests and endorse these important phases of people's struggle.

I believe now the debates, instead of focusing on the absence of Dalit female in male autobiographies should focus on the presence of Dalit males in women autobiographies and the representational justice rendered.

Works Cited

Baisantri, Kausalya. *Dohra Abhishaap*. New Delhi: Parmeshwari Prakashan, 2012. Print.

Bose, Lanjewar Aparna. "Dynamics of Self and the Rhetoric of Difference: Critiquing Marathi Dalit Women Autobiographies." *Literature of Small Cultures: An Assertion of Difference*. ed. Dharminder Singh Ubha and Deepinderjeet Randhawa, Zohra Printers: Patiala, 2010. Print.

Bose, Lanjewar Aparna. "Marathi Dalit Literary Criticism: A Critical Evaluation." *Creative Forum.* Vol. 26, No. 1, Jan-Jun 2013, pp. 125-144, Bahari Publications: New Delhi. Print.

_____"The Politics of Representation: Revisiting Dalit Feminism in Context to Dalit Women Autobiographies" – A Lecture Delivered as a Chief Resource Person at Kakatiya University, Warangal.

21

Religion, Caste and Identity: A Study of Bama's *Karukku*

Dr Narendra Kumar

Bama is a very famous Dalit woman writer who has moved the people with her depiction of Dalit people's poverty, exploitation and caste-discrimination. She is a Tamil woman whose pen-name is Bama. Her real name is Faustina Mary Fathima. She belongs to a converted Roman Catholic Family. She was born in 1958 at the village Wathirayiruppu, Puthupatty near Madurai. Her village is in the southern district of Tamil Nadu. Her father's name was Susairaj who was in the Indian Army as a soldier and her mother's name was Sebasthiamma. Her famous works are *Karukku* (1992) and *Sangati* (1998). She has published a series of short-stories and *Vanman* (2003). *Karukku* is her unconventional autobiography which was first published in 1992 in Tamil and later it was translated into English by Lakshmi Holmstrom. It has won the Crossword Award in 2000.

Bama was born in a Christian Dalit family. Thus, her Christian identity clashes with her Dalit identity.

Priyanka Jindal also observes the same thing when she writes, "Bama's Christian identity clashes with her 'Dalit' identity and forms a unique history in itself. It delineates the corrupt history enveloped in the structure of the church which itself is caste based. Her 'gender' clashes with her being a 'Dalit', for the oppression she faces is caste based as well as from the Dalit men" (Jindal, 226). Bama depicts in *Karukku* that Dalits have to live under the shadow of casteism and untouchability. It is about their traumatic experiences and a search for their identity as Sagita Patil Sharnappa writes, "Bama's *Karukku* represents the most traumatic and suffocating lives of Dalits. It is not an armchair reading, but transits mind and heart and makes the reader to introspect and brood over it. It is also a spiritual journey and quest for identity and integrity" (Sharnappa, 68). Bama had very bitter experiences in her village. She noticed that dalits were not allowed to touch the eatables of the high caste people. Dalits were considered untouchables in her village and they were not allowed to participate in any social activities and worked as servants under upper caste people. She tells many instances in her autobiography where she had to face the problem of caste discrimination. Bama narrates an experience of her childhood. One day she was returning from school. She saw an elder Dalit man who was carrying a packet of eatable. He was holding the packet by its string so that he may not be able to touch it. He was carrying it for an upper caste Naicker person in the village. At the first sight she laughed to see the packet in such a funny way. Her brother, Annan tells the truth to her. He tells her that was due to untouchability prevalent in their village. The lower caste people were not allowed to touch the eatables of the upper caste people. He tells her that due to this reason the old man was carrying the packet in such an odd manner. This incident numbed her and she felt very upset and grieved. From that day on she thought for improving the conditions of the Paraiyars. She has to thinks about her caste. She writes:

> What did it mean when they called "Paraiyar"? Had the name become that obscene? But we too are human beings. Our people should never run these petty errands for these fellows (Bama, 13).

Bama was highly motivated by her brother when she came to know the real positions of dalits in her village. She determined to come out of this caste. She thought that only education can bring her out from it. She tried to top in her class. Due to her education she developed friendship with many children. She writes, "In fact, because of that, many people become my friends, even though I am a Parachi" (Bama, 15). She faces the problem of casteism in her primary school. When she was in primary school upper caste students looked down upon her. That's why she went to the neighbouring town but her caste did not spare her. She faced humiliating situation there also. She had to face many hurdles in her studies but despite of all these obstacles, she stood first in SSLC examination. It was a big achievement for her. She faced the poverty conditions at her home to the extent that she had to pawn her earrings for her education. She completed her graduation with Maths and did her B. Ed. from St. Mary's College, Tuthukkudi. After that she joined the convent school as a teacher. She worked there for five years where she had to face many problems due to her caste.

During the British Empire many Christian missionaries came to India and they gave them donations and motivated them to become Christian. They won the hearts of the poor dalits people. They introduced Jesus to them and many Dalits embraced Christianity. Bama's family was one of these families. Bama has been an eye-witness of the discriminatory attitude prevalent in the church. Since her childhood, Bama goes to Catholic Church and she is impressed by the Christian scripture, the Bible. She thinks that church is a place of love and sacrifice where one can direct has relationships with God. But she feels much disappointed when she comes to know that bitter reality that the people are not like this in the church.

Bama's experiences discriminatory behaviour of the teachers and nuns towards the poor and Dalit students. She gets angry when she notices such kind of discriminatory behaviour. Due to this discriminatory behaviour she decides to be a nun. Bama narrates her experience that she was working in the convent where upper caste nuns and Tamil-Dalit nuns have different standards of living. Tamil Dalit nuns were considered at the lowest stage. She narrates, "I lamented inwardly that there was no place that was free of caste. And so at last I became a nun and was sent to a convent elsewhere" (22). This discrimination is further enunciated by Arulraja, "Those who commit atrocities against Dalits do not differentiate between Christian Dalits and non-Christian Dalits. For an Indian, a Dalit is a Dalit, whether Christian or not" (Arulraja, 9). In her autobiography she unravels the distorted mentality and the corrupt psychology of the chairing persons and the upper caste nuns who see the Dalit children with contempt. Bama dismantles the rotten mentality of such people who are the heads of institutions and still show discrimination and prejudice to the low caste people.

There was partiality among dalits also. Girls were not allowed to go to study and girls had to struggle for their education. They feared that they will face problem in their marriage if they get education. It was the only way to get equal status for the girls but they were not given any opportunity for education. Bama had to face the same problem. That's why she became a nun after the completion of her education. She wanted to serve the society by this profession. She had seen how the warden in the hostel commented on the low caste children, "Look at the Cheri children! When they stay here, they eat their fill and look as round as potatoes. But look at the state in which they come back from home — just skin and bone" (Bama, 17-18).

When she observes the behaviour of other teachers and nuns towards the children, she gets angry and keeps on arguing with them for the sake of poor children. This experience pushes her to think about becoming nun. "They said I could do far more useful work as a layperson than I would do as nun. They said that caste-difference counted for a great deal within convents." (Bama, 23)

She notices the discriminatory behaviour with Dalit and poor students. Many rich students come, spend their time and go happily while the Dalit students have to do all the sweeping and cleansing work and even after it they were not given any respect there. The other students still humiliated them. Bama get very angry but she had to suppress her anger just because she did not want to reveal her caste to them as she had fear that after knowing her caste those people would not give her same respect and they may not talk with her considering a Dalit. Bama shows her anger through her autobiography. She asks:

> Are Dalits not human beings? Do they not have common sense? Do they not have such attributes as a sense of honour and self-respect? Are they without any wisdom, beauty, dignity? What do we lack? (Bama, 27)

Bama's grandmother worked as a maid-servant for Naicker families. As a servant she did the cleansing the dirt, sweeping cowshed and she brought with her the leftover food of previous day given by those families. She worked in the fields and even the small children of these upper caste families called her by her name just because she was a Dalit woman. The same kind of treatment is meted out with Dalits. Omprakash Valmiki also describes the same attitude in his autobiography *Joothan* where even children also humiliate dalits by calling with their names or calling them by their caste. "Oh Chuhre". If the person was young or of the same age, then 'Abe Chuhre' was called (Valmiki, 2). Bama depicts that Paraiyar children had to work since their childhood so that they may earn something for their family. They work at construction sites, dig wells, carry loads, gather firewood, make match-boxes and make firecrackers in the factories by using chemicals. Bama narrates the pitiable plights of dalits how they are deprived of their right of education, "But these little ones' fate is the smell of match-box solution, not the smell of knowledge or learning. How can they afford to study, when it is such a struggle even to fill their bellies?" (Bama, 47) Boys had to graze cattle and the girls had to carry their younger sibling on their hips until they are age of ten or twelve years old. When they grow in age, they had to do all the household chores. During the time of harvest, the children had to do winnowing, thrashing and collecting the grain so that they may bring the collected grain at their home and sell it to the shopkeepers to purchase their daily use articles. Bama narrates that the women were so busy in the race of earning their breads that they were unable to give any time for their children. She writes:

> If you look at our streets, they are full of small children, their noses streaming, without even a scrap of clothing, rolling about and playing in the mud and mire, indistinguishable from puppies and piglets (Bama, 68).

Bama got a nutritious food, nice bed to sleep and a very comfortable life during her stay at the convent. She noticed that convent schools preferred to admit only rich and upper caste students. It was all due to donations, charity or sponsorships that the convents ran. Another thing she noticed was that the wealthy students did what they liked and all the nuns kept quiet even knowing their mistakes while the poor students got severe punishments for their petty mistakes. Bama felt very sad to know all this:

> All those people who had taught us, had taught us only that God is loving, kind, gentle, one who forgives sinners, patient, tender, humble, obedient. Nobody had ever insisted that God is just, righteous, is angered by

injustices, opposes falsehood, never countenances inequality. There is a great deal of difference between this Jesus and the Jesus who is made known through daily pieties. (Bama, 104)

P. Sivakami also narrates in her autobiography *The Grip of Change* through Thangam, a Dalit widow how Dalit women are considered untouchable by the upper caste people but whenever they get any chance they physically exploit them. In her autobiography *Viramma: Life of an Untouchable*, Viramma also describes that their holes attract the upper caste men than their wives. Whether it is a male or female autobiography caste spares none. Omprakash Valmiki also has to face the problem of untouchability in his life. He writes:

"Untouchability was so rampant that while it was considered all right to touch the dogs and cats or cows or buffaloes if one happened to touch a Chuhra, one got contaminated or pollution. The Chuhras were not seen as humans". (Valmiki, 2)

Bama felt very dissatisfied with her experience in the village or at the convent. She realised her mistake to adopt the profession of a nun in the convent. She thought that it was the place where she could serve the society very well but very soon she realised that she was wrong in her decision. She felt very disappointed. She writes, "Today I realise what an extremely foolish thing I did. But at that time I didn't understand in the least what I was doing. I was like one who was falling into a well, blindfolded" (Bama, 105).

Ultimately, she decided to return to her home. She was feeling humiliated when she travelled to her native place. She thought how enthusiastic she was feeling when she travelled to Jammu for her job as a nun. Bama felt frustrated and desperate to know the positions of Dalit in the hegemonic society. Indu observes, "The plight of the Dalit women is far more horrible in the Indian society as they are oppressed on the basis of caste, class and sex. They have to be subservient in all areas (Indu, 2).

As a conclusion, I would like to say that Bama's autobiography *Karukku* beautifully explores the pitiable plights of dalits. Dr Anil K. Aneja postulates, "Bama tells about the corruption and discrepancies inside the church and the discrimination on the name of caste" (Aneja, 28). Even children and women also have to suffer a lot due to their caste. Dalits are involved in petty jobs as they are not given the opportunity for their education. They cannot earn well that's why their women and children also have to work to feed their stomach. This circle of exploitation never ends and they remain always poor. They had to search for their identity in the dark well where there is nobody nearby to help them out.

Works Cited

Aneja, Anil K. "Forging Narrative of Identity in Bama's *Karukku.*" Ed. Singh, Bijender. *Indian Dalit Autobiographies: Marginalised Voices*. New Delhi: Authorspress, 2015: 21-29. Print.

Arulraja M.R. *Jesus The Dalit*. Jeevan Institute of Printing. Secunderabad, 1996. Print.

Faustina, Bama. *Karukku*: Trans. Laxmi Holmstrom, Oxford University Press: New Delhi, 2012. Print.

Jindal, Priyanka. "Inscribing Identity in History: A Study of Dalit and Afro-American Women Writings in Context of Bama's *Karukku* and Audre Lorde's *Zami: A New Spelling of My Name.*" *Lapis Lazuli: An International Literary Journal* www.pintersociety.com Vol. 5, No. 1, Spring 2015, pp. 224-235.

Indu, B.C. "Silence Speaks: A Study of Bama's *Karukku*". *The Criterion: An International Journal in English* Vol. IV. Issue III, June 2013. www.the-criterion.com.

Rajan B. and Shamsudeen, G. Syed. "Struggle for Empowerment: A Study of Bama's *Karukku, Sangati* and *Vannam.*" *International Journal of Human Resource and Industrial Research.* Vol.1, Issue 5, Sep-2014, pp. 01-06.

Sharnappa, Patil Sangita. "A Quest for Identity in Bama's *Karukku: An Unconventional Autobiography.*" Ed. Singh, Bijender. *Indian Dalit Literature: Critical Ruminations*. New Delhi: Authorspress, 2015: 61-69. Print.

Valmiki, Omprakash. *Joothan: A Dalit's Life*. Trans. Mukherjee, Arun Prabha. Kolkata: Samya, 2007. Print.

Index

A

Aaydaan, 211
Adiyar People, 146
African Women, 169
Age-Long Humiliation, 15
Age-Old
Atrocities, 57
  Caste Hierarchal Traditions, 57
All India
  Dalit Women Council, 223
  Dalit Women's Forum, 18
  Scheduled Castes Federation, 233
All India's Progressive Women's Organization, 174
Ambedkar, Dr. BR, 18, 52, 53, 101, 125, 126, 153, 216, 220, 223, 231, 236, 240
  And Savarkar, 213
  Baba Saheb, 105, 188, 229, 230, 233
  Ideology, 230
  Movement, 110
Ambedkarism, 231
Ambedkarite
  Movement, 19, 105, 114, 221, 223
  Thought, 231
Aryans, Colonized Indian Lands, 100
Asprishya Community, 185

B

Babasaheb's Ideology, 233
Baby Kamle, 19, 90, 199-129
Baby Kamle's Jina Amucha, 20, 101
Baisantri's Dohra Abhishap, 229
Bama, 10, 20, 58
  Ancesters in Hinduism to Christianity, 130
Born in Roman Catholic Family, 130
  Dalit Christian Girl, 130
  Dalit Paraiya Community, 132
  Faustine, 60
  Karukku, 161
  Real Name Faustina Mary Fathima, 130
  Renowned Tamil Writer, 161
  Sangati, 57-67
  School Teacher of Maths, 130
  Use of Tamil Nomenclature, 132
Bama's
  Christ Ideology, 248

Karukku, 120, 129-139, 226
Study, 247-254
Sangati-Autobiography of Dalit Community, 161-172
Bansode, Hira, 19, 53
Basu, Tapas, 177
Beauty Myth, Book, 42
Bhujan Mahila Mahasangha (BMM), 18
Bigamy, 186
Bio-Tech Advancement, 219
Black
Literature, 153
Protestants in America, 152
Women in America, 235
Brahmanic Hegemony, 125
Brahmanical
Feminism, 18
Literature, 15
Structure of Oppression, 57
Brahmanism, 69, 188
Brahmans,
Powerful Caste, 58
The Teacher, 100
Brain Storming, 154
Bride Price, 186
British
Colonization, 236
Policy of Exploitation, 146
Buddhism, 106, 114, 120, 236
Buddhist Religion, 215
Buffalo Fair, 101

C

Caste
Conflicts, 134
Discrimination, 59, 79, 126, 132, 248
Discrimination and Untouchability, 111
Hinduism, 232
Identity, 48
Issues, 18
Oppression, 18
Ridden Society, 95, 180
Stratified Society, 152
System, 120, 152, 165, 166
Casteism, 88, 93, 236
Classism or Sexism, 229-245
Casteless Gender, 19
Castes, 208
Ambattan, 208
Komurri, 208
Koravan or Ceri, 208
Mudaliar, 208
Reddiar, 208
Tuluppan, 208
Udaiyar, 208
Vaniyas, 208
Vannan, 208
Catholic Church, 248
Chaudhury, Madhu Karrao Master, 175
Chavan, Yashwant Rao, 179
Chekkote Forest Region, 141
Child Labour, 162, 171
Christian
Culture, 130
Dalit Communities, 168
Dalit Women, 168
Dalits, 250
Religion, 165
Closed Doors, 87-97
Coconut Plantations, 70
Communist Party, 147
Contemporary Art, 58
Crete, 138
Cultural Habits, 39
Culture of Education, 165

D

Daedalus and Icarus Myth, 130
Dalit
  And Tribal Rights, 144
  Bahujan, 144
  Buddhist Female Activists, 212
  Community (ies), 17, 20, 41, 59, 61, 62, 89, 120, 161, 163-165, 167, 168, 172, 174, 180, 184, 211, 230, 232, 233, 241
  Converts to Christianity, 232
  Culture, 168
  Domestic Violence, 166
  Exploitative System, 152
  Feminism, 95, 117, 162
  Ideology, 247
  Justice, 168
  Liberation Struggle, 18, 235
  Life Stories, 174
  Literary Movement, 41
  Literary Women Writers, 47
  Literature, 15, 16, 21, 59, 153
  Mahila Federation, 18
  Marginalization, 137, 138
  Modernity, 115
  Movement, 18, 53, 131, 144, 145, 152, 156
  Movement in India, 57
  Panchayat, 168
  Panthers, 152
  Parayar Writer, 80
  Patriarchy, 20, 151-160, 235
  Patriarchy Multifacet of-, 151-160
  People's Poverty, 247
  Society, 59, 80
  Subjugation, 15
  Various Names, (DVN), 67
    Adi Dravida, 67
    Adi Karnataka, 67
    Atisudra, 67
  Dasa, 67
  Dasyu, 67
    Panchama, 67
    Tirukutdba, 67
    Women (DW), 17, 18-21, , 41, 43, 48, 49, 55, 59, 62, 63, 64, 65, 66, 79, 80, 86, 90, 92, 93, 95, 97 101, 116, 119, 130, 155, 156, 161, 163, 166, 167, 172, 179, 184, 190, 193, 220, 234, 235, 236, 239, 241, 243, 247, 251
    Exploitation of-, 80
    Identity, 130
    Ideology, 153
    Issues, 154
    Marginalization and Subordination of-, 87-97
    Participation, 110
    Writers, 41, 57, 60, 107, 219, 220
    Women's
    Identity, 69-77
    Role of Marriage—, 69-77
    Oppression, 18
    Problems, 77
    Writings, 20
    Womenhood, 20
    Writers, 15-17, 41, 87
    Writing, 168
    —Fictional Writers, 41
    Social, Economic and Political Deprivation, 142
Dalitism, 114
Dalitization, 138, 156, 237
Dalitography, 132, 138

Datar, Usha Mehta Chhaya, 53
Daya Pawar, Batula, Social Claim (Auto), 16
Depressed Classes, 57
Dhup Chhava, 221
Discrimination, 39, 57, 62, 89, 90, 183, 183, 222
District
  Gaya, 120
  Jalaun, 194
  Ratnagiri, 109
  Wayanad, 141, 148
Dohra Abhishap, 183-191, 223
Domestic Violence (DV), 60, 162, 168, 233
Dowry, 167, 194

E

Early Marriage, 162
Economic
  And Socially Backward, 70
Exploitation, 64
  Insecurity, 146
Educated
  Dalit Women, 220
  Dalits, 106
Education Campaign, 144
Eklavya, 15, 104, 223
Emotional Trauma, 60
Exploitation Thinkers, 152
  Ambedkar, 152
  Narayan Guru, 152
  Periyar, 152
  Phule, 152

F

Family Planning, 186
  Measures, 232
Female Child, 165
Feminist
  And Dalit Issues, 156
  And Dalit Movements, 20
  Movement, 17, 18
  First Generation of Dalit Women, 220
Free Education, 166

G

Gadre, RSC, 53
Gandhi and Nehru, 125
Gayathri Mantra, 177
Gender
  Discrimination, 57-67, 115
  Issues, 64
Ghura Ka Purwa, Village, 194
Goddess Rukmayi, 127
Gods and Goddesses, 50
Gogoi, Bhaskar Jyoti, 76
Gopal Guru, 101, 154
Greek Legend, 138
Guru Nanak Dev, 113

H

Haldi Kum Ceremony, 239
Higher Education, 203
Hills of Appootti, 148
Hindu
  Caste Hierarchy, 151
  Caste System, 58
  Code Bill, 53
  Gods and Goddesses, 125
  Gods-Mythology, 145
  Philosophy, 102
  Religion, 105, 106, 168
  Religious Hierarchy, 144
  Varna, 113
  Varnashrama Dharma, 69
Hinduism, 101, 144, 145, 186
Human Rights, 141
Humanitarian Principles, 151

I

Identity Crisis, 214

Indian
- Army, 247
- Caste Struggle, 131
- Caste System, 129
- Civilization, 151
- Culture, 130
- Dalit Literature, 88
- Dalit Women, 58
- Regional Languages, 15
- Societies, 39
- Society, 15, 57, 82, 129
- Hypocrisy, 129

Inter-
- Regional Marriages, 233
- Dalit Conflicts, 138

J

Jagjivan Ram, 179
Jajmani System, 206
Jalso and Dalit Rangbhoomi, 231
JIna Amucha, 119
- Social Narratives, 101

Joothan, 90
Justice and Liberation, 162

K

Kakade, Laxmibai, 53
Kamle, Baby, 19
Kamle, Babytai, 235
Kamle, Shantibai, 235
Kandasamy, Meena, 155
Kangavalli and Nagamani, Wives of Kathamuthu, 157
Karat, Parakash, 53
Karna, Sootputra, Mahabharata, 93
Karukku, Bama's Autography, 131
Kaushalya, 183-191
Kaushik, Martand, 41
Kerala Aadivasi Movement, 141
King Minos, 138
Kishna, Village Pradhan, 197
Konkan Region, 109
Kshtriyas, The Warrior, 100

L

Lakshmi Holmstrom, 61, 162, 247
Land Acts, 148
Landless Labourers, 146
Laxman Bagni Mani's Upara, 16
Laxman Gaikwad's Uchalya: The Branded, 16
Liberation of Dalits, 88
- From Oppression and Injustices, 88

Life of Dalit Women, 163
Literacy
- Program, 144
- Societies, 55

Lokhande, PV Shashikant, 53
Lord
- Brahma, 69
- Buddha, 216

Low Caste Dalit People, 134

M

Mahabharata, 104
Mahad Satyagraha, 213
Mahar, 102, 104-106
- And Mang Children, 90
- And Mang Women, 92
- Caste, 230
- Community, 88, 89, 122, 123, 127, 231

Women, 94, 102-105, 115, 121, 122, 123
Maharashtra
- Dalit Sahitya Movement, 236

Dalit Women Sanghatana, (MDWS), 18
Maharishi Parsuram, 93
Mahars, 92, 93, 110, 119, 121, 124, 125, 126, 127, 175, 177, 230
  Caste, 175, 186
  Women, 119
Mahaswata Devi, 144
Mahila Mandal, 95
Malabr Hills, 141
Male-Dalit Writers, 110
Mang Communities, 89
Manuwadi Sanskriti, 18
Marathi Autographies, 16
Marathi
  Language, 109
  Sahitya Konkan Conference, 53
Marginalization, 130
  And Subordination of-, 87-97
Marginalized Communities, 134
Marriage Tradition, 166
Marxist Ideology, 134
Mary Fatima Rani, 60
Mary Fatima, 247
Minorities and Downtrodden, 79
Moon, Meenakshi, 19, 111
Moon, Vasad, 111
Mother Forest, CK Janu, 141-150
Mukherjee, Arun Prabha, 17
  Teacher, 190
Mukta Sarvagod's Closed Doors, 87-97
Multi-Cultural—Democracy, 220

N

Nadesan, Viramma's Father, 71
Naicker
  And Paraya Community, 13
  Caste, 248
  Women, 135, 227
Narada, 104
Narayan Guru, 18
Narendra Jadhav's Outcaste, 152
National Federation of Dalit Wome, 18
Nayar Sangati, 62
Nehru, Pandit, 179
Neo-Buddhist, 204
New Discriminations, 165
Nexus Between Caste and Masculinity, 20
Novels of Kaveri—Tara Pawar, 20

O

Om Prakash Valmiki, 251
  JOOTHAN, 88, 120
  Joothan—Kumud Pawde's Antaspot, 203, 204
  Joothan: A Dalit Life, 152
Ostracism, 50, 55
Other Backward Class (OBC), 144

P

P Sivakami, 19, 84
  Dalit Women, 80
  The Grip Of Change, 79, 86
Pallar and Parayar, 133
Pancher Movement, 106
Paraiya Women, 75, 162
  Community, 61
Paraiyas, 166

Parayar, 133, 206
And Chaaliyar Caste, 133
And Chaaliyar Community, 133
Party System, 147
Patriarchal, 18
Policy and Practices, 219, 220
Religions, 220
Rule, 135
Society, 186, 224
Structure, 59
System, 62
Patriarchy, 41, 104, 106, 235
And Caste, 117
Tradition, 57-67
Pattu, Viramma's Mother, 70, 72
Pawar, Tayabai, 53
Pawar, Urmila, 19, 47-56, 211-218
Dalit Women Writer, 109-117
Maharashtrian Literary Writer, 47
Married Harishchandra, 110
Pawar's
Love for Harishchandra, 217
Teacher-Diwakar, 111
Pawde, Kumud, 174
Mahar Family, 174
Pawde's Antaspot, 173-181
Pazhaiyana Kazhithalum, Tamil Novel, 41, 158
Periyar, 18
Phoolan Devi, 193-201
Female Don, 184
India's Bandit Queen, 193-201
Mother Moola Devi, 194
Rukmani, Sister, 195, 196
Uncle Bihari, 195, 196
Phule
And Ambedkar, 66
Jyotiba, 18, 125
Savitribai, 18
Phule-Ambedkar-Buddha Philosophy, 230
Plantations, 63
Plato, 156
Poverty and Illiteracy, 104
Professional Skills, 124
Pundit Maya, 47
Pune Pact, 221
Purity and Pollution, 152
Puthupathi Village in Tamil Nadu, 60

R

Ramayana, 104
Rao, Amipama, 19
Rege, Sharmila, 19, 54, 101, 112, 125, 156, 221, 222
Religious-Mystical—Theory, 70
Remarriage, 185
Revolutionary Indian Women, 228
Right To Education, 162
And Dalits, 16
Rigveda, 100
Or Purushasukta, 69

S

Samikkanu, 70
Sangati, 131, 247
Autobiographical Work of Dalit Writer Bama, 58
Bama's Second Work, 60
Collection of Autobiographic Stories, 162
Sanskritization, 180
Satchidananda Swamy, 40
Biography, 40

Sati Savitri, 104
Scheduled Castes Students Federation, 223, 232,
Scheduled Castes/Tribes, 204
Self-Determination, 53
Serf
  And Patriarchal Chain, 203, 209
  Family, 70
Sex Knows No Caste, 39-46
Sexism, 235
Sexual
  Abuse, 43, 45
  Lust, 157
  Molestation, 107
  Relationship, 42, 74
Sham Guka, 223
Shantabai Kamle's Majya Jalmachi—, 20
Shantibai Dani's Ratra Din Aamha—Teen Dagada Chi Chul, 221
Short Stories, 20
Shudras, Labourers and Service Providers, 100
Shweta Singh, 59, 175
Sikh Religion, 113
Slavery, 92
Social
  And Economic Traditions, 193
  Change, 152
  Cultural Hegemony, 58
  Exclusion, 88
  Injustices, 57-67
  Patriarchy, 20
  Rejection, 47-57
  System, 229
  Upliftment and Emancipation, 232
Socially Marginalized People, 40
Socio-Economic
  Deprivation, 141-150
Status, 66
Subjugated Communities, 59
Subjugation
  Of Dalit Women, 119-128
  Or Marginalization, 230
Sukharai, 223, 224
Superstitution, 185, 186
Suppression and Violence, 123

T

Tamil Dalit Christian Women, 131
Thangam, Widow, 43, 44, 155-157
The Grip of Change, 253
  P Sivakami, 151-160
The OUTCAST, 92
The Prisons We Broke, 100-108, 119-128
  Baby Kamle's Autobiography, 100-108
  Oppression and Resistance, 100-108
The Weave of My Life, Urmila Pawar's Autobiography, 109-117
Third World Countries, 142
Thread Ceremony, 177
Thulabai, Adivasi Gond Women, 232
Toddy and Arrack, 149
Traditional
  Patriarchal Society, 90
  Rituals, 101

Tribal
  Community, 141
  Rights, 148
Triple Exploitation, 219

U

Udayar, Paranjothi, 43, 44, 155-157
Underprivileged and Downtrodden, 69, 70
Untouchability, 132, 173, 174, 176, 220, 242, 244, 248, 253
Untouchable (s), 40, 42, 52
  Society, 232
Upper Caste Christian Community, 134
Urmila Pawar's The Weave of My Life, 211-218

V

Vaishyas, The Artisans and Merchants, 100
Varna, 100
  Hindu Society, 151
  Order, 125
Vyavashta, 100
Vedas, 175
Vedic Mantras, 177
Vellaiyamma, Kezhavi, 61
Vidya Bal, 53
Viramma's Viramma, 203-209
Viramna, —Dalit Member, 69-77
Viramna, Life of Untouchables, 69-77
Vrinda, 104

W

Women
  Beating, 217
  Liberation Movement, 156
Women's
  Liberation, 157
  Liberation Movement, 54
  Movement, 18